T0301626

Regional Economic Policy in Europe

INFER ADVANCES IN ECONOMIC RESEARCH

The *International Network for Economic Research* (*INFER*) was established in 1998 as an independent, non-profit research network. It supports high-profile research in all fields of economics and related areas through congresses, seminars, workshops and publications. The main objective of *INFER* is to foster interactions among academics, business practitioners and policy makers with a view to finding solutions to economic problems. Further details are available from the *INFER* web site at: www.infer-research.net

The *INFER* Advances in Economic Research series publishes cutting-edge research findings in all aspects of economics. A multi-stage referee process and a Scientific Advisory Board of distinguished academics, business practitioners and policy makers ensure the quality of the publications.

The *INFER* Advances in Economic Research series is edited on behalf of the Board of *INFER* by Michael Pickhardt.

Members of the Scientific Advisory Board:

John T. Addison
Moore School of Business
University of South Carolina, USA

Juergen G. Backhaus
University of Erfurt,
Erfurt, Germany

John Bradley
The Economic and Social Research Institute,
Dublin, Ireland

Inge Kaul
United Nations Development Programme
Office of Development Studies, New York, USA

Gordon Tullock
George Mason University
Fairfax, Virginia, USA

Regional Economic Policy in Europe

New Challenges for Theory, Empirics and Normative Interventions

Edited by

Ulrike Stierle-von Schütz, Michael H. Stierle,
Frederic B. Jennings, Jr. and Adrian T.H. Kuah

Edward Elgar
Cheltenham, UK · Northampton, MA, USA

Published by
Edward Elgar Publishing Limited
The Lypiatts
15 Lansdown Road
Cheltenham
Glos GL50 2JA
UK

Edward Elgar Publishing, Inc.
William Pratt House
9 Dewey Court
Northampton
Massachusetts 01060
USA

A catalogue record for this book
is available from the British Library

Library of Congress Control Number: 2008932887

ISBN 978 1 84844 038 8

Printed and bound in Great Britain by MPG Books Ltd, Bodmin, Cornwall

Contents

Editors

Ulrike Stierle-von Schütz studied at the University of Bristol and Trier University, from where she holds a degree in Economics. Currently, she is working as research and teaching assistant at RWTH Aachen University, Department of Public Economics. Her main fields of expertise are economic integration, regional economics and fiscal federalism. She is editor of several publication series of INFER, has served as an elected member of the INFER board in 2004/06 and is co-ordinator of the INFER Working Group Growth and Business Cycles.

Michael H. Stierle is economist at the European Commission, Directorate General Economic and Financial Affairs. He studied economics at Trier University and UNAM, Mexico City, and holds a PhD from Speyer University. He has worked in economic departments in the private financial sector as well as in academic research. He is a founding member and now Honorary Chair of INFER after chairing the network from 1998 to 2005. Michael's policy-oriented research is mostly concentrated on international economics, financial markets, growth and business cycles as well as regional economics.

Frederic B. Jennings, Jr. is president of the Center for Ecological Economic and Ethical Education (CEEEE) in Ipswich, Massachusetts. He holds a BA in economics from Harvard University, and an MA and a PhD in economics from Stanford University. His professional experience includes academic teaching and research at Tufts University and Bentley College in Massachusetts, and over twenty years as an economic consultant in economic litigation, transfer pricing analysis and other areas at Charles River Associates in Boston, Arthur Andersen in Washington, DC, and EconoLogistics in Ipswich, Massachusetts. Fred is an elected member of the INFER board.

Adrian T.H. Kuah is a faculty member of the Bradford University School of Management. He has international experience in organizations and improving business performance after working in the civil service and companies like Silicon Systems and AT&T. He holds a PhD in Business Administration from Manchester Business School and MBA from Strathclyde Graduate Business School, where he pursued his interest in analysing the

vii

competitiveness, strategies and characteristics of industry clusters. Currently, he lectures on strategic management and international competitiveness issues, and occasionally reviews for the *Academy of Management Journal* and *Business Ethics: A European Review.*

Contributors

Filip Abraham, Catholic University Leuven, Leuven, Belgium

John Bradley, Economic Modelling and Development Systems, Dublin, Ireland

Rafael Doménech, Universidad de Valencia, Valencia, Spain

Angel de la Fuente, Institute for Economic Analysis (IAE), Barcelona, Spain

Anita Halasz, European Commission, Brussels, Belgium

José A. Herce, FEDEA and Universidad Complutense of Madrid, Madrid, Spain

Pascal Hetze, University of Rostock, Rostock, Germany

Jan van Hove, European University College Brussels, Brussels and Catholic University Leuven, Leuven, Belgium

Frederic B. Jennings, Jr., Center for Ecological Economic and Ethical Education in Ipswich, MA, United States of America and INFER

Adrian T.H. Kuah, University of Bradford, Bradford, United Kingdom and INFER

Diego Martínez-López, Centro de Estudios Andaluces and University Pablo de Olavide, Seville, Spain

Santiago Lago-Peñas, University of Vigo, Ourense, Spain

Simón Sosvilla-Rivero, FEDEA and Universidad Complutense of Madrid, Madrid, Spain

Michael H. Stierle, European Commission, Brussels, Belgium and INFER

Ulrike Stierle-von Schütz, RWTH Aachen University, Aachen, Germany and INFER

Hailin Sun, University of Western Ontario, Stockton, Canada

Luoping Sun, Dalhousie University, Halifax, Canada

Gabriele Tondl, Vienna University of Economics and Business Administration, Vienna, Austria

Gerhard Untiedt, Gesellschaft für Finanz- und Regionalanalysen, Münster, Germany

Goran Vuksic, Institute of Public Finance, Zagreb, Croatia

Preface[*]

Regional policy in Europe is entering a new phase. After the enlargement of the European Union in 2004, the programming period 2007 to 2013 is the first in which these new economic challenges are being addressed by European regional policy. With the corresponding new regulation, more responsibility is being granted to national authorities to implement policy in many regions via substantially increased funding. At the same time, funding levels allocated to some regions are shrinking as a result of these regions' successful convergence and/or due to the new economic landscape in a newly enlarged European Union. For both types of regions, this change brings some substantial challenges concerning three main questions: How can national policy best support the effectiveness of the European funds? What is the best possible strategy to achieve a maximum impact on growth and employment? How should regional policy be implemented on all governmental administrative levels?

Against such a background, this collection presents a selection of policy, empirical and theoretical perspectives on contemporary dimensions of regional economic policy in the European Union. It concentrates on three areas: (a) the dissimilarities and resulting convergence of disparate regions within the European Union; (b) the localisation of economic activities and how regions can understand and manage them; and finally, (c) the experiences and lessons from European regional policy.

While exploring EU cohesion and regional development more generally, the book presents a variety of perspectives on their effects and examines some Spanish, Belgian and Eastern European experiences on growth, human capital, foreign investment and technological spillover. In this edition, we have included substantive contributions from renowned government and research institutes based in numerous European countries and the US, which offer a diverse array of vantages on the challenges for theory, empirics and normative interventions.

This collection will be of particular interest to policy makers, planners and researchers seeking to understand regional economic development issues, existing policies and their implementation, along with various Member State experiences in the European Union.

This book is a compilation from the 7th Annual Conference of the International Network for Economic Research (INFER), in London during the month of October 2005. Where appropriate, the papers have been updated before publication of this volume. We are indebted to all authors for their insightful contributions and for adhering to our tight deadlines in making this collection possible, as well as to Theresia van Reimersdahl for formatting this volume. We gratefully acknowledge the generous and important sponsorship from Carillion plc. Finally, we would like to thank all the participants in the conference for their fruitful contributions to intense discussions in a friendly and helpful atmosphere.

Ulrike Stierle-von Schütz, RWTH Aachen University
Michael H. Stierle, European Commission
Frederic B. Jennings, Jr., CEEEE and EconoLogistics
Adrian T.H. Kuah, University of Bradford

NOTE

* Opinions expressed here are exclusively those of the authors and do not necessarily reflect those of the corresponding institutions where the authors are employed.

PART ONE

Overview

1. New Challenges in Regional Economics: An Overview

Ulrike Stierle-von Schütz, Michael H. Stierle, Frederic B. Jennings, Jr. and Adrian T.H. Kuah*

INTRODUCTION

Since its beginnings, regional economics has tried to explain the uneven economic development across the spatial landscape, and the different behaviour of regions in response to local and global changes. The main challenges for this discipline are, thus, the identification of the sources of varying regional performances, and the provision of assistance to policy makers for dealing with social and economic problems arising from regional disparities.

Especially with the accession of twelve new Member States between 2004 and 2007, the disparities within the EU in economic, social and territorial terms have increased tremendously. For instance the GDP per capita in Luxembourg in purchasing power parities was, in 2006, more than 280 percent of the EU27 average, while Bulgaria and Romania were both about 60 percent below that average (Eurostat 2007). But also within single Member States, growth performance is concentrated in the most dynamic regions as, for example, capital regions and urban centres, and lagging behind in, above all, rural and peripheral areas.

Understanding the factors influencing the location of economic activities was a first step for regional science. (i) Completely or partially immobile production factors may easily provide reasons for the concentration of population and economic activities. With the inclusion of (ii) economies of scale at individual firms and locations as well as with the consideration of (iii) the level of transport and communication costs, locational analysis has succeeded in describing and explaining complex and modern agglomerations, building on the early work of Christaller, Lösch, von Thünen, Isard and others. The theoretical foundations of neoclassical and endogenous growth theories have provided main inputs for the analysis of regional long-run development. Here, the quality of human capital plays an important role for the ability of regions to catch up and to exploit technology spillovers. But regions do not act in isolation from each other. Thus, the investigation of the sources of (knowledge) spillovers in the spirit of Marshall (1920) and developments on the global scale have become more and more important for regional performance. Globalisation – specifically the closer integration of regions worldwide – has increased intra-industry trade and strong international competition from emerging economies, because mobile factors require the adjustment and modernisation of the regional production structure. Models of the new economic geography (NEG) (Fujita et al. 1999), starting with the core-periphery model of Krugman (1991a and 1991b), try to explain spatial concentration of economic activity in the presence of agglomeration externalities, imperfect competition and transport costs. Due to closer integration (often modelled as falling transport costs), regions will see different patterns emerging of industry concentration, which form clusters of economic activities (Porter, 1990). As if in a natural laboratory, regions in the integrating economic area of the European Union are indeed encountering falling costs of transport and communication as well as reduced trade barriers, and might specialise in a certain segment of a sector, as firms divide their production activities and take advantage of local economies of scale.

But this process may lead to an increase in inequality between regions and make those regions more prone to asymmetric shocks (Krugman and Venables 1993). The question then arises as to whether public policy may have an influence on the structural landscape and on how regional policy makers could respond and adapt to promote a more sustainable development. From a theoretical point of view, Baldwin et al. (2003) confront the NEG models with reflections on welfare implications, trade policy, tax competition and regional policy. From the models, it becomes clear that no simple answers or formulas for practical policy can be given, and that empirics will have to shed more light on the issue.

However, empirical investigation of regional issues is especially demanding in terms of capturing regional spillovers and externalities, given the problems with the availability and quality of data. New econometric and statistical tools have always had an important impact on regional economics and regional policy evaluation as, e.g., in cluster techniques, input-output analysis, spectral analysis, etc. In particular, spatial econometrics is increasingly playing a key role in the empirical modelling of locational interdependencies.

Based on these insights, regional policy tries to reduce regional disparities and to strengthen social, economic and territorial cohesion. Within the European Union, cohesion policy has become the most important EU policy area in budgetary terms. In the current Financial Perspectives from 2007 to

2013, up to 36 percent of the EU budget (i.e. EUR 347 billion in 2007 prices) will be devoted to regional cohesion. The largest financial assistance (81.5 percent) will be attributed to the convergence objective, concentrating on the lowest income areas. The second objective, regional competitiveness and employment, focussing on the capability of regions to pursue structural change and to develop their human capital, is supported by just below 16 percent of the total budgeted amount. The third objective seeks to strengthen cross-border, transnational and interregional cooperation in order to promote a balanced regional development, and this effort will be funded with 2.5 percent of the total allocation. While funding levels allocated to some regions are known to be shrinking as a result of convergence and enlargement, other regions will receive increased funding due to the new economic landscapes in the recently enlarged EU. Especially in the twelve new EU countries, preallocated transfers for 2007 are equivalent to 2.9 percent of the GDP (forecast) in 2007, on average reaching nearly 3.5 percent in Latvia and Lithuania. Since the principle of additionality applies, regional spending by the national government has to be added to those spending projections. Thus, as regional policy is devoting a significant amount of financing to the fostering of growth and convergence at the regional level, theory and empirics should help to make this policy effective to the highest possible degree by shedding analytical light on corresponding growth factors and potential impediments.

The remaining chapters of this book, a collection of theoretical, empirical and policy analyses, will now be briefly introduced. The book is organised into three parts: As a basis for the subsequent two parts, Part Two traces the economic landscape in Europe, displaying regional disparities and analysing catching-up and convergence processes; Part Three investigates the roles of clustering, technology, transaction costs and fiscal design for the localisation of economic activities and finally, Part Four reports on experiences from and lessons to be learned for European regional policy from different perspectives.

PART TWO: THE ECONOMIC LANDSCAPE IN EUROPE: REGIONAL DISPARITIES, CATCHING-UP, AND CONVERGENCE

Part Two of this book provides an overview of the current economic landscape in the enlarged European Union. The continued expansion of the EU regional integration bloc is stimulating growth and wealth in the Member States. The assimilation of Eastern European Member States increases the asymmetry of economies within the integration area. While regional inequalities are still a striking and persistent feature of many developed and less developed economies, how can regions better understand and manage such challenges? With an overview of inequalities existing in old Member States like Spain and new Member States like the Czech Republic and Hungary, this section provides a starting point for regional policy and for understanding the catching-up and convergence processes taking place. The various writers also suggest what can be done in order for certain regions to catch up and to converge in terms of endogenous growth, productivity and innovation. The role of human capital is highlighted as being of crucial importance also for the incumbent Member States while particularly for the New Member States supporting FDI and improving transport links to peripheral regions could help to facilitate human capital and technology spillovers.

Infrastructure investment and training schemes are some of the main instruments of regional policy implemented to increase internal cohesion within the EU. However, even within a country like Spain, there is still a considerable educational gap among its own territories, quite apart from its differences from other advanced EU Member States, despite the rising level of educational attainments since the 1960s. Ángel de la Fuente and Rafael Doménech, in Chapter 2, reveal that both schooling levels and infrastructure endowments are important determinants of income and growth. Education continues to yield the highest return in most of the poorer territories in Spain. There seems to be more room for reducing inequality through investment in human capital rather than in infrastructures. They also found that the returns from infrastructure investments are higher in the richer regions like Madrid, the Balearic Islands and Catalonia. The findings suggest that it may be possible to increase the effectiveness of both national and EU cohesion and growth policies by devoting greater resources to investment in human capital in poorer regions and by redirecting part of EU and national financing for infrastructures towards richer regions.

Gabriele Tondl and Goran Vuksic investigate growth factors of newer Member States in Chapter 3. Regional level studies in eastern Europe, as compared to country studies, are often neglected. This study is significant, as a number of regional governments are seeking to catch up and converge. The reason why certain Member States have undergone transition and recovery more effectively than others may also lie in the success of their regions. The authors investigate 36 regions of the Czech Republic, Slovakia, Hungary, Poland and Slovenia from 1995 to 2000, using important growth determinants such as the amount of foreign direct investment (FDIs) to these regions, their labour force participation, and their educational attainment.

Tondl and Vuksic find that FDI and – in line with de la Fuente and Deoménech – higher education in human capital are the main drivers of regional growth in the Eastern EU. Such growth is also coupled with access to the EU markets and higher growth areas surrounding capital cities and R&D hot spots. However, Tondl and Vuksic suspect that insufficient transport infrastructure may stifle the spatial effects beyond certain boundaries. They report that endogenous growth factors like innovation activity and human capital are important factors in regional growth, where regional policy can now play a crucial role. This chapter addresses how technology diffusion and innovation activities may help regions to attain progress.

PART THREE: LOCALISATION OF ECONOMIC ACTIVITIES: THE ROLE OF CLUSTERING, TECHNOLOGY, TRANSACTION COSTS AND FISCAL DESIGN

Part Three investigates the characteristics, benefits and concerns involved in the localisation of economic activities from a multi-perspective approach involving labour economics, public economics, institutional economics and economic geography. It contributes to the empirics based on recent developments in regional economic theory, in terms of technology spillovers, externalities and localisation of activities within a region. This collection of work addresses some issues of technology diffusion due to the integration of the EU and the impact of technological innovation on vertical and horizontal industry trade for a small and open EU economy. Externalities, in terms of vertical relationships in regional clusters, may reduce transaction costs, as empirics suggest.

Further, it will be discussed how technology diffusion, as a consequence of integration, may result in a need to employ skilled workers and may cause unemployment in some regions due to asymmetry. From the perspective of institutional economics, transaction costs in vertical relationships are analysed as external economies of scale in clusters. Finally, from the perspective of public economics, Part Three examines whether economic conditions and fiscal design in a region may reinforce the level of regional specialisation.

In Chapter 4, Pascal Hetze presents a theoretical endogenous growth model considering labour reallocation and trade in technologies within economic integration, such as a regional integration area like the EU. Economic integration, that can be biased towards technology or manufacturing, changes both the demand for and the supply of skilled labour. Hetze argues that technology diffusion results in a need to employ certain skilled workers in Member States and thus may cause unemployment in some Member States because of the shortage of skills. The diffusion of new technologies within the European Union is separate from the formation of skills. Based on his model, a symmetric economic integration may be non-optimal for some parts of Member States when there is a skill shortage. This may result in less innovation and higher unemployment in these areas. Hetze concludes that asymmetric integration could, therefore, be beneficial for both high productivity and low productivity countries. This chapter recommends that the technologically advanced Member States open their markets without demanding an equal openness in the less advanced economies.

Previous studies (Davis, 1995) indicate that economic integration leads to intra-industry trade owing to technological differences between regions. This is especially so for smaller economies that are not only influenced by domestic innovation but also by technological spillovers from the international communities. Filip Abraham and Jan van Hove look at the Belgian intra-industry trade in the manufacturing sector in Chapter 5. Because Belgium is a smaller, open economy within the European Union, the impact of domestic and international technological innovation on intra-industry trade may be important there. This chapter investigates the detailed sectoral panel data for Belgium's bilateral trade with 26 other countries. Abraham and van Hove found that related factor endowments are crucial for intra-industry trade. While they provide the first attempt to analyse the impact of technological spillovers on intra-industry trade, they demonstrate that high-quality vertical intra-industry trade is mostly driven by technological innovation and spillovers, while horizontal intra-industry trade and low-quality vertical intra-industry trade are driven by income similarity.

While works during the early 1990s (e.g. Krugman, 1991a and 1991b) focused on increasing returns to scale, and Porter (1990) considers localisation as constructing optimal relationships between firms and their customers and suppliers, Hailin Sun and Luoping Sun put forward the views of institutional economists and rethink the nature of transaction costs for regional economic development in Chapter 6. Sun and Sun construct a theoretical model to explore transaction costs at two locations for understanding vertical relationships as external economies of scale in clusters. They use transaction costs to provide a renewed focus on the role of market structure and they suggest that agglomeration increases opportunities for exchange and reduces transaction costs. Sun and Sun contend that, if the size of a cluster is below a critical value, then it will enjoy lower transaction costs from economies of scale.

In Chapter 7, Ulrike Stierle-von Schütz questions the role of public economics on regional production structures during the economic integration process. The possible role of public sector effects in a spatially changing production structure becomes an important issue in this chapter. Stierle-von Schütz investigates a panel of 13 Member States for 200 NUT2 regions in the European Union. Several determinants, such as market size and population density, are investigated. She finds that the organisation of the government, through a decentralisation indicator following the OECD's tax autonomy indicator, has an impact on the production structure and specialisation of a region. An autonomous region may try to diversify its production structures in order to insure against adverse shocks.

PART FOUR: EUROPEAN REGIONAL POLICY: EXPERIENCES AND LESSONS

Part Four of this book is devoted to experiences gained from and corresponding lessons to be learned for European regional policy. After a detailed description of the pros and cons of macro-modelling, John Bradley and Gerhard Untiedt present recent results showing a significant positive impact of European regional policy on economic growth and employment. Mainly agreeing with this finding, two economic analysts of the European Commission, who have been involved in the practical implementation of these policies, highlight the preconditions under which regional policy can be conducive to growth and employment. The last two chapters of the book provide an opportunity to compare two different approaches by assessing the impact of European regional policy on Spain – a key recipient of EU Structural Funds in recent decades. The conclusions of whether and how much the EU Structural Funds have benefited this Member State differ markedly with regard to the empirics – although neither finding directly contradicts the other.

In Chapter 8, John Bradley and Gerhard Untiedt focus on the impact assessments of European regional policy. They clearly warn against the simplistic evaluations and premature judgements frequently presented in the economic literature. Given the complexity of the Cohesion Policy design, the regional policy packages and the economic linkages, the authors argue in favour of a macro-modelling approach for the evaluation of EU economic policy effects on growth and employment. After a detailed description of all the pros, cons and caveats, recent evaluation results of different modelling approaches are presented and compared. While major differences arise particularly in the short term, both Quest and Hermin's model-based assessments show a significant positive long-term impact on economic growth stemming from positive supply-side effects even after a (hypothetical) termination of regional policy programmes.

In Chapter 9, Michael H. Stierle and Anita Halasz[1] provide an overview of the available empirical evidence and methods applied for assessing the contribution of European regional policy. They assess the conditions under which EU regional policy can make a contribution to convergence in Europe from partly non-publicly available information in order to give a fresh stimulus to the current academic debate. While concurring with Bradley's argument that sound and supportive national policies are an essential precondition for successful economic impact, they claim that, in addition, scarce financial means must be concentrated spatially, i.e. on the poorest Member States and regions. Stierle and Halasz conclude that the design of Structural Funds programmes must concentrate on expenditures that are likely to lead to growth and employment.

Chapter 10 is sceptical about the effectiveness of Structural Funds and supports the third condition of Stierle and Halasz, that the investment mix chosen by a Member State is of crucial importance in order to achieve real convergence via regional policy. Santiago Lago-Peñas and Diego Martínez-López provide an empirical analysis of the experiences on strategic design of Structural Funds in Spain. Being aware of the caveat that not all potential variables involved in the growth process have been analysed, they conclude that Spain's traditional approach based on infrastructure investment has not been able to reduce disparities across regions. Less conclusive are their findings concerning public investment for improving human capital, even if the schooling level has increased faster in poorer regions. Similarly, they do not find a significant relationship between R&D expenditure and Structural Funds support.

Chapter 11 by Simón Sosvilla-Rivero and José A. Herce provides another empirical evaluation of the macroeconomic effects in Spain of the EU regional policy in four successive programming periods, between 1989 and 2013, that involved an expenditure of almost EUR 138 billion. Based on a completely different approach from that of Chapter 10, using a macroeconomic model of Spain, Sosvilla-Rivero and Herce's conclusions differ markedly. The results indicate that these funds have significantly contributed to growth and to increased levels of income and employment. Compared with a baseline scenario without EU regional support, the successive programmes continue to lead to an average increase in the real production growth rate of more than 1½ percentage points, or in other terms, an average rise of almost 5 percentage points in the Spanish per capita income relative to the EU-15 average. In terms of the labour market, it is estimated that the EU aid has maintained, or generated, more than 250,000 jobs and reduced the unemployment rate by 0.13 percentage points. Finally, Sosvilla-Rivero and Herce's simulations suggest that the EU support has led to an increase in labour productivity by nearly 3 percentage points.

As Lago-Peñas and Martínez-López focus on the interregional catch-up effects, while Sosvilla-Rivero and Herce investigate the effects of real convergence of the Spanish economy towards the EU average, neither finding directly contradicts the other. In contrast, the empirical literature suggest that interregional differences have increased in recent decades at the same time as real convergence between countries has been achieved in Europe.[2] In addition, as Stierle and Halasz argue, in general, the positive results achieved using macro-economic models can be regarded as a potential impact, while the realised impact depends on the effective use of funds and an adequate investment mix.

NOTES

* Opinions expressed here are exclusively those of the authors and do not necessarily reflect those of the corresponding institutions where the authors are employed.
1. Both authors have been successively been involved in the economic design and evaluation of European Regional Policy as members of the economic evaluation team for regional policy in DG Economic and Financial Affairs of the European Commission. The chapter represents only the authors' personal views.
2. For a summary see e.g. European Commission 2004, chapter 2.

REFERENCES

Baldwin, R., R. Forslid, P. Martin, G. Ottaviano and F. Robert-Nicoud (2003), *Economic Geography and Public Policy*, Princeton, New Jersey: Princeton University Press.
Davis, D.R. (1995), 'Intra-industry trade: A Heckscher-Ohlin-Ricardo approach', in *Journal of International Economics*, **39** (3-4), pp. 201-226.
European Commission (2004), *The EU Economy 2004 Review*, European Economy 6/2004, Brussels.
Eurostat (2007), 'GDP per inhabitant in purchasing power standards', in *Eurostat news release* 179/2007, 17 December 2007, Luxembourg.
Fujita, M., P. Krugman, and A. Venables (1999), *The Spatial Economy, Cities, Regions, and International Trade*, Cambridge: The MIT Press.
Krugman, P. (1991a), 'Increasing returns and economic geography', in *Journal of Political Economy*, **99**, pp. 483-499.
Krugman, P. (1991b), *Geography and Trade*, Cambridge: MIT Press.
Krugman, P. and A. Venables (1993), *Integration, Specialization and Adjustment*, NBER Working Papers 4559, National Bureau of Economic Research, Inc.
Marshall, A. (1920), *Principles of Economics*, London: Macmillan (8th ed).
Porter, M.E. (1990), *The Competitive Advantage of Nations*, New York: Macmillan.

PART TWO

The Economic Landscape in Europe: Regional Disparities, Catching-up and Convergence

2. Human Capital, Growth and Inequality in the Spanish Regions

Angel de la Fuente and Rafael Doménech*

2.1 INTRODUCTION

Over the last few decades Spain's level of educational attainment has improved considerably. In 1960, over 10 percent of the country's adult population was illiterate and only a minority had finished primary education. In 2001, by contrast, the illiteracy rate had fallen below 3 percent and almost 60 percent of the population had some secondary or university training. As a result of this process of human capital accumulation, the average attainment of the adult population increased by approximately 70 percent between 1960 and 2000, from 4.97 to 8.19 years of schooling.

In spite of the considerable improvement illustrated by these figures, the educational situation of the country is still far from satisfactory. There remain in particular two structural problems that have been corrected only partially over the last decades: a considerable educational gap with other advanced countries and the existence of strong educational disparities across regions. If, as the economic literature on the subject suggests, the stock of human capital is an important determinant of the level of income and a strategic competitiveness factor in an economy that is becoming more and more knowledge intensive, the correction of these problems is likely to be a necessary condition for the desired convergence in income and welfare with our more advanced neighbours as well as for the achievement of internal cohesion.

This chapter is an extension to the Spanish case of some recent papers in which we have explored different aspects of the macroeconomics of education.[1] In it we analyze the determinants of regional productivity in Spain with special attention to the role of human capital. The results of this analysis are then used to quantify the importance of education as a source of regional income disparities, to estimate the social return to investment in different types of productive assets in each territory and to extract some tentative conclusions regarding the changes in our pattern of investment that may help speed up the growth of the country as a whole and to reduce internal inequality.

The chapter is organized as follows. In section 2.2 we present new estimates of average educational attainment in the Spanish regions. The series cover the period 1960-2000 and have been constructed using census data. In section 2.3 we develop a simple model of growth with human capital that will serve as a framework for the empirical analysis and derive a formula for the social return to investment in education. The empirical results and our estimates of the social rates of return to education, infrastructures and other physical capital are presented in sections 2.4 and 2.5. Finally, section 2.6 concludes with a summary of the main results of the chapter and a discussion of their implications for the formulation of growth and cohesion policies.

2.2 THE EVOLUTION OF SCHOOL ATTAINMENT LEVELS

In this section we use data from the national census and the municipal registers to construct new regional series of educational attainment covering the period 1960-2000. (See de la Fuente and Doménech (D&D, 2006b) for details). We provide estimates of the fraction of the population aged 25 and over that has started (but not necessarily completed) each of the following levels of education: illiterates (L0), primary schooling (L1), lower and upper secondary schooling (L2.1 and L2.2) and two levels of higher education (L3.1 and L3.2).

Table 2.1   Attainment levels and cumulative durations

code	level	Spanish equivalent	duration
L0	Illiterates		0
L1	Primary	primaria, graduado escolar	5
L2.1	Lower secondary	EGB, bachiller elemental, ESO	8
L2.2	Upper secondary	bachillerato, COU, FP I and FP II	12
L3.1	Higher education, first level	diplomatura, peritaje	14
L3.2	Higher education, second level	licenciatura	17

Table 2.1 lists the Spanish equivalents of the different attainment levels (which have changed over time) and their typical cumulative durations. Tables A.1-A.7 in the Appendix of D&D (2006b) contain detailed results on the composition of the adult population by educational level between 1960

and 2000. Using these data and the durations given in Table 2.1, we have estimated average years of attainment, which are shown in Table 2.2. The table shows normalized attainments, with the national average set to 100 in each period and the regions ordered by decreasing schooling in 2000. The last two rows show, respectively, average attainment in years for the country as a whole and the coefficient of variation across regions of relative attainment. Figure 2.1 shows the evolution of the educational gap relative to the US and the 15 members of the European Union before its recent enlargement (EU15).

Table 2.2 Normalized average years of schooling, Spain = 100

	1960	1965	1970	1975	1980	1985	1990	1995	2000
Madrid	120.9	120.2	119.6	120.2	120.7	118.5	116.8	114.9	114.2
P. Vasco	112.9	111.4	109.9	109.5	109.1	108.8	109.3	109.1	109.8
Navarra	108.3	108.6	108.8	108.0	107.3	106.7	106.9	106.9	108.0
Cantabria	112.1	110.0	108.0	107.0	106.1	104.8	104.3	103.8	104.2
Rioja	107.2	105.3	103.4	102.5	101.7	100.6	100.3	101.2	103.1
Cataluña	105.8	104.4	103.1	103.9	104.6	103.6	103.1	102.1	101.9
Aragón	102.1	102.0	101.8	101.0	100.3	100.1	100.7	100.9	101.9
Asturias	109.1	107.9	106.7	105.2	103.9	102.6	102.2	101.4	101.4
Baleares	98.0	98.4	98.8	99.0	99.1	99.5	100.6	100.1	100.3
Cast. y León	106.2	105.1	104.0	102.6	101.4	100.1	99.7	99.0	99.3
Canarias	91.9	94.4	96.8	97.1	97.4	98.1	99.5	98.4	97.9
Valencia	99.0	98.2	97.5	96.7	96.0	96.0	96.8	96.7	97.3
Murcia	93.2	92.6	92.0	90.8	89.7	91.5	94.3	94.7	95.4
Galicia	97.9	97.3	96.7	95.0	93.6	92.7	92.6	92.7	93.6
Andalucía	86.9	87.7	88.4	88.5	88.6	89.7	91.5	92.0	93.0
Cast.-Man.	86.7	87.0	87.2	85.8	84.4	84.9	86.2	86.7	87.6
Extremadura	85.6	86.1	86.5	85.3	84.3	84.9	86.3	86.4	87.0
Spain	100.0	100.0	100.0	100.0	100.0	100.0	100.0	100.0	100.0
Spain, years	4.97	5.08	5.19	5.53	5.87	6.35	6.84	7.52	8.19
coef. of var.	9.8%	9.2%	8.6%	8.9%	9.2%	8.5%	7.7%	7.3%	7.1%

Average educational attainment in Spain rose by over 60 percent between 1960 and 2000 while the dispersion of attainment levels across regions fell by 28 percent. Progress on both fronts was considerably faster during the second half of the sample period. Following some oscillations in the first two decades of the sample, regional attainment disparities decrease steadily after

1980 and the growth rate of years of attainment roughly doubles relative to the first half of the sample. During these last two decades the educational gap with the US and the EU15 has been significantly reduced, falling respectively from 35 to 22 points and from 54 to 36 points. No Spanish region, however, has managed to reach the average level of European attainment.[2]

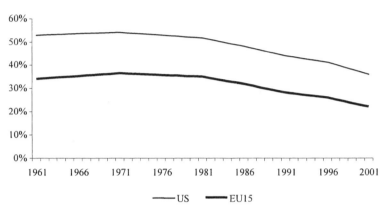

Notes:
Percentage difference in average years of schooling between each territory of reference and Spain. The data are taken from de la Fuente and Doménech (2006a). For some countries, the series have been extended from 1990 or 1995 to 2001 using the growth rates of average attainment implicit in the series constructed by Cohen and Soto (2001) for the relevant period.

Figure 2.1 Spain's educational gap relative to the US and the EU15

Using data for 1995, Figure 2.2 shows that educational attainment is closely related to income per capita. The correlation between relative income per capita and relative attainment (both measured in percentage deviations from the national mean) is 0.773 and the majority of the regions concentrate on the north-eastern and south-western quadrants of Figure 2.2, indicating that below-average income goes hand in hand with below-average attainment. In particular, all Objective 1 regions[3] but two (Asturias and Cantabria) have attainment levels below the national mean.

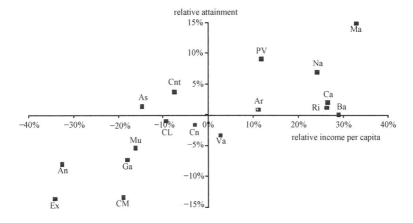

Notes:
Relative income per capita is GDP per capita in percentage deviations from the national average in 1995. The data used to calculate it are taken from Fundación BBV (2000).
Key: An = Andalucia; Ar = Aragón; As = Asturias; Ba = Baleares; Cn = Canarias; Cnt = Cantabria; CL = Castilla y León; CM = Castilla la Mancha; Cat = Cataluña; Ex = Extremadura; Ga = Galicia; Ma = Madrid; Mu = Murcia; Na = Navarra; PV = País Vasco; Ri = Rioja; Va = Valencia.

Figure 2.2 Relative attainment vs. relative GDP per capita in 1995

2.3 THEORETICAL FRAMEWORK

In the rest of this chapter we will attempt to quantify the impact of schooling on regional income and to estimate the social return to investment in education. For both exercises we will need a model that describes the relationship between average schooling and aggregate output. In this section we develop a simple model of growth with human capital that incorporates the two mechanisms identified in the theoretical literature on the subject, called *level* and *rate* effects. First, the *level* of output is assumed to be an increasing function of average attainment through a standard aggregate production function with human capital as an input. And second, the model assumes that the rate of technical progress is also an increasing function of average schooling through an external effect that cannot be privately appropriated by individuals in the form of higher wages.

The model has two components: an aggregate production function and a technical progress function. The production function will be assumed to be of the Cobb-Douglas type:

(1) $Y_{it} = A_{it} K_{it}^{\alpha_k} S_{it}^{\alpha_S} L_{it}^{\alpha_l}$

where Y_{it} denotes the aggregate output of region i at time t, L_{it} is the level of employment, K_{it} the stock of physical capital, S_{it} the average stock of human capital per worker, measured by the average years of schooling of the adult population, and A_{it} an index of technical efficiency or total factor productivity (TFP) which summarizes the current state of the technology and, possibly, the influence of omitted factors such as geographical location, climate, institutions and endowments of natural resources. The coefficients α_i (with $i = k, s, l$) measure the elasticity of output with respect to the stocks of the different factors. An increase of 1 percent in the stock of human capital per worker, for instance, would increase output by α_S% holding constant the stocks of the other factors and the level of technical efficiency.

Under the standard assumption that (1) displays constant returns to scale in capital, labour and total human capital, LS (i.e. that $\alpha_k + \alpha_l = 1$), we can define a per capita production function that will relate average productivity to average schooling and the stock of capital per worker. Letting $Q = Y/L$ denote output per worker, $Z = K/L$ the stock of capital per worker, and dividing both sides of (1) by total employment, L, we have:

(2) $Q = A f(S) = A Z^{\alpha_k} S^{\alpha_S}$

In what follows, it will be useful to define the aggregate Mincerian returns parameter, ρ, by

(3) $\rho = \dfrac{A f'(S)}{A f(S)} = \dfrac{A Z^{\alpha_k} \alpha_S S^{\alpha_S - 1}}{A Z^{\alpha_k} S^{\alpha_S}} = \dfrac{\alpha_S}{S}$

This parameter measures the percentage increase in output resulting from a one-year increase in average attainment.

The technical progress function describes the determinants of the growth rate of total factor productivity. We will assume that region i's TFP level can be written in the form:

(4) $A_{it} = B_t X_{it}$

where B_t denotes the national 'technological frontier' (i.e. the maximum attainable level of efficiency in production given the current state of scientific and technological knowledge in the country) and $X_{it} = A_{it}/B_t$ the 'technological gap' between territory i and the frontier. It will be assumed that B_t grows at a constant and exogenous rate, g, and that the growth rate of X_{it} is given by

(5) $\Delta x_{it} = \gamma_{io} - \lambda x_{it} + \gamma S_{it}$

where x_{it} is the log of X_{it} and γ_{io} a fixed regional effect that helps control for omitted variables such as R&D investment. Notice that this specification incorporates a technological diffusion or catch-up effect. If $\lambda > 0$, regions that are closer to the technological frontier will experience lower rates of TFP growth. As a result, relative TFP levels will tend to stabilize over time and their steady-state values will be an increasing function of the level of schooling.

The allocation of resources to the educational system can be considered an investment decision since it involves a trade-off between current costs and future benefits that take the form of an increase in output due to the increased level of skill of the workforce. As in the case of more standard investment projects, the economic payoff to an additional year of schooling can be quantified by computing its internal rate of return. This variable is formally defined as the discount rate that equates the present value of the flow of additional output generated by a marginal increase in average attainment with the present value of the relevant costs, including the loss of current output due to the at least partial withdrawal from the labour market of individuals while they receive training.

Working within the framework of the model we have just developed, it is possible to derive an almost closed-form expression that can be used to approximate the social return to investment in education.[4] We will consider the effects of a marginal increase in the educational attainment of a representative 'young' individual belonging to a given generation, keeping constant the level of education of older workers and future generations. We will assume that our agent of reference spends the first S years of his adult life in school and retires at time U. It will also be assumed that the total cost of each year of schooling is a constant fraction μ of the output of an adult worker endowed with the average attainment level for the country as a whole, which will be denoted by S_O. The productivity of the representative individual after completing his studies will be given by the per capita production function introduced above,

(2') $Q_t = A_t(S)f(S)$

where the notation emphasizes the fact that the level of technical efficiency, S, is also a function of the level of schooling through the technical progress function given in equation (5). We will assume, finally, that probability of employment is also an increasing function of schooling. We will denote by $p(S)$ the function describing this relation for the case of an adult worker seeking full-time employment, and by $p_s(S) = \eta p(S)$ the analogous function for a student seeking part-time employment for a fraction $1-\phi$ of the standard working hours. Hence, η is an adjustment coefficient that corrects for the differential employment probability of students and ϕ can be interpreted as the fraction of useful time devoted to school attendance.

Under these assumptions we can define a function $V(S)$ that measures the present value of the contribution of a given cohort to aggregate output, net of the costs incurred in its training, as a function of its average attainment. We have, in particular,

$$(6) \quad V(S) = J(S) + I(S) - C(S) + W(S)$$
$$= \int_0^S (1-\phi)\eta p(t) A_t f(t) e^{-rt} dt + \int_S^U p(S) A_t S) f(S) e^{-rt} dt$$
$$- \int_0^S \mu A_t f(S_O) e^{-rt} dt + \int_U^\infty p(S_O) A_t(S) f(S_O) e^{-rt} dt$$

where S denotes the average schooling of the reference cohort while S_O is the observed average attainment of the current population, which we will attribute both to already trained adults and to all future generations. The functions $J()$, $I()$ and $C()$ that appear in this expression capture, respectively, the present value of the output produced by the agent while he is attending school and working part-time, his expected production during his adult life as a full-time worker and the direct costs of schooling. The function $W()$, finally, measures the present value of the output of all future generations, which is a function of S only through the initial value (at time U) of the index of technical efficiency, A_t.

The marginal social product of an increase in attainment will be given by the derivative of this function with respect to S, $V'(S_O)$. To facilitate the calculations, we will assume that we start out from the steady-state value of the technological gap variable, X, that corresponds to the observed level of schooling, S_O. Next, we set the result of the calculation equal to zero and solve the resulting equation for the value of the discount rate to obtain the value of r that equates the present value of the streams of costs and benefits associated with a marginal increase in educational attainment.

Proceeding in this manner, it can be shown that the social rate of return to schooling, r_S, is given by

$$(7) \quad r_S = R_S + g$$

where g is the rate of exogenous productivity growth at the frontier and R_S the value of R that solves the following equation:

$$(8) \quad \frac{R}{1-e^{-RH}} = \frac{\rho + \varepsilon + \gamma/(R+\lambda)}{1-(1-\phi)\eta + \mu/p_0} \equiv \frac{\rho + \varepsilon + EXT}{OPPC + DIRC}$$

where μ is the total direct cost of a year of schooling measured as a fraction of average output per worker, ρ is the aggregate Mincerian returns coefficient, γ the rate effects parameter that captures the contribution of schooling to technical progress, λ the rate of technological diffusion, $\varepsilon = p'(S_O)/p(S_O)$ the curvature of the function $p(S)$ that describes the probabability of employment as a function of educational attainment, $p_O = p(S_O)$ the average employment probability of an adult worker and

$$(9) \quad H = U - S_O$$

the average duration in years of the working life of the representative individual, defined as the difference between the average retirement age and the average school-leaving age.

To interpret equation (8), notice that its left-hand side is an increasing function of R where the term $1-e^{-RH}$ that appears in the denominator serves to adjust for the fact that the 'useful life' of the asset (the working life of the representative individual) is finite. The right-hand side is simply the ratio of the marginal benefits derived from an additional year of schooling (which we can interpret as the 'dividend' paid by human capital) to its cost, with all the terms expressed as fractions of the output of an adult worker with average education. The first term in the numerator (ρ) captures the expected increase in output as a result of the level effect holding the probability of employment constant, the second one (ε) the expected gain in output that comes from the increase in the probability of employment as a result of higher attainment and the third (EXT) captures the externalities that operate through the rate effects of human capital. The denominator measures the total cost of an additional year of schooling as the sum of two terms. The first one ($OPPC$) is the opportunity cost of school attendance in terms of foregone output, and the second one ($DIRC$) the direct costs of the educational system.

2.4 EDUCATIONAL ATTAINMENT AND REGIONAL PRODUCTIVITY

In this section we estimate a version of the model developed above using panel data for the Spanish regions. The equation we estimate is of the form

$$(10) \quad \Delta q_{it} = \Gamma + \mu_i + \eta_t + \lambda b_{it} + \alpha_k \Delta k_{it} + \alpha_x \Delta x_{it} + \beta \Delta s_{it} + \varepsilon_{it}$$

where Δ denotes annual growth rates (over the subperiod starting at time t), q_{it} is the log of output per employed worker in region i at time t, k and x the logs of the stocks of (non-infrastructure) physical capital and infrastructures per employed worker, s the log of the average number of years of schooling of the adult population and b_{it} a technological gap measure that enters the equation as a determinant of the rate of technical progress in order to allow for a catch-up effect. This term is the Hicks-neutral TFP gap between each region and Madrid (M) at the beginning of each subperiod, given by

$$(11) \quad b_{it} = (q_{Mt} - \alpha_k k_{Mt} - \alpha_x x_{Mt} - \beta s_{Mt}) - (q_{it} - \alpha_k k_{it} - \alpha_x x_{it} - \beta s_{it}).$$

To estimate this specification we substitute (11) into (10) and use non-linear least squares with data on both factor stocks and their growth rates. In this specification the parameter λ measures the rate of (conditional) convergence in relative TFP levels. Notice that if this parameter is positive, relative TFP levels eventually stabilize, signalling a common asymptotic rate of technical progress for all territories, and the regional fixed effects μ_i capture permanent differences in relative total factor productivity that will presumably reflect differences in R&D investment and other omitted variables.

The estimated model is identical to the one developed in the previous section except that (i) the specification of the production function given in (1) is extended to incorporate the stock of infrastructures as a separate input and (ii) the level of education has been omitted from the technical progress function given in equation (5). This last change implies that our empirical specification does not allow for rate effects from education. The reason for this omission is that a preliminary attempt to estimate the 'full model' produced unsatisfactory results.[5] In spite of this, and for reasons that will be discussed later, we will return to the theoretical framework developed in the previous section for the calculation of the social return to schooling and we will interpret our results under the hypothesis that the only schooling coefficient we estimate in this section picks up both level and rate effects from human capital. To underline this fact and avoid any possible confusion, we have used β (rather than α_s) to denote the coefficient of schooling in equations (10) and (11).

The data on regional employment (number of jobs) and output (gross value added, GVA, at factor cost) are taken from Fundación BBV (1999 and 2000). GVA is measured in pesetas of 1986 and excludes the value added of the building rental sector, which includes imputed rents on owner-occupied buildings. Employment in this sector, which is very small, is also deducted from overall employment. The series of infrastructure and non-infrastructure capital stocks have been constructed by Mas, Pérez and Uriel (2002). The (net) stock of physical capital, which is also measured in 1986 pesetas, is broken down into two components. The infrastructure component (x) includes publicly financed transportation networks (roads and highways, ports, airports and railways), waterworks, sewage, urban structures and privately-financed toll highways. The stock of non-infrastructure capital (k) includes private capital, net of the stock of residential housing, and the stock of public capital associated with the provision of education, health and general administrative services. These last three items are aggregated with the capital stock of the private sector because our output measure includes government-provided services.[6] For shortness, we will at times speak of *private* and *public* capital to refer to the infrastructure and non-infrastructure components of the stock of physical capital. It should be kept in mind, however, that this is not entirely accurate.

As a proxy for the stock of human capital, we use our own attainment series and an alternative estimate of average years of schooling constructed using a series from Mas et al. (MPUSS, 2002) on the composition of the working-age population by attainment level which is, in turn, based on *Labour Force Survey* data. Section 2 of the Appendix to D&D (2006b) gives estimates of reliability ratios for these two schooling series. This variable is a statistical indicator of the information content of a given data set that can be used to gauge the size of the downward bias caused by measurement error in the estimation of the growth effects of human capital.[7]

The results obtained with both schooling series are reported in Table 2.3. All equations contain period dummies. Equations [1] and [2] contain a full set of regional dummies, and equations [3] and [4] retain only those regional fixed effects that were significant in the first iteration. Inspection of the table and a comparison with other studies reveals a number of interesting results. First, the coefficient of human capital (β) goes from being insignificant based on the MPUSS (2002) data to having a large and significant value with our attainment series. This result is consistent with our estimates of the information content of the two series, as the relevant reliability ratio is 0.900 for our data and only 0.035 for MPUSS's attainment series when both are measured in logarithmic differences. Second, our estimate of β in this chapter

(0.835) is higher than those obtained with cross-country data by de la Fuente and Doménech (D&D 2006a) using similar specifications (0.540 with a full set of country dummies and 0.394 when only the significant fixed effects are retained). Again, the explanation seems to lie at least partly in the information content of the different data sets (the relevant reliability ratio for the cross-country attainment series in D&D was 0.246). In fact, our estimate of β in this chapter lies well within the range (and somewhat below the average value) of the meta-estimates obtained by D&D (2006) after correcting for measurement error.

Table 2.3 Growth estimates with alternative schooling series and specifications

	[1]	[2]	[3]	[4]
S data from:	MPUSS	D&D	MPUSS	D&D
α_k	0.161	0.171	0.161	0.171
	(3.05)	(3.27)	(3.24)	(3.50)
α_x	0.062	0.0567	0.062	0.0560
	(3.52)	(3.25)	(4.33)	(3.88)
β	−0.013	0.835	−0.013	0.835
	(0.11)	(2.04)	(0.11)	(4.13)
λ	0.048	0.045	0.048	0.045
	(3.27)	(3.30)	(7.96)	(6.36)
adj. R^2	0.749	0.753	0.757	0.763
std. error reg.	0.0097	0.0096	0.0095	0.0094
no. of observ.	255	255	255	255
regional effects	all	all	signif.	signif.

Notes:
All equations include period dummies.
White's heteroscedasticity-consistent t ratios in parentheses below each coefficient.
The employment ratio has been dropped from the equation due to its lack of significance.

Our estimate of β implies that human capital accounts for a substantial fraction of cross-regional productivity disparities. Figure 2.3 shows the contribution of schooling to the relative productivity of the Spanish regions. Relative productivity is defined as the log of real output per job measured in deviations from the (unweighted) sample average of the same variable. Using regression weights to average the different regions, we find that the share of schooling in average productivity was 39.86 percent in 1995 – so that for the typical Spanish region schooling accounts for 4/10 of the productivity gap with the sample average.[8]

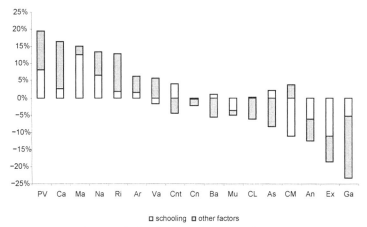

□ schooling □ other factors

Figure 2.3 Contribution of schooling to relative productivity in 1995

Taken literally, our results also imply private returns to education (measured by the wage increase induced by an additional year of schooling) that are well above those obtained through the estimation of wage equations with individual data.[9] That is, the estimated value of β is too high to capture only the direct level effects of human capital that should translate into higher wages. This discrepancy can be interpreted as evidence of the existence of externalities linked to the accumulation of human capital.[10] In the following section we will assume that these externalities take the form of rate effects, just as in the model developed in section 2.3. We have made this assumption for two reasons. The first one is that in our opinion the most plausible source of human capital externalities identified in the literature has to do with the positive incidence of this factor on the rate of technical progress. The second reason is that this is indeed a rather conservative assumption because it implies that externalities materialize only gradually over time and must be discounted accordingly. When this is done, the contribution of externalities to the social return to education (which we will calculate in the following section) is considerably smaller than under the alternative hypothesis that they have an immediate effect on the level of output.

Turning to the remaining coefficients of the model, we find that both the private capital stock and the stock of infrastructures enter the equation with positive and significant coefficients. On the other hand, both of these coefficients are smaller than those obtained in previous studies that have made use of similar regional data including in some cases the MPUSS schooling series.[11] The sum of these two coefficients is about 25 percent below capital's share of national income, whose average value over the last decade in our sample was 31.4 percent.[12] To be on the safe side when comparing the social returns to different assets, we will scale up the coefficient of private capital (α_k) so that the sum $\alpha_k + \alpha_x$ is equal to the share of capital in national income. This ad-hoc correction yields a baseline value of α_k of 0.258.[13]

Using our corrected estimates of the parameters of the production function, Figure 2.4 shows the shares of schooling and private and public capital in the relative productivity of a typical Spanish region in 1965 and 1995. The figure shows that differences in schooling have become relatively more important over time as a source of (shrinking) productivity disparities across regions, making this variable a potentially very powerful instrument of regional redistribution. By contrast, remaining differences in stocks of private capital account for only 10 percent of observed productivity disparities in the last year of our sample, and infrastructure stocks display a slightly negative correlation with relative productivity.

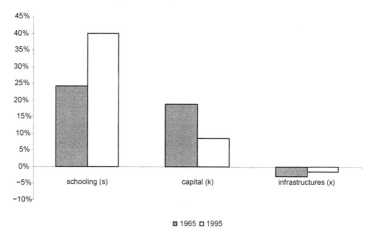

Figure 2.4 Shares of different factors in relative productivity

2.5 THE SOCIAL RETURN TO SCHOOLING AND THE OPTIMAL PATTERN OF INVESTMENT

In this section we will present estimates of the social return to schooling in the Spanish regions. These estimates are obtained by applying the social returns formula derived in section 2.3 to a representative individual endowed with the average level of attainment observed in each territory in 1995. In subsections 2.5.1 and 2.5.2 we discuss the values assigned to the parameters of the underlying model and the data used in the exercise. In subsection 2.5.3 we present the results. In subsection 2.5.4, finally, the estimated returns to human capital are compared to those of investment in infrastructures and in other physical capital in order to evaluate the optimality of the pattern of investment observed in the different regions.

To interpret correctly the results presented below, it is important to keep in mind that the social rates of return we calculate measure the returns to educational investment in a very specific and restrictive sense. These rates capture, in particular, the expected economic return to an increase in the quantity of schooling, holding cost and quality constant at their existing levels. They do not tell us anything, however, about the returns to expenditure on improvements in the quality of the educational system. The problem here is empirical rather than conceptual: although it is easy to derive the required formula, we do not have in the literature reliable estimates of the impact of school inputs on the quality of the educational system or about the contribution of quality improvements to productivity growth. This is an important limitation because this is undoubtedly the more relevant margin in the long run and because the literature does suggest that there are good reasons to think that the quality of schooling could be at least as important as its quantity.[14]

The procedure used to estimate the social return to schooling also has other limitations that should be kept in mind. One of the key inputs for the social returns calculation is an econometric estimate of the contribution of school attainment to productivity which essentially measures the strength of this connection in the case of a hypothetical average region. This raises two problems. The first one is that the results for each region are very sensitive to the specification of the production function. Since this is not the case for sample averages, the results we obtain for Spain as a whole should be much more reliable than those for individual regions.[15] The second problem is that the econometric model implicitly assumes that the quality of a year of schooling is the same everywhere, irrespective of its cost or indeed of any other factor. This implies that our calculations will understate the aggregate return to schooling in regions with educational systems of above-average quality. If quality is positively correlated with resource input (an issue that remains controversial, as discussed in de la Fuente and Ciccone (D&C 2003), our results will also underestimate the returns to education in territories with high expenditure per student.

A final limitation of our rate of return estimates is that they only incorporate those components of the social return to schooling that 'go through the market' and translate into increases in regional output. This leaves out a number of important things that are difficult to measure, including the contribution of education to personal development and its returns in leisure and in home production as well as its effect on social cohesion. Hence the results we present are very likely to underestimate the true returns to education by an amount that may be large but is extremely difficult to measure with precision.

2.5.1 Choice of Parameter Values

Table 2.4 lists the values or ranges of values of the parameters that will be used below to compute the social return to investment in human and physical capital, with our baseline estimates shown in italics.

Table 2.4   Parameter values used in the calculations

Human capital	
level effects: α_S	0.394-0.587
rate effects: γ	0-0.15%
Others	
physical capital: α_k	0.171-0.258
infrastructures: α_x	0.056
technological diffusion: λ	0.045
rate of tech. progress: g	0.015
time used in school: ϕ	0.80
retirement age: U	60.5
depreciation of ph. cap.: δ_k	7.86%
depreciation of infrastr.: δ_p	4.33%

Following Jones (2002), we assume an exogenous (steady-state) rate of productivity growth of 1.5 percent per annum. The depreciation rates for infrastructures and for non-infrastructure physical capital have been recovered from the corresponding investment and capital stock series using the data from Mas et al. (2002) discussed in section 2.4. The estimates of δ_k and δ_p given in the table are average values over the last 10 years in our sample of the depreciation rates for Spain as a whole. The parameter (ϕ) that measures the opportunity cost of training (through the fraction of time devoted to schooling) has been set to a value of ϕ equal to 0.8. This implies that the potential labour supply of a student is 20 percent of the standard workweek.[16] The retirement age *(U)* refers to the entire country in 1995 and is calculated by averaging the estimates for males and females reported by Blöndal and Scarpetta (1999), weighting them by the share of each sex in total employment (using Eurostat's *Labour Force Survey* data for 2000 referring to the age group 25-64).

The remaining coefficients shown in the table are the key parameters of the growth model outlined in section 2.3 once the production function has been extended to include infrastructures as an additional input separate from other physical capital. The values of λ, α_x and α_k are taken from section 2.4. As we have already indicated, the reference value of α_k has been obtained by correcting the estimated value of this parameter so that the sum of the coefficients of the stocks of infrastructures and other physical capital is equal to the observed share of capital in gross value added (which is 31.4 percent). The main problem we face S at this stage is that of assigning values to the two human capital parameters that appear in the theoretical model (that is, the level effects coefficient, α_S, and the rate effects parameter, γ) on the basis of the single schooling coefficient (β) estimated in section 2.4. One possibility would be to set $\alpha_S = \beta$ and $\gamma = 0$. This would amount to assuming that there are no rate effects and that our estimate captures only a pure level effect. While this would be the simplest way to proceed, for reasons already discussed in the previous section we have preferred to work with the more plausible and more conservative assumption that the strong externalities that are implicit in our estimate of β involve long gestation lags. We have assumed in particular that our estimate of β captures the long-term effects of human capital on productivity (that is, the sum of level and rate effects in the steady state of the equation that describes the evolution of the technological gap relative to the frontier). This assumption implies the following relationship between the parameters of interest:

$$(12) \quad \frac{\beta}{S} = \frac{\alpha_S}{S} + \frac{\gamma}{\lambda}$$

which we have used to solve for the reference value of γ given in Table 2.4 using the estimated values of β and λ and an outside estimate α_S that will be discussed shortly. The value of S used in this calculation is average attainment for Spain as a whole in 1995.

The range of values of α_S shown in Table 2.4 has been set drawing on the results of de la Fuente and Doménech (D&D, 2002a) for a sample of OECD countries and on microeconometric estimates of the private returns to schooling at the individual level. Our reference value for α_S (0.587) is the smallest of all meta-estimates of this parameter obtained by D&D (2002a) after correcting the attenuation bias induced by measurement error. This figure is also consistent with the microeconometric evidence on the individual returns to schooling in Europe. It implies a value of the individual

Mincerian returns to schooling parameter of 9.06 percent for the average OECD country, which is halfway between the average value of this parameter (8.06 percent) estimated by Harmon et al. (2001) for a sample of EU countries, and their average estimate of 10.62 percent for Anglo Saxon countries where the estimated returns to schooling presumably reflect the contribution of education to productivity more accurately than in continental Europe due to the greater flexibility of their labour markets. The minimum value of α_S given in Table 2.4 is also taken from D&D (2002a) and corresponds to an estimate that has not been corrected for measurement error bias.

2.5.2 Data and Sources

Table 2.5 defines the variables that enter the social rate of return formula and Table 2.6 shows the relevant data. Our two estimates of the aggregate Mincerian returns parameter (ρ and ρ_{min}) are obtained by dividing our reference and minimum estimates of the level effects coefficient (α_S) by average attainment in each region, as discussed in section 2.3. The expected duration of the working life of the representative individual (H) is calculated as the difference between the expected retirement age and the age at which an individual of average attainment would have completed his schooling (provided this is at least 14 years). Average attainment figures correspond to 1995 and are taken from section 2.2.

Our estimates of the direct cost of schooling (μ) are based on data on private and public expenditure on secondary and university education taken from several sources of the National Statistical Institute and the Ministry of Education (see de la Fuente, Doménech and Jimeno, 2005, for additional details). Our indicator attempts to approximate the average cost per student (including both privately and publicly financed costs) of a marginal increase in the enrolment rate in post-compulsory education. The cost of university education excludes research expenditures. We also exclude public transfers to households to finance living expenses and other non-tuition costs. The cost indicator μ is a weighted average of average expenditure per student at the secondary and tertiary levels, measured as a fraction of average output per employed worker. We use weights of 2/3 and 1/3 for secondary and tertiary studies to approximate the impact of a marginal increase in upper secondary enrolment under the assumption that half of the new graduates will enter a university.

The variables p_O, η and $\varepsilon = p'(S_O)/p_O$ capture the total probability of employment of adult workers, the correction factor for students who seek part time employment, and the sensibility of the probability of employment to educational attainment, taking into account its effects on both participation probabilities and employment rates. The three variables are constructed using the results of the estimation with individual data from the Labour Force Survey of a participation and an employment equation using a two-stage specification à la Heckman (1979) to correct the likely selection bias in the second equation (for additional details, see DDJ, 2005).

Table 2.5   Variables used in the calculation of the social rate of return on schooling and sources of the data

---

ρ, ρ_{min} = macroeconomic Mincerian returns to schooling parameter. It measures the average (log) increase in output per employed worker resulting from an additional year of schooling of the adult population. It is obtained by dividing the estimated elasticity of output with respect to the stock of human capital (α_S) by average attainment in each region (S_O). Our reference value for ρ is based on an estimate of α_S that is corrected for measurement error bias, but we also use an uncorrected estimate to obtain a lower bound on the value of ρ, which is denoted by ρ_{min}.

S_O = average years of school attainment of the adult (over 25) population in 1995. Source: Section 2.2.

$H = U - Max(6+S_O, 14)$ = estimated length of the (post-school) working life of the representative individual.

μ = total costs of schooling (private + public) per student measured as a fraction of GDP per employed worker. Source: de la Fuente, Doménech and Jimeno (DDJ, 2005).

$p_O = p(S_O)$ = total probability of employment after leaving school, taking into account the probabilities of employment and labour force participation. Source: DDJ (2005).

η = correction factor capturing lower student labour force participation and employment rates. Source: DDJ (2005).

$\varepsilon = p'(S_O)/p(S_O)$ = sensitivity of the total probability of employment to the level of schooling. Source: DDJ (2005).

An important problem is that our original estimate of $p'(S_O)$ captures the effects of schooling on employment at the individual level (in partial equilibrium), holding constant average attainment at the aggregate level, rather than the aggregate general-equilibrium effects that would be relevant for the calculation of social returns, which are likely to be significantly smaller. To try to correct the resulting bias, in an admittedly very rough way, we have divided by three the estimated value of $p'(S_0)$ before calculating the value of ε that is shown in Table 2.6.

Table 2.6   Data used in the calculation of the social rate of return to schooling

	S_0	$\rho\,\%$	$\rho_{min}\,\%$	$\mu\,\%$	$P_0\,\%$	$\varepsilon\,\%$	η
Andalucía	6.91	8.49	5.70	7.50	45.87	2.93	0.149
Aragón	7.58	7.74	5.20	9.03	63.40	1.70	0.300
Asturias	7.62	7.70	5.17	8.72	46.48	2.64	0.030
Baleares	7.52	7.80	5.24	7.14	66.39	1.26	0.233
Canarias	7.40	7.93	5.33	9.38	54.11	2.40	0.294
Cantabria	7.80	7.53	5.05	9.25	49.27	1.98	0.024
Cast. y León	7.44	7.89	5.29	8.67	56.38	2.33	0.216
Cast.-Mancha	6.51	9.01	6.05	8.54	56.15	2.44	0.176
Cataluña	7.67	7.65	5.14	8.84	66.37	1.80	0.289
Valencia	7.27	8.07	5.42	9.47	59.45	1.95	0.267
Extremadura	6.50	9.04	6.07	8.79	50.26	2.79	0.109
Galicia	6.97	8.42	5.65	10.57	53.32	2.14	0.123
Madrid	8.64	6.80	4.56	6.94	59.06	1.69	0.103
Murcia	7.12	8.25	5.54	8.86	54.40	1.95	0.178
Navarra	8.04	7.30	4.90	9.37	65.75	1.65	0.242
P. Vasco	8.20	7.16	4.80	9.71	58.17	2.13	0.206
Rioja	7.61	7.72	5.18	10.47	58.10	1.75	0.036
Spain	7.52	7.81	5.24	8.40	55.38	2.30	0.189

2.5.3 Results

Figure 2.5 shows two alternative estimates of the social rate of return to schooling (r_S) in the Spanish regions. Both sets of figures are estimates that take into account rate effects (using our baseline estimate of 0.15 percent for γ) as well as induced changes in employment. The only difference between them has to do with the assumed value of the level effects parameter (α_S), which is corrected for measurement error bias in one case (labelled *baseline* in the figure) but not in the other (*min*).

    According to our baseline estimates, the social rate of return to schooling ranges from 10.10 percent in Madrid to 12.55 percent in Extremadura, with an average value of 11.41 percent for the entire country. Under the more pessimistic (*min*) assumption on the size of the level effects, the average return drops to 9.15 percent and the lowest value of r_S to 8.07 percent. Under both assumptions, estimated returns to human capital are highest in the poorest regions (Castilla la Mancha, Extremadura and Andalucía) and lowest in Madrid, Cantabria and Rioja.

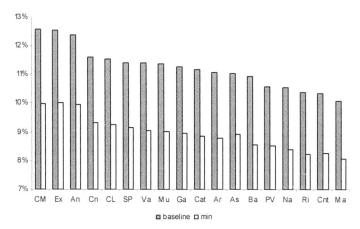

Figure 2.5 Social rate of return to schooling in Spain

It will be convenient to recalculate the rate of return to schooling under a variety of scenarios in order to isolate the contribution of different factors to this return and to check the sensitivity of the results to various assumptions. Using the two alternative assumptions about the size of level effects discussed above, we will construct *baseline* and *min* estimates of the return to schooling under three different scenarios. The first one (*level*) considers only the direct level effects of human capital on average productivity. In the second one (*employment*), we introduce employment effects and in the third one (*OBS*) we add rate effects under the assumption that $\gamma = 0.15$ percent to obtain the all-in estimates that correspond to Figure 2.5.

Figure 2.6 summarizes the findings for Spain as a whole. The bulk of the return to human capital can be traced back to its direct (level) effects on productivity. Considering only this factor, the baseline estimate of r_S goes from 7.23 percent in the Madrid to 9.36 percent in Castilla la Mancha with a national average of 8.19 percent.

For the country as a whole, the sequential introduction of employment and rate effects adds 2.24 and 0.98 percentage points respectively to the baseline returns arising from level effects.

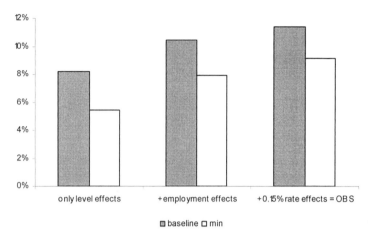

Figure 2.6 Social returns to schooling under different scenarios in Spain as a whole

2.5.4 The Relative Returns to Investment in Schooling and in Physical Capital

In this section we will compare the social return to schooling (using our *baseline* estimates) with the returns to non-infrastructure physical capital and to infrastructures (r_k and r_x). Our estimates of r_k and r_x are calculated as $r_i = MP_i - \delta_i + g$ where MP_i is the marginal product of factor i, δ_i its rate of depreciation and g the rate of technical progress (which is assumed to be 1.5 percent as in the previous sections).[17] For these calculations we use the data on regional output and factor stocks in 1995 discussed in section 2.4 and our baseline estimates of the relevant output elasticities and depreciation rates given in Table 2.4.

Figure 2.7 summarizes the results of this section and the previous one for the case of the entire country. If we exclude the lowest bound scenario (our *min* estimate when only level effects are considered), our calculations suggest that, at the national level, the economic returns on human capital are at least comparable to and probably slightly higher than those on non-infrastructure physical capital.

On the other hand, the estimated return to infrastructure investment appears to be significantly higher than those on private and human capital.[17]

The situation, however, varies greatly across regions, particularly in terms of the relative returns to education and infrastructures. Figure 2.8 displays two estimates of the *social premium on human capital* relative to both private capital and to infrastructures. These social premia are defined as the difference between the social rate of return on schooling and the expected returns to the two (private and infrastructure) components of the stock of physical capital. For each of these two factors, we show two estimates of the human capital premium that are obtained by comparing, respectively, our *baseline* and *min* estimates of the return to human capital with the estimated (baseline) returns on the other assets.

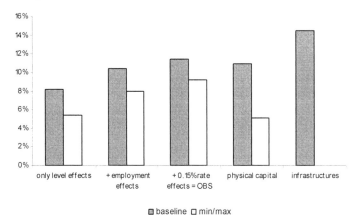

Notes: The 'min' estimate of the return on physical capital makes use of the direct estimate of α_k given in Table 2.3.

Figure 2.7 Social rate of return to schooling under different scenarios and returns on physical capital and infrastructures in Spain

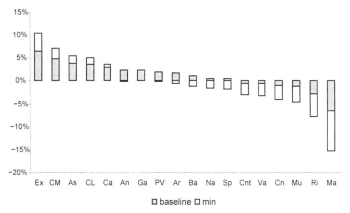

Figure 2.8a Social premium on human capital relative to non-infrastructure physical capital

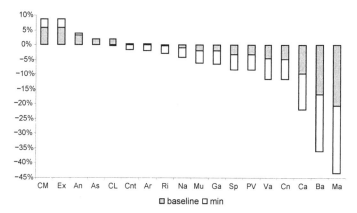

Figure 2.8b   Social premium on human capital relative to infrastructures

Turning to infrastructures, the situation is reversed: according to our baseline estimates, the return on public capital exceeds that on human capital in ten out of seventeen regions. Education, however, continues to yield the highest return in most of the poorer territories. This is illustrated in Figure 2.9, which plots the human capital premium relative to infrastructures against relative income per capita in 1995.

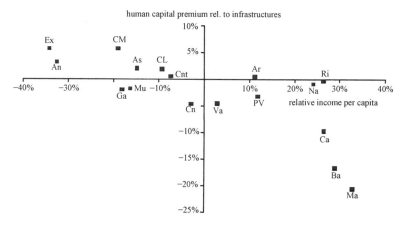

Figure 2.9 Human capital premium relative to infrastructures vs. relative income per capita in 1995

For the richest Spanish regions (Madrid, Baleares and Cataluña) the expected returns on infrastructure investment are extremely high and exceed those on education by over ten percentage points. For the rest of the regions the differences in estimated returns are much lower and the human capital premium is generally positive in the poorer regions and tends to decline with income per capita. This suggests that public investment strategies should differ across regions. Infrastructure stocks appear to be the critical bottleneck at the top of the income distribution, while increasing educational attainment seems to be crucial for low-income regions.

2.6 CONCLUSION

Infrastructure investment and training schemes, together with location incentives for private investment, have traditionally been the main instruments of regional policy and have played a key role in EU efforts to increase internal cohesion. Our results indicate that both schooling levels and infrastructure endowments are significant and quantitatively important determinants of income. One direct implication is that investment in both education and infrastructures can be effective in reducing internal disequilibria within Spain and in promoting the country's convergence toward average EU income levels.

Our results also suggest that there are important differences in the role that these two types of investment can and should play in achieving these two objectives. First, there seems to be more room for reducing internal inequality through investment in human capital than in infrastructures. Differences in schooling levels account for around 40 percent of productivity differentials across regions, while the distribution of infrastructure stocks contributes very little to such differences and actually reduces them marginally. Second, the pattern of returns across regions is very different for the two factors. While the expected returns to infrastructure are generally higher in the richer regions and reach extremely high levels in Madrid, Baleares and Cataluña, the return to education tends to be higher in the poorest territories, where it also exceeds that on infrastructures. Hence, a conflict between the two goals of cohesion policy, national convergence to EU income levels and the reduction of internal disparities, arises in relation to infrastructures but not with regard to education.

These considerations suggest that it may be possible to increase the effectiveness of both national and EU cohesion and growth policies by devoting greater resources to investment in human capital in poorer regions and by redirecting part of EU and national financing for infrastructures towards richer regions. As one of us has argued elsewhere (see de la Fuente,

2004c), a shift in the pattern of infrastructure investment in this direction, by itself, is likely to generate a net welfare gain because the operation of the standard mechanisms for personal redistribution within Spain will channel a substantial part of the resulting output gains back to the poorer regions and to the needier segments of the population. If part of the reduction in infrastructure investment in Objective 1 regions is compensated by an increase in educational funding, the net welfare gains are likely to be considerably larger, for aggregate output will rise faster without a substantial increase in internal inequality.

NOTES

*   This chapter is a (somewhat shortened) translation of an article (de la Fuente and Doménech, 2006b) published in the Spanish journal *Moneda y Crédito* and is reprinted here with permission from its editors.
1. See in particular de la Fuente and Doménech (2002a, 2002b and 2006a) and de la Fuente (2004a).
2. Spain's educational deficit is smaller but still worrisome if we focus on the younger cohorts. In 2003, 63.4 percent of the Spanish population aged between 20 and 24 years had completed at least upper secondary schooling. This figure is over ten points below the EU15 average and leaves Spain in the penultimate position within this group of countries, only ahead of Portugal. (See Eurostat, 2005.)
3. Valencia (Va) and all the regions located to its left in Figure 2.3 were Objective 1 regions in 1995.
4. It is only an approximation because, as we will see shortly, the calculation implicitly assumes that a one-year increase in average attainment will be obtained by keeping everybody in school a year longer rather than by gradually raising the attainment of younger cohorts.
5. This is a rather common problem in the literature (see for instance de la Fuente, 2004b) and may be due in part to multicollinearity problems since the correlation between the level of schooling and its growth rate is often fairly high. On the other hand, the distinction between level and rate effects becomes diluted in models than incorporate technological diffusion. In this context, an increase in the stock of human capital increases the rate of technical progress, but this effect gradually dies off as the country gets closer to the technological frontier and the growth rate of TFP stabilizes. As a result, the rate effect becomes a level effect in the medium or long run and, if convergence to the technological steady state is sufficiently fast, it becomes difficult to separate the two effects.
6. The results are very similar when we exclude the output of the public sector from our productivity measure and the non-infrastructure component of public capital from k.
7. Let X be the (unobservable) variable of interest and P a noisy proxy for it so that $P = X + \varepsilon$, where ε is a random measurement error. The reliability ratio of P is defined as the ratio between the signal and the sum of signal and noise contained in the data, that is, as $r \equiv (\text{var}X/\text{var}P) = [\text{var } X/(\text{var}X + \text{var}\varepsilon)]$ where var$X$ measures the signal contained in the series and var ε the noise that distorts it. (Notice that we have implicitly assumed that the measurement error term, ε, is not correlated with X. When several noisy proxies are available for a given variable of interest, their respective reliability ratios can be estimated by regressing each of the proxies on the rest following the procedure proposed by Krueger and Lindhal (2001). See also section 2 of the Appendix to de la Fuente and Doménech (2006a).
8. We define the relative productivity of region i ($qrel_i$) as the difference between the region's log output per employed worker and the average value of the same variable in the sample. The contribution of human capital to relative productivity (cs_i) is obtained multiplying the coefficient of this factor, β by the relative level of schooling (measured in log differences

with the geometric sample mean). After constructing these two variables for each region, we estimate a regression of the form $cs_i = aqrel_i + e_i$ where e_i is a random disturbance. The coefficient obtained in this manner, $a \equiv cs_i/qrel_i$, measures the fraction of the observed productivity differential that can be attributed to human capital in the sample as a whole.

9. De la Fuente (2004) derives a formula that approximates the relationship between the individual mincerian returns to schooling through higher wages (θ) and the macroeconometric parameter that measures the contribution of schooling to aggregate output. Assuming perfect competition, constant returns and the absence of externalities, θ (which measures the percentage increase in the average wage associated with an additional year of schooling) would be given by $\theta = (\beta/S)/(1-\pi)$ where S is average attainment in years and π the share of capital in national income. With our data and results, using the average value of S in Spain as a whole in 1995, the expected value of θ would be 16 percent. This figure is much higher than the value of this parameter (8.38 percent) estimated directly by de la Fuente et al. (2005) using individual level data taken from the Encuesta de Estructura Salarial for 1995.

10. Another possibility is of course the endogeneity bias arising from reverse causation from income to schooling. With our specification, however, it seems unlikely that such a bias can be important. Since the two-year periods over which growth rates are calculated are very short, there is not enough time for shocks to the growth rate of productivity to affect the educational stock of the adult population which, unlike enrolment rates, will respond to rising income only with a considerable lag.

11. See for instance Mas et al. (1995), de la Fuente and Vives (1995), González-Páramo and Argimón (1997), Dabán and Lamo (1999) and de la Fuente (2002b).

12. The share of capital in output is measured as the ratio between gross operating surplus and GVA for Spain as a whole after excluding the building rental sector. For this calculation we use Fundación BBV data and estimate total labour costs by imputing to non-salaried employees the average compensation of salaried employees in the same sector, except for the fisheries sector where this would yield a negative operating surplus. For this sector, we impute to non-salaried employees 1/2 of the labour cost per salaried employee.

13. We scale up α_k alone, rather than α_k and α_x together while respecting their ratio, because this yields a more plausible pattern of relative returns. The coefficient estimates shown in Table 2.3 imply rates of return of 5.09 percent and 14.46 percent for private and public capital respectively in Spain as a whole. With our correction, the return to private capital rises to 10.91 percent.

14. See de la Fuente (2004b).

15. Our calculations are based on the estimation of a Cobb-Douglas function in years of schooling. With this specification, the elasticity of output with respect to human capital, α_s, is constant and the aggregate Mincerian returns parameter, $\rho = \alpha_s/S$, varies across regions in inverse proportion to attainment. An alternative Mincerian specification that has often been used in the recent literature, by contrast, imposes a common value of ρ for the whole sample. This makes little difference when we are interested in drawing conclusions for a hypothetical average region but becomes crucial when we want to compare rates of return across territories. While we find the Cobb-Douglas specification intuitively more appealing than the Mincerian functional form and have found that it fits the OECD data better, it may still be too restrictive. If this is the case, cross-regional results may be distorted in a way that will depend on the true sensitivity of ρ to average attainment.

16. This figure is probably too low if we interpret it literally as a measure of the potential supply of labour time, but it may be reasonable as an estimate of the potential income of students relative to full-time adult workers with the same level of schooling.

17. The contribution of infrastructures to productivity has been an extremely controversial issue in the literature. Recent evidence for the US states suggests that the economic returns to infrastructure investment have been rather low or even negligible over the last three decades, but practically all the evidence available for Spain points to the opposite conclusion. One possible explanation for these contrasting results is that the payoff to infrastructures may fall sharply once the stock of this factor becomes large enough to adequately serve the needs of a given territory. If this is the case, existing results suggest that Spain has not yet reached this 'saturation' point. See de la Fuente (2002a) for a survey of the relevant literature.

REFERENCES

Blöndal, S. and S. Scarpetta (1999), *The retirement decision in OECD countries*, OECD Economics Department Working Paper 202.

Cohen, D. and M. Soto (2001), *Growth and human capital: good data, good results*, CEPR Discussion Paper 3025, London.

Dabán, T. and A. Lamo (1999), *Convergence and public investment allocation, Spain 1980-93*, Documento de Trabajo D-99001, Dir. Gral. de Análisis y Programación Presupuestaria, Ministerio de Economía y Hacienda, Madrid.

de la Fuente, A. (2002a), *Infrastructures and productivity: a survey*, mimeo, Instituto de Análisis Económico, CSIC, Barcelona.

de la Fuente, A. (2002b), *The effect of Structural Fund spending on the Spanish regions: an assessment of the 1994-99 Objective 1 CSF*, CEPR Discussion Paper 3673, London.

de la Fuente, A. (2003), *Human capital in a global and knowledge-based economy, Part II: assessment at the EU country level*, Final report for the European Commission, Brussels.

de la Fuente, A. (2004a), *La rentabilidad privada y social de la educación: un panorama y resultados para la UE*, Documento de Economía 21, Fundación Caixa Galicia, Santiago de Compostela.

de la Fuente, A. (2004b), 'Educación y crecimiento: un panorama', *Revista Asturiana de Economía*, 31, pp. 7-49.

de la Fuente, A. (2004c), 'Second-best redistribution through public investment: a characterization, an empirical test and an application to the case of Spain', *Regional Science and Urban Economics*, 34, pp. 489-503.

de la Fuente, A. and A. Ciccone (D&C, 2003), *Human capital in a global and knowledge-based economy*, Final report to the European Commission, Brussels.

de la Fuente, A. and R. Doménech (D&D, 2002a), *Human capital in growth regressions: how much difference does data quality make? An update and further results*, CEPR Discussion Paper 3587, London.

de la Fuente, A. and R. Doménech (D&D, 2002b), *Educational attainment in the OECD, 1960-90*, CEPR Discussion Paper 3390.

de la Fuente, A. and R. Doménech (D&D, 2006a), 'Human capital in growth regressions: how much difference does data quality make?', *Journal of the European Economic Association*, 4(1), pp 1-36.

de la Fuente, A. and R. Doménech (D&D, 2006b), 'Capital humano, crecimiento y desigualdad en las regiones españolas', *Moneda y Crédito*, 222, pp. 13-56.

de la Fuente, A. and X. Vives (1995), 'Infrastructure and education as instruments of regional policy: evidence from Spain', *Economic Policy*, 20, April, pp. 11-54.

Eurostat (2005), Structural indicators database, available at: http://epp.eurostat.ec.europa.eu/.

de la Fuente, A., R. Doménech and J.F. Jimeno (2005), *Capital Humano, Crecimiento y Empleo en las Regiones Españolas*, Documento de Economía 24. Fundación Caixa Galicia.

Fundación BBV (1999), *Renta nacional de España y su distribución provincial. Serie homogénea. Años 1955 a 1993 y avances 1994 a 1997. Tomo I*, Bilbao.

Fundación BBV (2000), *Renta nacional de España y su distribución provincial. Año 1995 y avances 1996-1999*, Bilbao.

González-Páramo, J.M. and I. Argimón (1997), 'Efectos de la inversión en infraestructuras sobre la productividad y la renta de las CC.AA.', in E. Pérez Touriño (ed.), *Infraestructuras y desarrollo regional: Efectos económicos de la Autopista del Atlántico*, Editorial Civitas, Colección Economía, Madrid.

Harmon, C., I. Walker and N. Westergaard-Nielsen (2001), 'Introduction', in C. Harmon, I. Walker and N. Westergaard-Nielsen (eds), *Education and earnings in Europe. A cross-country analysis of the returns to education*. Edward Elgar, Cheltenham, UK and Northampton, MA, USA, pp. 1-37.

Heckman, J. (1979), 'Sample Selection Bias as a Specification Error'. *Econometrica*, **47**, pp. 153-161.

Jones, C. (2002). 'Sources of U.S. economic growth in a world of ideas', *American Economic Review*, **92**(1), pp. 220-239.

Krueger, A. and M. Lindahl (2001), 'Education for growth: why and for whom?', *Journal of Economic Literature*, **39**, pp. 1101-1136.

Mas, M., F. Pérez and E. Uriel (2002), *El stock de capital en España y su distribución territorial*, Fundación BBVA, Bilbao.

Mas, M., J. Maudos, F. Pérez and E. Uriel (1995), *Infrastructures and productivity in the Spanish regions: a long-run perspective*, mimeo, IVIE, Valencia.

Mas, M., F. Pérez, E. Uriel, L. Serrano and A. Soler (2002), 'Capital humano, series 1964-2001', *Capital humano y actividad económica* (CD-ROM), Fundación Bancaja, Valencia.

3. What Helps Regions in Eastern Europe Catch Up? The Role of Foreign Investment, Human Capital and Geography

Gabriele Tondl and Goran Vuksic*

3.1 INTRODUCTION

The objective of this chapter is to investigate the determinants of regional growth in the EU's new member states in Eastern Europe. Since their economic prospects are characterized by a process of catching up, growth is an issue of primary concern for these countries.

Since the mid-1990s, we have observed superior growth performance in Eastern European countries vis-à-vis Western Europe, providing evidence that the process of catching up is well underway. However, it is also evident that there are major internal growth differences within Eastern European countries. From this perspective, the question arises as to why growth rates differ across regions within these countries. Why do some Eastern regions show highly dynamic growth, while others only enjoy weak growth?

Economic growth theory offers a number of hypotheses with respect to the determinants of growth, about which a vast quantity of empirical literature emerged in the 1990s. Some researchers investigated growth factors within large sets of countries worldwide (e.g., Sachs and Warner 1995; Sala-i-Martin 1997; Gallup et al. 1998), while others looked at growth factors within OECD economies (e.g., de la Fuente 1995; Bassanini et al. 2001). A number of studies also examined growth factors at the regional level in the EU (e.g., Fagerberg and Verspagen 1996; Fagerberg et al. 1997; Vanhoudt et al. 2000; Paci et al. 2001; Tondl 2001; Badinger and Tondl 2003). For Eastern Europe, on the other hand, only a few studies which investigate multiple growth factors have been carried out at the country level (e.g., Campos and Kinoshita 2002), but there are practically no growth factor studies at the regional level.[1]

So far, most country studies on Eastern European growth have focused on exploring the causes of why some countries have undergone transition and recovery more quickly than others, and therefore they have investigated particular factors which are likely to influence growth in transition. Thus many growth studies have focused on the significance of institutional reform and market liberalization for growth in Eastern Europe (Hernández-Cáta 1997; Fischer et al. 1998; Havrylyshyn and van Rooden 2000; Fidrmuc 2000; Falcetti et al. 2002) or the role of economic policies (Barlow and Radulescu 2002). Only a few studies have investigated growth factors which are relevant in the post-transition stage, such as investment, foreign direct investment (FDI) and education (Fidrmuc 2000; Campos and Kinoshita 2002).

As the transition process has been completed and regional differences have manifested themselves in the catching-up process in Eastern Europe, however, a general interest has arisen in knowing which factors are important for the catching-up process. In this respect, our chapter aims to fill a gap in Eastern European regional growth analysis.

In light of this objective, we investigate regional growth in a sample comprising 36 regions from the Czech Republic, Slovakia, Hungary, Poland and Slovenia for the period from 1995 to 2000, a time when those countries had left transition behind and their economies had generally begun to catch up (WIIW 2002). For this purpose, we created a comprehensive regional database, EAST RegStat, compiled from national statistical data. Investigating the drivers of regional growth in the post-transition period, we look at a variety of factors which seem to be particularly relevant in Eastern European countries, namely: capital accumulation and foreign direct investment, which reached rather high levels in this period; labour force participation, which decreased due to mounting unemployment; educational attainment at the secondary and higher levels, in which a number of Eastern European countries rank fairly high; and innovation. In addition, we investigate the role of geographical factors such as spatial dependencies among regions and potential access to EU markets. Another particular concern of this study is to investigate factors which may explain technological progress, manifested by a strong increase in productivity in Eastern European regions in this period. Therefore, we look at the role of innovation activity and technology diffusion in achieving technological progress.

The results indicate that foreign direct investment and higher education are most important for regional growth in Eastern Europe. Regions with better market access exhibit superior growth. Moreover, spatial dependencies suggest a tendency toward emerging growth clusters in Eastern Europe. The areas around capital cities outperform in all factors and are at the forefront of the catching-up process.

The rest of the chapter is organized as follows: Section 3.2 reviews the literature and puts forward our hypotheses with respect to growth factors in Eastern European regions. Section 3.3 defines the theoretical model to be tested. Section 3.4 describes our data set, EAST RegStat, and gives initial insights into regional developments on the basis of these data. Section 3.5 then explains the estimation procedure and reports the results of our estimations. Section 3.6 presents our conclusions.

3.2 LIKELY SOURCES OF GROWTH IN EASTERN EUROPEAN REGIONS IN THE POST-TRANSITION PERIOD

In 1995, Eastern European economies entered a very specific situation of economic development where basically the downsizing measures of transformation had been completed and the process of rebuilding and modernizing started. On average, regional per capita income growth amounted to four percent annually in the period from 1995 to 2000, except in the Czech Republic where it was fairly weak. In particular, capital city areas showed higher growth, even twice the average in the Czech Republic and in Poland. These growth differences raise the question of why some regions saw higher growth rates than others, meaning that they would catch up faster in terms of income.

Using the arguments of growth theory and the findings of empirical growth research as our point of departure (e.g., see Fagerberg et al. 1997; Vanhoudt et al. 2000; Badinger and Tondl 2003 for an investigation of growth factors in EU-15 regions), we propose that investment, the labour market participation rate, educational attainment, innovation activity, the stock of FDI as well as spatial dependencies and location factors may be factors which explain Eastern European regional growth. What arguments have been made in favour of these growth factors, and what findings has the existing growth literature on Eastern Europe come to?

First of all, with respect to investment we have to note that due to massive privatization, capital accumulation has been higher in Eastern Europe than in the EU since the mid-1990s (25 percent versus 19 percent on average between 1994 and 1997; Dobrinsky 2001; Campos and Coricelli 2002), with foreign direct investment playing an important role (13 percent of investment in 1997/99; Campos and Coricelli 2002). On the regional level, investment activity differed significantly. In the period from 1996 to 2000, regional investment rates ranged from 20 percent in Poland to almost 40 percent in

Slovakia. In capital city areas, investment was two thirds higher. In Bratislava, it even reached 70 percent of gross value added (GVA). To what extent can investment explain growth in Eastern European regions? In one of the few empirical studies of economic growth in Eastern Europe, Campos and Kinoshita (2002) propose that capital formation has had a significantly positive effect on growth in Eastern European countries.

Furthermore, we assume that in the latter part of the 1990s regional growth in Eastern Europe was related to labour market developments. In the first five years of transformation, labour participation rates, that is, the ratio of employed persons to total population, had significantly declined in general (Boeri 2000), but it largely stabilized in the latter half of the 1990s (except in many regions of the Czech Republic and Slovakia). Demographic and labour market developments are responsible for this decline. Emigration and early retirement were important factors contributing to the decline in participation rates in Eastern Europe. Skill mismatches and labour-saving productivity increases also led to higher unemployment and thus to lower participation rates. Unemployment rates had increased steadily in Eastern Europe until 1994, then showed a tendency to decline until 1998 (Burda 1998), but increased again thereafter (Eurostat 2000). After a short period of expansion after 1994, employment dropped again in the Czech Republic, Slovakia and Poland (WIIW 2002). Falling participation rates reduce the growth prospects of a region, as produced output has to be shared with a larger inactive share of the population. The question arises to what extent participation was important for regional growth in the post-1995 period.

Education, which is given primary significance in endogenous growth models, may have played an important role in regional growth in Eastern Europe because of the relatively high attainment rates in secondary education. In the period in question, 55 percent of the population had finished secondary school in the Czech Republic, 48 percent in the Slovak Republic, 43 percent in Poland and Slovenia and 37 percent in Hungary. Within countries, attainment rates were fairly consistent. In the richer regions of the EU this rate stood at 41 percent, and in the less developed regions of the cohesion countries (Spain, Portugal, Greece, Ireland) the rate was only 25 percent. Attainment rates in higher education are less striking in Eastern Europe: 6 to 9 percent of the population had finished a degree in higher education, again with a high concentration in capital city areas, whereas the rate is 10 percent in the cohesion countries and 16 percent in the richer EU regions.

Given the arguments of growth theory, which postulate that on the one hand education provides knowledge and skills which contribute to the production process (Lucas 1988; Mankiw et al. 1992) and on the other hand has a direct impact on research capacity (Romer 1990), differences in education levels across Eastern European regions should make a difference in terms of growth. The existing growth regressions for Eastern European countries provide mixed evidence. Fidrmuc (2000) found that secondary education has a positive impact on growth, whereas Campos and Kinoshita (2002) found a negative impact.

Recent growth literature emphasizes that productivity increases have become the most important source of growth in advanced economies (Easterly and Levine 2001). Given the large productivity gap of Eastern countries, productivity growth should also be highly important in Eastern European regions and should play a central role in maintaining the momentum of the catching-up process. In a growth-accounting exercise, Dobrinsky (2001) demonstrated that total factor productivity growth showed signs of becoming a driving force for growth in these countries after the mid-1990s.

In principle, productivity growth can be generated either by improving knowledge and skills through education (see above), or by technological progress which either stems from internal R&D or results from technology transfer. On average, regional R&D rates are fairly modest in the accession countries. Only in Slovenia and the Czech Republic do they reach fairly high values: 1.6 and 1.3 percent, respectively. Like higher education, R&D activity is concentrated in capital city areas, where R&D expenditures account for 1.5 to 2.4 percent of GVA.

Technology transfer may play an important role in Eastern European regions: One primary source of technology transfer may be FDI, which has reached substantial levels in Eastern European countries, not least because of lower wage costs, generous tax concessions for foreign investors, and the prospect of EU integration (Altomonte and Resmini 2001; Klazar et al. 2001). FDI levels in Eastern European regions reached 32 percent of GVA in Hungary and 26 percent in the Czech Republic; in the other countries, FDI accounted only for 10 to 15 percent of GVA. In this context, the level of FDI was on average twice as high in capital city regions. With FDI technology incorporated into capital goods, process knowledge and managerial skills are transferred to the host region. A number of recent studies have attempted to test for technology spillovers through FDI, either on the microeconomic or on the macroeconomic level. In this context, a direct effect of productivity increases in the plant where FDI was received and an indirect effect on the productivity of other firms in the same location or same sector have been observed (Baldwin et al. 1999). Indirect productivity spillovers may take place through the labour force (Fosfuri et al. 2001) or through upstream and downstream interfirm relationships (Blomström and Kokko 1998; Markusen and Venables 1999). Technology spillovers are contingent on social capabilities at the local level (Abramowitz 1986), in particular on the education level of the local workforce (Borensztein et al. 1998). The results of studies using firm-level data for Eastern European countries are mixed. Kinoshita (2000) tests for technology spillovers due to FDI on local firms in the Czech Republic and finds that these spillovers depend on the extent of the local firms' own R&D activities. In contrast, Djankov and Hoekman (2000), who do not account for the absorption capacity of local firms, find no clear evidence of spillovers from FDI in the Czech Republic. Macroeconomic and sectoral studies which directly assess the growth impact of FDI on the economy or sector come to a positive assessment of FDI's growth effects. Thus, Altomonte and Resmini (2001) were able to verify the positive growth impact of foreign-owned firms on downstream and upstream domestic firms in Poland. Similarly, Hunya (2002) as well as Campos and Kinoshita (2002) found that FDI has a positive effect on growth. The latter show that this effect depends on the level of human capital in the recipient country.

As described by Resmini (2000), FDI in Eastern European countries is not focused on labour-intensive sectors, rather on capital-intensive and even science-based sectors. In combination with a relatively high educational level, this should facilitate technology transfers through FDI. Consequently, we propose the hypothesis that FDI is an excellent channel for technology transfer in Eastern European regions and should thus have led to higher growth in regions with high FDI stocks.

Given our focus on regional economies, it is appropriate that we also check growth differences in light of economic geography and spatial effects. First, we shall examine spatial dependencies among regions in Eastern Europe. An obvious way to check for general spatial dependencies is to look at growth spillovers between regions. Such spillovers may result from a variety of interactions between regions, such as interregional trade flows, labour market interactions, productivity spillovers, etc. A number of regional growth analyses, for example Rey and Montouri (1999), Fingleton (2001), Niebuhr (2001), and Kosfeld et al. (2002), have detected growth spillovers in other geographical areas. There are also studies in the literature which explicitly analyse the interactions underlying such growth spillovers. For example, Cheshire and Magrini (2000) analyse interregional migration flows, Paci and Pigliaru (2001) analyse productivity spillovers across EU regions, and Paci and Usai (2001) and Funke and Niebuhr (2001) analyse regional R&D spillovers. Nevertheless, since we wish to account for the overall spillover effects between regions (rather than individual effects, for which data are not always available), we shall focus on growth spillovers. The implication of growth spillovers is straightforward. Evidence of such spillovers indicates that a region's growth depends on that of bordering regions, that is, a region surrounded by high-growth regions will also show high growth, and a region surrounded by low-growth regions will show poor growth. This means that high-growth and low-growth clusters will appear. It is very difficult for a region in a low-growth cluster to move to a more dynamic growth path. This effect will be analysed using a spatial econometric model as suggested in spatial econometrics literature (Anselin 1988; Anselin and Florax 1995; Kelejian and Prucha 1998).

Second, we shall test the relevance of peripherality (agglomeration) effects in Eastern European regions. More precisely, we shall look at access to demand in EU markets, where such access is a function of distance and quality of transport. Thus we shall test the argument that regions which are geographically closer to EU centres with high demand and better transportation links to these centres enjoy superior growth.

Third, and alternatively to the second proposition, we shall directly test the question to which extent regions located along the EU border and capital regions register higher growth.

Of course, there are a number of other factors which may have a significant influence on growth. First, as we know from country-level statistics, foreign trade (above all with the EU) has become very important in Eastern Europe. However, we can assume that various regions trade to a different extent. Therefore, it would be interesting to find out whether differences in trade intensity have led to growth differences. Intensive trade usually leads to higher growth since it unleashes pro-competitive effects and facilitates technology transfer. Furthermore, as country-level studies have shown, differences in socio-political and institutional factors were responsible for early growth differences in Eastern Europe. These factors can be expected to vary even more across regions and could therefore be important in explaining growth differences. Unfortunately, there are no regional statistics on either factor, therefore we cannot test for their effects.

3.3 SPECIFICATIONS FOR THE ESTIMATION

In order to test the hypotheses proposed in the previous section, we shall use a cross-section growth-accounting framework which has become the standard in empirical growth literature (see Temple 1999). We do not use a catching-up model since we are not interested in the convergence dynamics within the group of Eastern European regions but in the factors influencing growth in those regions. Without deriving a fully specified growth model (which is not the focus of this chapter), we develop a model following the approach of Benhabib and Spiegel (1994).

The starting point is an augmented Solow model of economic growth as specified by Mankiw et al. (1992):

(1) $Y = AK^\alpha H^\beta L^\gamma$

where Y is income, K is physical capital, H human capital, L labour and A the total factor productivity. α, β and γ are elasticities of output with respect to physical capital, human capital and labour. We assume constant returns to scale, so that $\alpha + \beta + \gamma = 1$.
Equation (1) becomes

(2) $Y = AK^\alpha H^\beta (POP \cdot PART)^\gamma$

if population POP is different from the labour force L, and $PART$ represents the participation rate L/POP.
In intensive form, equation (2) becomes

(3) $y = Ak^\alpha h^\beta PART^\gamma$

where per capita income $y = Y/POP$, per capita capital $k = K/POP$, and the stock of human capital per person $h = H/POP$.

Since the objective is to examine the causes of changes in per capita income, we express the model in log differences and use these directly for estimation (Benhabib and Spiegel 1994). All variables except for human capital (see below) will be considered in terms of these differences.

(4) $\Delta \ln y = \Delta \ln A + \alpha \ln k + \beta h + \gamma \ln PART$

We use the investment rate INV as a proxy for capital accumulation $\Delta \ln k$; h is the average educational attainment rate in the population, $\Delta \ln PART$ is the change in the participation rate and $\Delta \ln A$ is technological progress measured in terms of productivity growth.

At first, education is considered a factor of production, representing knowledge that determines the efficiency of production. Changes in educational attainment should therefore lead to higher growth. In another respect, however, the level of education also determines the capacity to generate technological progress, that is, productivity growth (Benhabib and Spiegel 1994, 2003; Temple 1999). Finally, education can also be a conditioning factor for technology diffusion (see below).

In empirical growth literature, many authors (e.g., Benhabib and Spiegel 1994; Pritchett 1996) consider the level of education – and not its changes – to be the factor determining growth. The reasons for this choice of variable are diverse and also involve problems of data accuracy (de la Fuente and Doménech 2000 and their paper in this volume). Since we observe the growth process over a fairly short time period, changes in human capital are unlikely to determine growth. Therefore, we consider the level of education in a region. Two types of education will be considered: First, we look at secondary educational attainment, in which respect Eastern European countries rank fairly high in country comparisons. Second, we look at higher educational attainment, which is average in these countries.

We consider several possibilities of how technological progress $\Delta \ln A$ is generated. In line with endogenous growth theory, innovation activity should be the primary source of technological progress. Furthermore, technological progress can happen by means of technological diffusion, which is clearly more important in developing and transition economies which do not yet possess a large R&D sector. FDI may therefore be a particularly important channel for technology diffusion.

As to the first source of technological progress (innovation), we measure R&D activity in the tradition of Romer (1990) as well as Aghion and Howitt (1992) in terms of the resources devoted to R&D, or R&D expenditures $R\&D_{exp}$. In line with the critique put forward by Jones (1995) that the absolute scale of R&D resources shows little correlation with technological advancement, and in light of recent suggestions of R&D activity indicators used in empirical research (Fagerberg et al. 1997; Bassanini et al. 2001), we use a relative indicator: $R\&D_{exp}/Y$ refers to expenditures in percent of GVA, as well as the number of employed persons in R&D activities relative to total employment $R\&D_{pers}/L$. Thus we can express the equation as follows:

(5.1) $\Delta \ln A = \delta_{11}(R\&D_{exp}/Y)$
(5.2) $\Delta \ln A = \delta_{12}(R\&D_{pers}/L)$

Note that according to the arguments on education presented above, higher education in particular should also be a direct variable for innovation capacity.

As to the second source of technological progress, technology diffusion, we start from Nelson and Phelps (1966) and Benhabib and Spiegel (2003) and consider the potential of technology diffusion to be a positive function of the technology gap in a region. The technology gap GAP is represented by the productivity gap of region i with respect to the EU average:

(6.1) $GAP_i = [(Y/L)_{EU} - (Y/L)_i]/(Y/L)$

meaning that

(6.2) $\Delta \ln A = \delta_{21} GAP$ and
(6.3) $\Delta \ln A = \delta_{22} GAP * h$

if we assume that the availability of human capital in the region is a precondition for technology diffusion, as suggested by Nelson and Phelps (1966) and specified by Benhabib and Spiegel (1994, 2003).

Finally, we postulate that the presence of foreign direct investment enables technology transfer, meaning that

(7.1) $\Delta \ln A = \varphi_1 FDI$
(7.2) $\Delta \ln A = \varphi_2 FDI*h$

where FDI refers to the stock of foreign direct investment as a share of regional GVA. Alternatively, technology transfer through FDI may be subject to the absorption capacity of the region, which may be determined by its human capital, as argued by Borenzstein et al. (1998) in the tradition of Nelson and Phelps (1966).

Finally, we include spatial aspects and new economic geography aspects in our model.

We assume that there are regional growth spillovers, which means that a region's growth is determined by the growth of its surrounding regions.

(8) $\Delta \ln y_t = \mathbf{W} \Delta \ln y_t$

where $\mathbf{W}$ is the $N \times N$ spatial weights matrix of the dimension equivalent to the number of regions N of our sample with elements w_{ij}, which describes the interaction between region i and region j. We choose a contiguity spatial weights matrix where $w_{ij} = 1$ if regions i and j have a common border and $w_{ij} = 0$ if they do not.[2] If growth spillovers can be verified, this indicates the existence of growth clusters.

The effect of access to market demand was tested by the following market access indicator (Schürmann and Talaat 2000):

(9) $ACCESS_i = \sum_{j=1}^{N} Y_j^{\psi} \cdot \exp(-\tau \cdot t_{ij})$

The market access of region i is determined by the market size (GDP) of all other regions j located either in the EU or in Eastern Europe, Y_j. t_{ij} is the time required for transport by lorry from region i to region j. The closer a region is to market demand, the higher its market access. ψ and τ are weighting parameters. Y_j thus indicates the market potential. t_{ij} is an impedance function. The weight of market potential (ψ) is usually assumed to be one, but it can be larger than one if agglomerations are assumed to be more attractive. The parameter τ indicates the importance of distant regions. If τ is large, distant regions are less important. If market access turns out to be important for growth, this would mean that there are tendencies of agglomeration in the sense of New Economic Geography models (Krugman 1991). Those Eastern regions with high market access to the EU are then considered potential parts of the European core.

In summary, we can specify the following variants of the model to be estimated:

(10)

$$\Delta \ln y = a + \Delta \ln A \qquad + \qquad \alpha\Delta\ln k + \beta\ln h + \gamma\Delta\ln PART + W\Delta\ln y + u_{it}$$

$$= a + \delta_{11}(R\&D_{exp}/Y) + \qquad\qquad K$$

$$= a + \delta_{12}(R\&D_{pers}/L) \qquad + \qquad K$$

$$= K \qquad\qquad + \delta_{21}GAP \quad + \qquad K$$

$$= K \qquad\qquad + \delta_{22}GAP^*h + \qquad K$$

$$= K \qquad\qquad + \phi_1 FDI \quad + \qquad K$$

$$= K \qquad\qquad + \phi_2 FDI^*h \ + \qquad K$$

$$= K \qquad\qquad + \quad K \quad + \qquad K \qquad + EUborder \qquad + u_{it}$$

$$= K \qquad\qquad + \quad K \quad + \qquad K \qquad + capital \qquad + u_{it}$$

$$= K \qquad\qquad + \quad K \quad + \qquad K \qquad + EU\text{--}ACCESS \ + u_{it}$$

3.4 DATA ISSUES AND A FIRST LOOK AT EMPIRICAL DEVELOPMENTS IN THE REGIONS

A unique dataset was created for this study: EAST RegStat, for which a substantial amount of data from national statistical offices were compiled and used along with data from Eurostat. The dataset covers 36 NUTS II level regions in Central and Eastern Europe, that is, regions in the Czech Republic, Slovakia, Hungary, Poland and Slovenia which is not divided into NUTS II regions in the Eurostat regional system. In general, the data collected cover the period from 1995 to 2000. For most indicators, Eurostat data were taken as the principal data source. Some missing values were taken from national statistics, if available, with due checks for the trend consistency of time series. For several indicators, however, national statistics were the main data source. In a number of series, data for one or two missing values had to be filled by extrapolation, with consistency being checked in various ways, for example by application of country level data to regions.

The following indicators are used in our analysis:[3]

   (i)   average annual real growth of GVA per capita, 1995-2000
   (ii) average gross fixed capital formation (all sectors), 1996-2000
   (iii) average annual change in the labour participation rate, 1995-2000
   (iv) average secondary and higher educational attainment, 1996-2000
         (percent of population which has completed secondary/higher
         education)
   (v)   average annual change in educational attainment rates, 1995-2000
   (vi) average level of FDI as a percentage of GVA, 1996-2000
   (vii) market access indicator, 1997.[4]

As in any empirical research on Eastern European economies, one needs
to account for the fact that the quality of the data in this study has certain
limitations. The reliability of employment data is certainly not very good,
since there is a large shadow economy in these countries. Furthermore, it may
be difficult to compare education data across countries because quality
standards differ. There are also weaknesses in the registration of citizens, so
that people may live and work in different locations than where they are
registered.

3.5 RESULTS OF THE ESTIMATION

In this section, we estimate a spatial lag model assuming a contiguity matrix
in order to model spatial dependencies.

From an econometric point of view, the model can be expressed as follows:

(11) $y = \rho_1 \mathbf{W} y + \mathbf{X} \beta + u_{it}$
      $u_{it} = \rho_2 \mathbf{W} u + \varepsilon_{it}$
      where $|\rho_1| < 1, \ |\rho_2| < 1$

and where y (N × 1) is the dependent, endogenous variable, $\mathbf{X}$ (N × K) is the
vector of K explanatory variables, and $\mathbf{W}$ is the contiguity N × N spatial
weights matrix containing spatial weights for all regions in the sample. ρ_1 and
ρ_2 are (scalar) spatial correlation parameters, and the vector β (K × 1)
contains the parameters of the explanatory variables. u_{it} is a non-spherical
disturbance term, while ε_{it} is assumed to be distributed NID (0, σ^2).

Since $\mathbf{W}y$ is endogenous, the OLS estimator is biased and inconsistent.
Spatial econometrics offers estimation procedures that address this problem.
We employ the feasible general spatial two stage least squares estimator
(FGS2SLS) developed by Kelejian and Prucha (1998), which is

computationally simpler than the ML estimator (Anselin 1988) and which is also considered to be an unbiased estimator. Its asymptotic properties are proven (Debabrata et al. 2003). Moreover, Kelejian and Prucha (1999) examined the small sample properties of the estimator in Monte Carlo simulations and found that the small sample bias is negligible.

The Kelejian and Prucha procedure involves two steps:

- In order to deal with the endogeneity problem of $\mathbf{W}y$, an instrumental variable estimator (2SLS) is applied. Starting from the reduced form of equation (11),

$$(12) \quad y = (I - \rho_1 W)^{-1} X\beta + (I - \rho_1 W)^{-1}(I - \rho_2 W)^{-1}\varepsilon$$

and given the conditional expectation in reduced form

$$(13) \quad E(Wy/X) = W(I - \rho_1 W)^{-1} X\beta = WX\beta + W^2 X(\rho_1\beta) + W^3 X(\rho_1^2\beta) + ...$$

X, WX and W^2X are used as instruments. The exogenous variable X (which is always an instrument) as well as its spatial lags are used as instruments for $\mathbf{W}y$.

- However, this IV estimation does not account for the spatial correlation in the error term $u \approx (0, \sigma^2\Omega), \Omega = (I - \rho_2 W)^{-1}(I - \rho_2 W')^{-1}$ and therefore leads to inefficient parameter estimates and biased estimates of standard errors. The solution is a feasible GLS estimation, which means running unweighted least squares on the transformed series $y^* = (I - \rho_2\mathbf{W})y$, $\mathbf{W}y^* = (I - \rho_2\mathbf{W})\mathbf{W}y$, and $\mathbf{X}^* = (I - \rho_2\mathbf{W})\mathbf{X}$; for the estimation of ρ_2, we use the GM estimator of Kelejian and Prucha (1999), which is based on the residuals u obtained in the first step. Once again, (the same) instruments are used for $\mathbf{W}y^*$.

Estimation is effected with an Eviews program developed in Badinger and Tondl (2003). As a test for spatial dependence, we use the standardized Moran's I statistic. We test for the form of spatial dependence (spatial error versus spatial lag model) with the LM_{ERR} and LM_{LAG} test statistics (see Anselin and Rey 1991; Anselin and Florax 1995; Anselin and Bera 1998).

It should be noted that the estimation constitutes a cross-section analysis. Since we regard a short time period, no other specification is reasonable.

Once the correct estimator is found for the spatial model, it is also important to account for possible simultaneity issues and multicollinearity between regressor variables. It is likely that simultaneity is encountered between the dependent variable and investment, and to a lesser degree between the dependent variable and the level of FDI.[5] To circumvent this problem, we use the initial values of these regressors instead of period averages, an approach used frequently in growth literature (Temple 1999; Levine and Zervos 1998). Furthermore, the estimated models need to account for the multicollinearity of regressors. From the correlation matrix[6] we see that there is high correlation between the capital city region status and investment, FDI, higher-level human capital and research. Taking initial values of investment and FDI also solves the endogeneity problem between these variables and the capital dummy variable, human capital and R&D. There is also the possibility of endogeneity between the participation rate and output, which we cannot treat properly. Therefore, the results must be interpreted with some caution.

Below we estimate a sequence of different specifications. In all specifications, however, we estimate a spatial lag model. Table 3.1 contains the results derived from a core model (Model 1), which includes as explanatory variables regional investment, changes in the participation rate and a spatial lag of growth measuring growth spillovers from neighbouring regions. As discussed above, the initial values of the investment variable are employed to alleviate the endogeneity problem. Only the spatial lag of growth turned out to be significant in this simple specification with a positive sign, and this result remains robust in all other specifications as well. The LM_{LAG} statistic suggests that the spatial lag model is the correct form for modelling spatial dependencies. This indicates that regional growth rates are highly influenced by those of neighbouring regions. The coefficient also remains fairly stable in all ensuing estimations. Almost one fifth of a region's growth is explained by growth in neighbouring regions, which should give rise to growth clusters.

Given the results of the basic model, we are first interested in the extent to which location factors can explain growth differences. As argued for example in Petrakos (1996), capital city areas and regions adjacent to EU regions have a location advantage due to better endowments, infrastructures or proximity to EU markets which should result in higher growth. In order to test this hypothesis, we use a dummy variable for capital city regions, for regions bordering the EU, and the accessibility variable. The capital city dummy variable turns out to be highly significant, confirming the impression given by the statistics in Section 3.2 that capital cities enjoyed substantially higher growth than other regions in the period under review. The correlation matrix of variables indicates that FDI, higher education and research are closely correlated with the capital city region status. These factors determine the high growth of capital city regions. Also capital city areas host more advanced sectors as shown in Smith (2003). As indicated by the insignificant coefficient of the EU border dummy variable, regions geographically close to EU areas surprisingly do not show higher growth. What is important, in contrast, is access to demand in EU markets as shown by the significantly positive coefficient of the access variable. Remember from Section 3.3 that market access is determined by the travel time to markets.[7] This indicates that Eastern European regions with a better infrastructure link to EU markets also have better growth prospects. The simple status as a region bordering the EU is not sufficient.

Table 3.1   Estimation results – basic model and location factors

	Dependent variable: Δy							
	Model 1		Model 2		Model 3		Model 4	
intercept	−0.598	(−0.29)	0.478	(0.28)	−0.869	(−0.44)	−0.067	(−0.04)
inv	0.048	(1.06)	−0.012	(−0.29)	0.036	(0.80)	0.045	(1.10)
$\Delta part$	0.246	(1.69)	0.139	(1.11)	0.283	(1.99)	0.273	(2.50)
						*		**
capital			3.474	(3.73)				
			***					
EU					0.882	(1.04)		
border								
access							0.031	(1.81)
							*	
DCZ							−3.946	(−4.06)
							***	
lag Δy	0.170	(2.39)	0.165	(2.94)	0.186	(2.78)	0.125	(2.10)
	***		***		***		**	
ρ_2	0.170		0.165		0.186		0.125	
$z(I)$	1.81		1.40		1.83		0.11	
LM_{ERR}	1.37		0.65		1.30		0.24	
LM_{LAG}	4.50		5.41		4.95		1.10	
	**		**		**			
adj. R^2	0.33		0.51		0.46		0.76	
no. obs.	36		36		36		36	

Notes:
Estimated using the general spatial two stage least squares procedure given in Kelejian and Prucha (1998), *t*-statistics in parentheses, $z(I)$ is the standardized *z*-value of Moran's *I*, LM_{ERR} is the Lagrange multiplier test for residual spatial autocorrelation, LM_{LAG} is the Lagrange multiplier test for endogenous spatial lag, *** significant at the 1% level, ** significant at the 5% level, * significant at the 10% level.

Note that a dummy variable for Czech regions is used in Model 4. We also tried dummy variables for other countries to account for country-specific effects such as national growth differences or national institutional characteristics. Only the Czech dummy variables turned out to be significant. We decided not to use country-specific dummy variables in further specifications since they dominate over spatial dependencies and thus introduce a bias into the otherwise appropriate spatial lag model.

Note that investment is never found to be a significant growth factor in the core model. The labour participation rate becomes significant only in some specifications, most notably in the one with the Czech dummy variable, which indicates that participation may be of some importance in regions outside of the Czech Republic. Lower participation rates may have been problematic under the perspective of increasing welfare in terms of per capita income. Low participation serves to limit income growth.

In Table 3.2, we present the results of estimations in which endogenous growth factors are included in the core model.

Table 3.2 Estimation results – model with the endogenous factors human capital and innovation

	Dependent variable: Δy					
	Model 5		Model 6		Model 7	
intercept	−0.235	(−0.08)	4.615	(1.37)	3.208	(0.98)
inv	−0.013	(−0.28)	0.063	(1.45)	0.031	(0.61)
$\Delta part$	0.084	(0.66)	0.100	(0.71)	0.141	(0.99)
hc_m	−0.044	(−0.80)	−0.148 **	(−2.14)	−0.090	(−1.40)
hc_h	0.504 ***	(3.56)				
R&D_exp			1.287 **	(2.44)		
R&D_ls					1.066 *	(2.02)
lag Δy	0.160 ***	(3.28)	0.188 ***	(3.21)	0.159 **	(2.69)
ρ_2	0.160		0.188		0.157	
$z(I)$	0.39		1.92		1.27	
LM_{ERR}	0.06		1.16		0.23	
LM_{LAG}	4.96 **		5.22 **		3.98 **	
adj. R^2	0.66		0.43		0.48	
no. obs.	36		36		36	

Notes:
Estimated using the general spatial two stage least squares procedure given in Kelejian and Prucha (1998), t-statistics in parentheses, $z(I)$ is the standardized z-value of Moran's I, LM_{ERR} is the Lagrange multiplier test for residual spatial autocorrelation, LM_{LAG} is the Lagrange multiplier test for endogenous spatial lag, *** significant at the 1% level, ** significant at the 5% level, * significant at the 10% level.

First we consider a specification with human capital – secondary and higher educational attainment – in addition to investment, labour participation and a spatial lag of growth. While the coefficient of higher education is highly significant in this and later estimations, that of secondary education is generally not. This suggests that only differences in higher education attainment rates can explain growth differences. Since higher education is correlated with further variables that will be tested subsequently (R&D, FDI), it will not be included in the ensuing estimates. Further estimates (not shown here) with higher-level human capital and additional non-correlated variables (EU border, Czech dummy variable) showed that the coefficient of higher education is very stable.

The insignificance of the coefficient of medium-level human capital, which – contrary to expectations – even becomes significantly negative in one estimation, may have something to do with a skill mismatch between educational standards and labour market requirements. As Boeri (2000) points out, qualifications in the East tend to be very narrowly specified and are often not transferable to new jobs. Similar puzzling evidence such as found in our estimation appeared in a study conducted by Campos and Kinoshita (2002), who investigated the growth impact of human capital (measured in terms of the average number of years of schooling in the population) and found that it was negative in the period from 1990 to 1998. They argue that human capital was artificially high in Eastern European countries and largely did not coincide with actual qualification standards, thus it may not be such an important variable in the growth process. Next, we aim to test the extent to which innovation activity was important for growth. Two indicators are used to measure innovation activity: R&D expenditures and the share of R&D personnel in the labour force. Both variables show a significantly positive coefficient, suggesting that innovating regions do, in fact, have better growth prospects. In all models with endogenous growth factors, the spatial lag of growth remains significant.

Table 3.3 shows the results of estimations with variables describing technology diffusion. First we tested whether the potential for technology diffusion given by the productivity gap is related to regional growth. A positive coefficient would indicate that regions with a high productivity gap benefit from technology diffusion and have higher growth rates. The results of the estimations confirm this hypothesis only if the gap is caused by a higher education level in the region. In such cases, the coefficient is significantly positive. Regions with a well-educated labour force are more likely to benefit from technology transfer. Alternatively, we include the regional FDI stock in our basic model, also including medium-level education but not higher education because of the high correlation between FDI and higher education. The results suggest that FDI has been a significant variable in growth promotion over the observed period. Note that in general investment includes private and public investment and may partly be financed by FDI. However, our FDI variable does not interfere with investment since we consider the level of FDI as a stock variable. While the spatial growth lag proves to be significant as well, none of the other variables are.

Table 3.3　Estimation results – model with technology diffusion (technology gap, FDI)

	Dependent variable: Δy							
	Model 8		Model 9		Model 10		Model 11	
intercept	1.153	(0.27)	−0.724	(−0.24)	−0.376	(−0.10)	0.871	(0.25)
inv	0.006	(0.12)	−0.004	(−0.06)	0.063	(1.40)	0.054	(1.21)
$\Delta part$	0.074	(0.56)	0.221 *	(1.74)	0.151	(1.07)	0.146	(1.06)
hc_m	−0.058	(−0.92)	−0.026	(−0.44)	-0.046	(−0.61)	−0.058	(−0.84)
hc_h	0.439 **	(2.55)						
GAP	−0.351	(−0.56)						
GAP*hc_h			0.153 **	(2.07)				
FDI					8.024 **	(2.24)		
FDI*hc_h							0.666 **	(2.47)
lag Δy	0.174 ***	(3.47)	0.161 ***	(3.17)	0.215 ***	(3.44)	0.204 ***	(3.47)
ρ_2	0.174		0.161		0.215		0.204	
z(I)	0.51		0.60		1.99		1.88	
LM_{ERR}	0.01		0.00		1.17		1.06	
LM_{LAG}	5.11 **		3.87 **		5.26 **		5.35 **	
adj. R^2	0.62		0.73		0.38		0.45	
no. obs.	36		36		36		36	

Notes:
Estimated using the general spatial two stage least squares procedure given in Kelejian and Prucha (1998), t-statistics in parentheses, z(I) is the standardized z-value of Moran's I, LM_{ERR} is the Lagrange multiplier test for residual spatial autocorrelation, LM_{LAG} is the Lagrange multiplier test for endogenous spatial lag, *** significant at the 1% level, ** significant at the 5% level, * significant at the 10% level.

In addition, the impact of FDI was tested as contingent on a region's absorption capacity, indicated by the extent of higher educational attainment. This interactive term (FDI*hc_h) is considered to measure the possible technology spillovers through FDI when contingent on the educational level in the region. We find that medium-level education is not an important factor to benefit from FDI, whereas higher education is a decisive factor. This interactive term (*FDI*hc_h*) turns out to be highly significant and a positive determinant of growth. The significance of other variables from the first specification remains unchanged.

In summary, we can draw the following conclusions:

(i)   Our estimations suggest that the strong inflow of foreign direct investment is an important determinant of high growth in Eastern European regions. Increased capital accumulation as such is far less important.

(ii)   In addition to a high level of FDI, human capital (specifically higher education) and innovation activity are the most important growth factors in Eastern European regions. Higher education is also a very important factor because it is a determinant of technology transfer and technology spillovers from FDI. Surprisingly, secondary education does not play an important role. There can even be a negative relationship between the share of secondary education and growth if the quality of education is inadequate.

(iii)   Moreover, there are significant spatial dependencies between closely located regions, meaning that a region's growth is significantly more likely to be higher if the region is close to other high-growth regions. About one fifth of a region's growth is determined by that of the surrounding regions. This indicates a tendency toward growth clusters in Eastern Europe.

(iv)   Capital city areas are best endowed in terms of essential growth factors (FDI, human capital, R&D), which explains their outstanding growth performance. Growth of capital city regions is likely to be self-reinforcing (see Fazekas 2000) resulting in increasing national disparities.

(v)   There is little evidence that differences in the labour participation rate play a significant role in growth. Other factors are far more important.

(vi)   Access to EU markets has become important for growth.

(vii)   Regions in Eastern Europe surrounded by low-growth regions with a low stock of FDI, a low level of higher education, no R&D and poor infrastructure links with EU markets had no chance to catch up in terms of income levels in the period from 1995 to 2000.

3.6 CONCLUSIONS

This chapter has attempted to shed some light on the determinants of regional growth in Eastern Europe in the latter half of the 1990s, a period when transformation was largely completed and the process of catching up with the EU varied considerably across different Eastern European regions.

We based our hypotheses on growth factors in an economic growth model and argued that the high capital accumulation and high education level in Eastern Europe might have been important for growth in dynamic regions. Furthermore, we expected that technology transfer, in particular through FDI, might have played an important role. In addition, we supposed that location factors and spatial dependencies mattered for growth.

We carried out our empirical analysis with a sample of 36 NUTS II level regions from the Czech Republic, Slovakia, Hungary, Poland and Slovenia for the period from 1995 to 2000. In order to take likely spatial dependencies into account, we set up our growth regressions in a spatial econometric framework. It turned out that a spatial lag model in which per capita income growth is also dependent on the growth of surrounding regions was the most appropriate for our objectives. For the purpose of estimation, we used the general spatial two stage least squares procedure suggested by Kelejian and Prucha (1998), a two-stage instrumental variable estimator which is considered to be an unbiased estimator for the spatial context with established asymptotic properties.

Our results partly prove the proposed hypotheses and partly reveal new, surprising aspects.

First, we find that Eastern European capital city areas clearly enjoy agglomeration advantages and have better resources in all respects (human capital, FDI, research), which makes them growth leaders. Second, foreign direct investment in particular – and not capital accumulation as such – was the main driving factor behind regional growth in Eastern Europe. Third, human capital, specifically higher education, is the second most important growth factor in Eastern European regions after FDI. Fourth, regions with a high R&D rate are leaders in terms of growth. Fifth, we can observe a regional clustering of growth, as regions surrounded by high-growth areas showed high-growth performance themselves. However, as our experiments with spatial weighting matrices have shown, spatial effects are still rather limited geographically, which is probably evidence of insufficient transport infrastructure. We also found that access to EU markets matters for growth in Eastern European regions, indicating that peripheral regions with poor infrastructure links have worse growth prospects. Sixth, we find no clear evidence that labour market participation rates and attainment rates in secondary education play a significant role in the growth of Eastern regions. A high secondary education attainment rate may even be an impediment to growth if qualification standards do not match the requested profiles.

Evidently, endogenous growth factors such as innovation activity and human capital are important factors in regional growth. In this regard,

Eastern European regions and EU regions rely on similar growth factors However, technology transfer is also a main source of productivity growth in Eastern European regions. Testing the technology gap model with human capital as a conditioning factor, we find that this was a highly relevant means of technology transfer. Above all, however, FDI has to be considered a main channel of technology spillovers, especially if combined with human capital from higher education.

We should expect the regional disparities between Eastern European regions to remain, specifically due to the ongoing basis for growth in capital city areas, the restriction of spatial interactions between neighbouring regions, and the peripheral characteristics of many regions. The task of both national and EU regional policymakers will be the development of transport infrastructure to overcome location disadvantages. Upgrading human capital, improving both medium-level and higher education, and promoting innovation activity will be prerequisites for regions outside of agglomerations to improve their growth prospects. Education will also be key to attracting foreign direct investment, which will remain crucial for growth. National and EU regional policy should consider the fact that human resources and innovation are highly important factors in establishing endogenously driven, high-quality growth. Finally, policymakers must consider the fact that FDI is the most regional prominent factor in catching up. Policies that would discourage FDI would endanger regional growth.

APPENDIX

EAST RegStat Data and Definitions

36 NUTS II level regions from Czech Republic, Slovakia, Hungary, Poland, Slovenia; time period: 1995-2000

	Definition	Source
Gross Value Added	Nominal and real GVA in euro, at 1995 prices and 1995 exchange rates.	1995-1999 Eurostat. 2000 GUS, SURS, CSU, KSH and Infostat.
Population	Total population.	CZ, HU, SI: 1995-1999 Eurostat, 2000 extrapolation. PL: 1995, 1998-1999 Eurostat, 1996 and 2000 GUS. SK: 1996-1999 Eurostat, 1995, 2000 Infostat.
Employment	Total employment. Number of persons employed.	CZ and HU: Eurostat. PL: GUS. SI: SURS. SK: 1997-2000 Infostat, 1995-1996 extrapolation based on GDP trend.

R&D expenditures	Total expenditures for research and development in business sector, government sector and higher education sector.	CZ: 1995-1997 Eurostat, 1998-2000 extrapolation. HU: KSH. PL: GUS. SI: EUROSTAT. SK: 1995-1997 Eurostat, 1998-2000 INFOSTAT.
R&D employment	Total employment in research and development in business sector, government sector and higher education sector.	CZ: 1995-1997 Eurostat, 1998-2000 extrapolation. HU: KSH. PL: GUS. SI: Eurostat. SK: 1995-1997 Eurostat, 1998-2000 Infostat.
Gross Fixed Capital Formation	Gross fixed capital formation in euro, at 1995 prices and 1995 exchange rates.	CZ: 1995-1999 Eurostat, 2000 allocation of country investment. HU: KSH. PL: 1998-1999 Eurostat, 1995-1997 and 2000 extrapolation, allocation of country investment. SI: SURS. SK: 1995-1999 Eurostat, 2000 from country data.
Foreign Direct Investment	Stock of foreign direct investment in euro, at 1995 prices and 1995 exchange rates.	CZ: 1998-2000 CNB, 1995-1997 extrapolation based on allocation of country FDI stock. HU: calculated using regional data from KSH and allocation of country FDI stock. PL: calculated, based on regional FDI flows and allocation of country FDI stock. SI: WIIW. SK: 1996-2000 NBS, 1995 calculated from country FDI stock.
Education	Educational attainment. Number of persons who have completed secondary and higher education. Secondary education includes ISCED-97 Sectors 3 and 4. Entrance is at age 15-16 after compulsory schooling. It comprises general education in preparation for university entrance, vocational schools as well as upper secondary-level apprenticeship programmes under the dual system in Germany. Higher education corresponds to ISCED-97 Sectors 5 and 6. Sector 5 includes short degree programmes such as bachelor's (UK), Fachhochschule (D) and laurea breve (I), but also longer higher education programmes such as	Eurostat Labour Force Survey for CZ: 1998-2000, HU: 1997-2000, PL: 1998-2000, SI: 1996-2000, SK: 1999-2000. Other years extrapolation.

	Diplom (D) and master's (UK) programmes. Education in Section 6 awards an advanced research qualification, such as PhD programmes and doctoral studies. (See OECD, *Education at a Glance 2002*, Paris, OECD)	
Market access	Market access indicator: The *market size* and the *distance* of the destination region are taken into account. Market size is represented by regional population or GDP. Distance corresponds to travel time between two regions by different modes of transport.	Institute for Spatial Planning (IRPUD), University of Dortmund. For details see: Schürmann and Talaat (2000).

Notes:
CZ – Czech Republic, HU – Hungary, PL – Poland, SI – Slovenia, SK – Slovak Republic.
Data sources:
CNB – Czech National Bank, CSU – Czech Statistical Office, Eurostat – Statistical Office of the EC, GUS – Polish Official Statistics, Infostat – Institute of Informatics and Statistics Slovakia, KSH – Hungarian Central Statistical Office, NBS – National Bank of Slovakia, SURS – Statistical Office of the Republic of Slovenia, WIIW – Vienna Institute for International Economic Studies.

List of Variables Used in Estimations

Δy	average growth in real GVA per capita, 1995-2000, in percent
lag Δy	spatial lag of growth in real GVA per capita
$\Delta part$	average growth in participation rate (employment/population), 1995-2000, in percent
inv	initial value of investment rate (investment/GVA), 1995, in percent
RD_e	R&D expenditures in percent of GVA, 1996-2000 average
RD_ls	R&D employment in percent of total employment, 1996-2000 average
hc_m	percent of population (all ages) with secondary educational attainment in total population, 1996-2000 average
hc_h	percent of population (all ages) with higher educational attainment in total population, 1996-2000 average
GAP	productivity gap in relation to EU average in 1995. $GAP_i = (\text{productivity}_{EU} - \text{productivity}_i)/\text{productivity}_i$, whereby i indicates the region
GAP*hc_h	interaction term GAP and higher level educational attainment
GAP*hc_m	interaction term GAP and secondary level educational attainment

FDI_s   initial value of stock of FDI in percent of GVA, 1995
FDI_s*hc_m   interaction term FDI and secondary educational attainment rate
FDI_s*hc_h   interaction term FDI and higher education
ACCESS   indicator of market access to EU regions using GDP as
                 measure for market size, ranges from 0-100, where 100 = best
                 access.
EU border   Dummy variable for regions located at the border with the EU.
capital   Dummy variable for capital city regions.
DCZ   Dummy variable for Czech regions.

NOTES

*   Research for this paper was conducted under the auspices of the OeNB Anniversary Fund,
     Project No. 8869, 'EU integration and regional development: Prospects for Eastern Europe'
     financed by the Austrian central bank (Oesterreichische Nationalbank).
1.   There are, however, some studies which address the issue of regional specialization and
     employment dynamics in Eastern European countries, e.g. Resmini (2002), Traistaru and
     Wolff (2002), Traistaru et al. (2002) and Smith (2003).
2.   As an alternative to the contiguity matrix, we used two weights matrix specifications where
     the influence of other regions' growth declined with increasing distance. One took the form
     $w_{ij} = d_{ij}^{-\delta}$, where d_{ij} denotes the distance between the centres of two regions and δ is the
     distance decay parameter, which can be varied (see also Fingleton 2001; Badinger and
     Tondl 2003). Another took the form $w_{ij} = \exp(-\delta\, d_{ij})$, where again various values were tried
     for δ. In both cases, a high value had to be taken for δ in order to obtain a correctly specified
     spatial econometric model. This indicates that spatial dependencies diminish very quickly
     between Eastern European regions. Therefore, we selected a contiguity matrix as a spatial
     weights matrix.
3.   Precise data definitions and sources are given in the Appendix. Note that we calculated the
     average growth rate by regressing annual logs of GVA on a constant trend over time rather
     than computing growth from GVA from the beginning and end of the period. This should
     yield growth rates which are less influenced by short-term instability, as explained in
     Temple (1999). Growth rates for other indicators are calculated in the same fashion.
4.   We thank Carsten Schürmann, Ahmed Talaat and Michael Wegener for kindly granting
     permission to use their access indicator statistics.
5.   With FDI the likelihood of simultaneity is less severe than suggested, for example, in
     Fazekas (2000), because we use FDI stock and not flow data. In addition, this potential
     problem may be less serious than with the variable investment. A large part of FDI inflows
     motivated by higher growth rates are market-seeking investments which either represent
     'tariff jumping' or seek proximity to markets due to high transportation costs. However,
     these potential trade obstacles (i.e. motives for investment) are not so strong at the regional
     level if regions are relatively small, which is the case in our study. It may not be necessary
     to invest directly in the fastest-growing region in order to gain easy access to its market, that
     is, it may be enough to produce in any region within the national borders (in the case of
     administrative trade barriers) or – if transport costs are high – in the neighbouring region.
6.   The correlation matrix can be made available on request.
7.   Several combinations of weighting parameters were tested for the EU ACCESS variable.
     The parameter ψ for market size was assigned the values 0.5, 1 and 2. A value of 0.5
     indicates no particular attractiveness in agglomerations, whereas with $\psi = 2$ agglomerations
     are more attractive than other regions. The weighting parameter for transport time, τ, takes
     the values 0.01, 0.003 and 0.001, and the impact of distant regions decreases as τ increases.

REFERENCES

Abramowitz, M. (1986), 'Catching-up, forging ahead or falling behind', *Journal of Economic History*, **46**, pp. 385-406.

Aghion, P. and Howitt, P. (1992), 'A model of growth through creative destruction', *Econometrica*, **60**, pp. 323-351.

Altomonte, C. and L. Resmini (2001), *Multinational Corporations as Catalyst for Industrial Development: The Case of Poland*, William Davidson Institute Working Paper 368.

Anselin, L. (1988), *Spatial econometrics: Methods and models*, Dordrecht: Kluwer.

Anselin L. and A.K. Bera (1998), 'Spatial dependence in linear regression models with an introduction to spatial econometrics', in D. Giles and A. Ullaah (eds) *Handbook of applied economic statistics*, New York: Dekker, pp. 237-289.

Anselin, L. and J.G.M. Florax (1995), *New directions in spatial econometrics*, Berlin et al.: Springer.

Anselin, L. and Rey S. (1991), 'Properties of tests for spatial dependence in linear regression models', *Geographic Analysis*, **23**, pp. 112-131.

Badinger, H. and G. Tondl (2003), 'Trade, human capital and innovation. The engines of European regional growth in the 1990s', in B. Fingleton (ed.), *European regional growth*, Series: Advances in Spatial Science, Heidelberg: Springer, pp. 215-240.

Baldwin, R., H. Braconier and R. Forslid (1999), *Multinationals, endogenous growth and technology spillovers: Theory and evidence*, CEPR Discussion Paper 2155, London.

Barlow, D. and R. Radulescu (2002), 'The relationship between policies and growth in transition countries', *Economics of Transition*, **10** (3), pp. 719-745.

Bassanini, A., S. Scarpetta and P. Hemmings (2001), *Economic Growth: The role of policies and institutions. Panel data evidence from OECD countries*, OECD Economics Department Working Paper 283, Paris: OECD.

Benhabib, J. and M.M. Spiegel (1994), 'The role of human capital in economic development: Evidence from aggregate cross-country data', *Journal of Monetary Economics*, **34** (2), pp. 143-173.

Benhabib, J. and M.M. Spiegel (2003), *Human capital and technology diffusion*, Working Paper No. 2003/02, Federal Reserve Bank, San Francisco.

Blomström, M. and A. Kokko (1998), 'Multinational Corporations and Spillovers', *Journal of Economic Surveys*, **12** (3), pp. 247-277.

Boeri, T. (2000), *Structural change, welfare systems, and labour reallocation: Lessons from the transition of formerly planned economies*, New York and Oxford: Oxford University Press.

Borensztein, E., J. De Gregorio and J.W. Lee (1998), 'How does foreign direct investment affect economic growth?', *Journal of International Economics*, **45** (1), pp. 115-135.

Burda, M.C. (1998), *The Consequences of EU Enlargement for Central and Eastern European Labour Markets*, CEPR Discussion Paper 1881, London.

Campos, N.F. and F. Coricelli (2002), 'Growth in Transition: What We Know, What We Don't and What We Should', *Journal of Economic Literature*, **40** (3), pp. 793-836.

Campos, N.F. and Y. Kinoshita (2002), *Foreign Direct Investment as Technology Transferred: Some Panel Evidence from the Transition Economies*, William Davidson Institute Working Paper 438.

Cheshire, P. and S. Magrini (2000), 'Endogenous processes in European regional growth: convergence and policy', *Growth and Change*, **31** (4), pp. 455-479.

Debabrata, D., H. Kelejian and I. Prucha (2003), 'Finite sample properties of estimators of spatial autoregressive models with autoregressive disturbances', *Papers in Regional Science*, **82** (1), pp. 1-26.

de la Fuente, A. (1995), *Catch-up, Growth and Convergence in the OECD*, CEPR Discussion Paper 1274, London.

de la Fuente, A. and R. Doménech (2000), *Human Capital in Growth Regressions: How much difference does data quality make?*, CEPR Discussion Paper 2466, London.

Djankov, S. and B.M. Hoekman. (2000), 'Foreign investment and productivity growth in Czech enterprises', *World Bank Economic Review*, **14** (1), pp. 49-64.

Dobrinsky, R. (2001), *Convergence in per capita income levels, productivity dynamics and real exchange rates in the candidate countries on the way to EU accession*, Interim Report No. IR-01-038, IIASA – International Institute for Applied Systems Analysis, Laxenburg.

Easterly, W. and R. Levine (2001), 'It's not factor accumulation: Stylized facts and growth models', *World Bank Economic Review*, **15** (2), pp. 177-219.

Eurostat (2000), 'Educating young Europeans. Similarities and differences between the EU member states and the Phare countries', *Statistics in focus*, theme 3 – 14/2000.

Fagerberg, J. and B. Verspagen (1996), 'Heading for divergence? Regional growth in Europe reconsidered', *Journal of Common Market Studies*, **34** (3), pp. 431-448.

Fagerberg, J., B. Verspagen and M. Caniels (1997), 'Technology, growth and unemployment across European regions', *Regional Studies*, **31** (5), pp. 457-466.

Falcetti, E., M. Raiser and P. Sanfey (2002), 'Defying the odds: Initial conditions, reforms, and growth in the first decade of transition', *Journal of Comparative Economics*, **30** (2), pp. 229-250.

Fazekas, K. (2000), *The Impact of Foreign Direct Investment on Regional Labour Markets in Hungary*, Budapest Working Paper on the Labour Market, Hungarian Academy of Sciences, Budapest.

Fidrmuc, J. (2000), *Liberalization, Democracy and Economic Performance during Transition*, ZEI Economic Policy Papers B05-2000, Bonn: Centre for European Integration Studies.

Fingleton, B. (2001), 'Theoretical economic geography and spatial econometrics: dynamic perspectives', *Journal of Economic Geography*, **1**, pp. 201-225.

Fischer, S., R. Sahay and C.A. Vegh (1998), *How Far is Eastern Europe from Brussels?*, IMF Working Paper No. 98/53, Washington: International Monetary Fund.

Fosfuri, A., M. Motta and T. Ronde (2001), 'Foreign direct investment and spillovers through workers' mobility', *Journal of International Economics*, **53** (1), pp. 205-222.

Funke, M. and A. Niebuhr (2001), *Spatial R&D Spillovers and Economic Growth – Evidence from West Germany*, HWWA Discussion Paper 98, Hamburg, Hamburgisches Weltwirtschafts-Archiv.

Gallup, J.L., J.D. Sachs and A.D. Mellinger (1998), *Geography and Economic Development*, NBER Working Paper 6849, Cambridge, MA: National Bureau of Economic Research.

Havrylyshyn, O. and R. van Rooden (2000), *Institutions Matter in Transition, but so do Policies*, IMF Policy Working Paper 00/70, Washington: International Monetary Fund.

Hernández-Catá, E. (1997), *Liberalization and the Behavior of Output During the Transition from Plan to Market*, IMF Working Paper 97/53, Washington: International Monetary Fund.

Hunya, G. (2002), *Recent Impacts of Foreign Direct Investment on Growth and Restructuring in Central European Transition Countries*, WIIW Research Report 284, Vienna: WIIW.

Jones, C.I. (1995), 'R&D-based models of economic growth', *Journal of Political Economy*, **103** (4), pp. 759-784.

Kelejian, H. and I. Prucha (1998), 'A generalized two-stage least squares procedure for estimating a spatial autoregressive model with autoregressive disturbances', *Journal of Real State Finance and Economics*, **17**, pp. 99-121.

Kelejian H. and I. Prucha (1999), 'A generalized moments estimator for the autoregressive parameter in a spatial model', *International Economic Review*, **40** (2), pp. 509-533

Kinoshita, Y. (2000), *R&D and Technology Spillovers via FDI: Innovation and Absorptive Capacity*, William Davidson Institute Working Paper 349.

Klazar, S., M. Sedmihradsky and A. Vancurova (2001), 'Returns of education in the Czech Republic', *International Tax and Public Finance*, **8** (4), pp. 609-620.

Kosfeld, R., H.F. Eckey and C. Dreger (2002), 'Regional convergence in unified Germany: A spatial econometric perspective', *Volkswirtschaftliche Diskussionsbeiträge* 41/02, Universität Kassel.

Krugman, P. (1991), 'Increasing returns and economic geography', *Journal of Political Economy*, **99** (3), pp. 483-499.

Levine, R. and S. Zervos (1998), 'Stock markets, banks and economic growth', *American Economic Review*, **88** (3), pp. 537-558.

Lucas, R.E. (1988), 'On the mechanics of economic development', *Journal of Monetary Economics*, **22** (1), pp. 3-42.

Mankiw, G., D. Romer and D. Weil (1992), 'A contribution to the empirics of economic growth', *Quarterly Journal of Economics*, **107**, pp. 407-437.

Markusen, J.R. and A.J. Venables (1999), 'Foreign direct investment as a catalyst for industrial development', *European Economic Review*, **43** (2), pp. 335-356.

Nelson R.R. and E.S. Phelps (1966), 'Investment in humans, technological diffusion, and economic growth', *American Economic Review*, **56** (2), pp. 69-75.

Niebuhr, A. (2001), 'Convergence and the effects of spatial interaction', *Jahrbuch für Regionalwissenschaft*, **21**, pp. 113-133.

Paci, R. and S. Usai (2000), 'Externalities, knowledge spillovers and the spatial distribution of innovation', *GeoJournal*, 49 (4), pp. 381-390.

Paci, R. and F. Pigliaru (2001), *Technological Diffusion, Spatial Spillovers and Regional Convergence in Europe*, CRENoS Working Paper 01/01, University of Cagliari.

Paci, R., F. Pigliaru and M. Pugno (2001), *Disparities in Economic Growth And Unemployment Across The European Regions: A Sectoral Perspective*, CRENoS Working Paper 01/3, University of Cagliari.

Petrakos, G.C. (1996), 'The regional dimension of transition in Central and Eastern European Countries', *Eastern European Economics*, **34** (5), pp. 5-38.

Pritchett, L. (1996), *Where Has All the Education Gone?*, World Bank Working Papers 1581.

Resmini, L. (2000), 'The determinants of foreign direct investment in the CEECs: New evidence from sectoral patterns', *Economics of Transition*, **8** (3), pp. 665-689.

Resmini, L. (2002), *Specialization and Growth Patterns in Border Regions of Accession Countries*, ZEI Working Paper B17-2002, Bonn: Centre for European Integration studies.

Rey, S. and B. Montouri (1999), 'US regional income convergence: A spatial econometric perspective', *Regional Studies*, **33** (2), pp. 145-156.

Romer, P. (1990), 'Endogenous technological change', *Journal of Political Economy*, **98** (5), pp. 71-102.

Sachs, J.D. and A. Warner (1995), *Economic Convergence and Economic Policies*, NBER Working Paper 5039, Cambridge, MA: National Bureau of Economic Research.

Sala-i-Martin, X. (1997), 'I just ran two million regressions', *American Economic Review*, **87** (2), pp. 178-183.

Schürmann, C. and A. Talaat (2000), *Towards a European Peripherality Index. Final Report*, Report for General Directorate XVI Regional Policy of the European Commission, Dortmund: IRPUD.

Smith, A. (2003), 'Territorial inequality, regional productivity, and industrial change in Postcommunism: Regional transformations in Slovakia', *Environment and Planning*, **35** (6), pp. 1111-1135.

Temple, J. (1999), 'The new growth evidence', *Journal of Economic Literature*, **37** (1), pp. 112-156.

Tondl, G. (2001), *Convergence After Divergence? Regional Growth in Europe*, Springer, Wien, Heidelberg, New York: Springer.

Traistaru, I. and G.B. Wolff (2002), *Regional Specialization and Employment Dynamics in Transition Countries*, ZEI Working Paper B18-2002, Bonn: Centre for European Integration Studies.

Traistaru, I., P. Nijkamp and S. Longhi (2002), *Regional Specialization and Concentration of Industrial Activity in Accession Countries*, ZEI Working Paper B16-2002, Bonn: Centre for European Integration Studies.

Vanhoudt, P., T. Matha and B. Smid (2000), 'How productive are capital investments in Europe?', *EIB Papers*, 5 (2), pp. 81-106.

WIIW (2002), *Countries in Transition 2002*, WIIW Handbook of Statistics, Vienna: WIIW.

PART THREE

Localisation of Economic Activities:
The Role of Technology Spillovers,
Clusters and Fiscal Policy

4. Asymmetric Economic Integration in a Two-Region Model and the Effects on Unemployment and Growth

Pascal Hetze

4.1 INTRODUCTION

The enlargement of a regional integration bloc (NAFTA, EU, and others) is supposed to stimulate growth and wealth in both the old and new member states. However, the assimilation of some East-European countries into the EU and Mexico into NAFTA increases the economic differences within the integration blocs. In particular, there will be more diversity with respect to skill endowments in the labor force and in the output of research and development (R&D), even if the partner countries agree on equal steps in economic integration (maybe with the exception of labor mobility). However, it is not clear whether the symmetric removal of trade barriers produces the best results for both partners if the old and new members differ in their economic and technological structure. This chapter investigates possible effects of structural adjustments arising from integration on unemployment and innovation. It can be shown that asymmetric integration with one-way openness to foreign R&D products is preferred under the assumption of skill shortages in one country.

The main argument for economic integration is that it opens up productivity potentials through efficient resource reallocation or technology spillovers. Models of growth through innovation in the tradition of Rivera-Batiz and Romer (1991) show that free technology exchange between the economies leads to high rates of economic growth as integrated economies enlarge the scope of available R&D products.[1] Driving forces behind the productivity and technology effects of integration can be spatially confined knowledge spillovers, as described in Jaffe et al. (1993) and Audretsch and Feldman (1996). The positive effect of openness on innovation and productivity growth is supported by various empirical studies. For example, Keller (2002) concludes that R&D conducted in neighboring countries contributes up to 20 percent of productivity increases in domestic industries.

Holod and Reed (2004) show that regional cooperation rather than global integration leads to gains from increased economic openness.[2]

However, the effects of economic integration on technological change and growth are mixed if we consider economies with structural differences. Economic integration may enlarge these differences due to its impact on resource reallocation. Depending on initial resource endowments, one country might specialize in highly productive activities while the other ends up with less productive industries. This implies lower growth prospects for the relatively poorer economy (Grossman and Helpman, 1990; Rivera-Batiz and Xie, 1993; and Feenstra, 1996). Other negative consequences of economic integration can arise in the labor market. Economic integration with skill-biased effects may result in wage inequality (Bretschger, 1997), unemployment (Davis, 1998), or both (Şener, 2001).

The objective of this chapter is to investigate the effects of regional technology exchange on economic growth and unemployment. The novelty in the approach is the consideration of the employment effects of regional technology on jobs. We construct a two-sector, two-country model, in which growth is driven by R&D at home and abroad, where technological change has effects on the level of unemployment via labor reallocation.[3] Economic integration tends to stimulate technological change and structural adjustments in more integrated economies. As a consequence, the extent of labor reallocation increases. Unemployment then results from economic integration due to frictions in the process of labor reallocation. The shortage of skilled labor may be one source of such frictions.

The main results of this chapter are that the enlargement of an integration bloc and the resulting regional technology trade leads to more job destruction and an increasing availability of technologies. However, in contrast to the standard approach it is unclear whether the combined R&D output increases or decreases. Finally, growth can be higher or lower after integration. Furthermore, integration can be biased towards R&D for one country and towards manufacturing for the other country. In this case, the benefits and costs of integration are unequally distributed among the two economies. While at least one country is better off after integration as long as skilled labor is abundant, more regional technology trade can have negative effects on both economies in the case of skill shortages. However, in such cases, economies can agree on asymmetric economic integration in order to realize more gains from technological exchange.[4]

The chapter is organized as follows. Section 4.2 introduces the model with endogenous technological innovation and explains how it is related to job destruction, job creation and equilibrium unemployment. In section 4.3, we present the effects of economic integration under the assumption of regional technology trade. Finally, section 4.4 concludes the chapter.

4.2 THE MODEL

The model considers the joint formation of technologies and skills and analyzes how this affects the matching of labor demand and supply under an assumption of technology-skill complementarity and technology spillovers between two neighboring countries. From this we derive how economic integration affects growth and employment. We construct a two-country, two-sector model with manufacturing and R&D. Growth is driven by domestic and foreign technological innovations and may be restricted by skill shortages. Unemployment occurs as a symptom of this growth restriction. According to the two-country analysis, we identify variables for country $j \in [h,f]$, where h denotes the home country and f the foreign one. To keep the exposition simple, we refer to the home country if no subscript occurs.

We consider economies populated by a mass L_j of infinitely long-lived individuals. The individuals are endowed with one unit of labor which they supply inelastically. Accordingly, L_j equals the total labor supply in country j. Labor is employed in either manufacturing or R&D, or remains unemployed. Labor allocation depends on relative income opportunities and the employment level is subject to frictions in labor reallocation. The degree of economic integration has effects on both labor allocation and the level of employment.

The subsequent analysis involves two stages. First, we develop the equilibrium labor allocation between R&D and manufacturing, in a growth framework which follows the literature on growth via endogenous technological progress based on Aghion and Howitt (1992). Then, we introduce the reallocation of labor with endogenous job creation and job destruction, and demonstrate how skill shortages change equilibrium labor allocation and thus influence the level of unemployment.

4.2.1 Technological Progress

Technological progress is the only source of equilibrium growth. At any time t, R&D in both countries forms new technologies and shifts the national technology frontier $0, \tau_{j,t}^{\max}$. As soon as a research unit develops an innovation this adds a new technology τ to the current number of available technologies in the interval $[0, \tau_{j,t}^{\max}]$. Hence, the span of production possibilities increases over time. By each innovation the productivity level A_τ of the corresponding technology increases by λ:

(1) $A_\tau = \lambda A_{\tau-1}$

Technological progress spreads out the productivity gains of innovations within a country and across the borders. However, institutional and technological barriers, such as tariffs and different technological standards, or geographical distance may prevent innovations from a full diffusion abroad. Let $\sigma_{j,j}$ denote the degree of technology exchange, where $\sigma_{h,h} = \sigma_{f,f} = 1$ and $0 \leq \sigma_{h,f}$, $\sigma_{f,h} \leq 1$. While the access to domestic technologies at home is unrestricted, diffusion barriers restrict the flows across borders and partly exclude one country from the use of innovations developed abroad. Hence, $\sigma_{h,f}$ measures the share of foreign innovative technologies which are available at home (and $\sigma_{f,h}$ for the other way around). The range of full variation is between the closed economy case, $\sigma_{h,f}$, $\sigma_{f,h} = 0$ and the fully integrated economy, $\sigma_{h,f}$, $\sigma_{f,h} = 1$.

The total number of domestic and foreign R&D units is $L_{R,h} + L_{R,f}$. Each unit has a Poisson-distributed arrival rate ε_j of being the next innovator. We allow for structural differences between the two R&D sectors, which means that $\varepsilon_h \leq \varepsilon_f$. A high ε_j may stand for a high educational level in the j R&D sector or high capital endowments of the j research units. The total number of R&D units together with their research productivity and the degree of openness yields the result that the productivity of the technology frontier increases by $\lambda^{\varepsilon_h \cdot L \cdot R, h + \sigma_{h,f} \varepsilon_f L \cdot R, f}$ per time unit. Consequently, the maximum productivity level evolves according to:[5]

$$(2) \quad g_{A_h} = \ln(\lambda) \sum_{j=h,f} \sigma_{h,j} \varepsilon_j L_{R,j}.$$

Technological progress is endogenous, because the size of the R&D sector in terms of sector employment, $L_{R,j}$, is the result of labor allocation between R&D and manufacturing. How many workers are employed in each sector depends on their relative income opportunities in manufacturing and R&D. Foreign demand and competition from abroad also affect the employment levels in each country.

4.2.2 The Final Good Production

There exist different firms in manufacturing. Each one has its own productivity level based on their technological vintage, but all produce the same final good Y. Hence, τ defines a certain technology used by a manufacturing firm. Technological progress implies that manufacturing firms differ in productivity levels. Relative productivity is given by $a_\tau = A_\tau / A_{\tau^{max}}$, which equals unity in τ_t^{max} and falls between zero and one in all other vintages. A new firm in manufacturing appears whenever there is a new technology available. The new firm chooses the current τ_t^{max} but no updating is possible afterwards. This implies a relative productivity loss in subsequent periods, as newer embodied technologies appear, such that the specific a_τ declines as further technological innovation provides a higher productivity level to newer manufacturing firms. We also assume that there is a maximum divergence from the current maximum productivity $A_{t^{max}}$ which characterizes a minimum sustainable relative productivity $a_{t^{min}}$. Consequently, the gradual increase in $A_{t^{max}}$ as a result of technological progress leads to the technological obsolescence of vintages below τ_t^{min}. This means that although there is a wider range of available technologies, only those surpassing the minimum productivity level are actually used. While the range of vintages is fixed to $[\tau_t^{min}, \tau_t^{max}]$, each vintage starts with τ^{max} and ends with τ^{min} some periods later. In this model, the manufacturing sector undergoes a continuous structural change with the progressive emergence and disappearance of different technological vintages.

It takes two steps for a manufacturing firm to produce its output Y_τ. First, it has to employ labor to transform basic inputs into an intermediate good to be used for production. We assume for simplicity that this transformation has a simple linear technology, in which one worker transforms a fraction $1/\gamma$ of one unit of the intermediate good x_τ. Hence, given the optimal number of intermediates, labor demand is:

(3) $L_{M,\tau} = x_\tau \gamma$

In the second step, the final good is formed from the intermediate goods at a decreasing rate of return α and at the productivity level A_τ. This transformation produces some overhead costs δ_τ, with $\delta_\tau = \delta A_\tau$. The vintage production function therefore yields:

(4) $Y_\tau = A_\tau x_\tau^\alpha - \delta_\tau$.

However, only vintages which fulfil $A_\tau \geq a_{t^{min}} A_{t^{max}}$ contribute to the production of total output $Y_t = \sum_{\tau^{min}}^{\tau^{max}} Y_\tau$ as they have a productivity level which represents a technology above the minimum level.

The demand for the intermediate good and labor are the result of profit maximization in manufacturing. As long as a vintage remains viable, it earns a flow of profits $\pi_{M,\tau}$. To produce the final good, the firm has to pay p_τ for one unit of the intermediate good. The subsequent transformation into the final good causes labor costs γ times the wage rate w_τ and overhead costs δ_τ. Hence, the consequent profit equation is:

(5) $\pi_{M,\tau} = A_\tau x_\tau^\alpha - (p_\tau + \gamma w_\tau) x_\tau - \delta_\tau$

The maximization of (5) over x_τ yields as a first-order condition the demand for the intermediate good,

$$(6) \quad x_\tau = \left(\frac{\alpha a_\tau A_{\tau_t^{max}}}{p_\tau + \gamma w_\tau} \right)^{\frac{1}{1-\alpha}},$$

and the demand for labor which is γx_τ. Firms from different technological vintages vary in labor demand and demand for the intermediate good. Highly productive technologies imply, *ceteris paribus*, a higher demand for inputs.

Wages are set exogenously, for example, in a bargaining process affected by productivity increases in manufacturing. In contrast to production technologies, labor is homogenous and we therefore assume that all manufacturing workers receive the same wage w_t. Hence, the wage rate is proportional to $A_{\tau_t^{max}}$ with β_j as a measure for the amount of income that goes to labor:

$$(7) \quad w_{j,t} = \beta_j A_{j,\tau_t^{max}}.$$

The share β_j is assumed to be determined in such a way that, in absence of labor market frictions (to be modeled later), total labor supply and total labor demand are in equilibrium.

While manufacturing workers earn w_t, the competitive manufacturing firms earn zero profits over their technological lifetime. Market entry is associated with the implementation of a technology, which is the maximum available at time t. The costs of implementation are F_τ. The manufacturing sector is competitive so that the flow of profits over the firm's technological lifetime only covers implementation costs. Define $\bar{t}$ as the date of market entry and let T denote the point in time when the firm closes due to technological obsolescence. Then the zero-profit condition implies that $\int_{t=\bar{t}}^{t=T} e^{-r(t-\bar{t})} \pi_{M,\tau,t} dt = F_\tau$

4.2.3 R&D and the Intermediate Good Production

The units in the R&D sector produce the intermediate good and develop technological innovations, which allow provision of intermediate goods with a higher level of productivity A_τ. Various R&D units compete in the development of the next innovation. As soon as an innovator appears with a new maximum technology τ_t^{max} it sells the innovation in form of intermediate goods to the manufacturing sector. The consequent flow of profits determines the value of an innovation. This value then yields the return to labor of an R&D unit, which is the alternative income to the wage rate in manufacturing. The R&D units produce the intermediate good at constant marginal costs $c_\tau = cA_\tau$, which are proportional to the technology level. The previous technology becomes common knowledge as soon as an innovation occurs. As a result, different firms compete in the supply of the intermediate good so that they set the price equal to marginal costs. Hence, no profits arise for these intermediate good suppliers. However, only the innovator has the knowledge about the leading technology τ_t^{max}. Hence, there is no competition in the supply of technology τ_t^{max} and its supplier earns monopolistic profits. The innovator replaces the previous monopoly and then sets the profit-maximizing price and output. Profits of the R&D unit therefore arise from serving the part of the manufacturing sector at home and abroad that uses the highest technology level $\tau_{j,t}^{max}$:

$$(8) \quad \pi_{R,t} = \sum_{j=h,f} \sigma_{h,j}(p_{j,\tau_t^{max}} - c_{j,\tau_t^{max}})x_{j,\tau_t^{max}} \ .$$

The R&D monopoly chooses the profit-maximizing quantity of output and sets the corresponding $p_{\tau_t^{max}}$. The R&D unit faces the inverse demand function of the manufacturing vintage τ_t^{max}, which results from the demand function (6). With the corresponding solution for $P_{j,\tau_t^{max}}$ the first-order condition of the maximization program $\max \pi_{R,\tau_t^{max}}$ produces the profit-maximizing quantity of the intermediate good

$$(9) \quad x_{j,\tau_t^{max}} = \left(\frac{\alpha^2}{\gamma\omega_{j,\tau_t^{max}} + c} \right)^{\frac{1}{1-\alpha}} ,$$

where $\omega_\tau = w_t/A_\tau$ denotes the productivity-adjusted wage. The consequent price of the intermediate good can then be written as:

$$(10) \quad P_{j,\tau_t^{max}} = \frac{c_{\tau_t^{max}}}{\alpha} + \left(\frac{1}{\alpha} - 1 \right)\gamma w_{j,t} \ .$$

The monopolist sets the price by imposing a two-fold mark-up over marginal costs. First, $1/\alpha$ represents the usual mark-up according to the price elasticity of demand. The second part of the mark-up term comes from the transformation technology in manufacturing, which connects the demand for labor to the demand for the intermediate good in a fixed proportion. High wages then reduce the demand for the intermediate good. However, according to the inverse demand function, a small quantity of output corresponds to a high price for the intermediate goods.

The value $p_{j,\tau_l^{max}} x_{j,\tau_l^{max}}$ is the recurring income of the R&D unit as long as it can realize the monopolistic profits. However, competitors continually undertake efforts to replace the incumbent technological maximum. This means that the flow of excess monopoly profits immediately stops as soon as a better technology is developed. The replacement emerges stochastically at probability ε_h and $\sigma_{h,f}\varepsilon_f$ per labor unit in a number of $L_{R,j}$ R&D units at home and abroad, which employ one worker each. Thus, the expected present value J_τ of an innovation takes account of the flow of profits and the probability of a total loss of the asset value, by being defined as:

$$(11) \quad rJ_\tau = \pi_{R,\tau} - J_\tau \sum_{j=h,f} \sigma_{h,j}\varepsilon_j L_{R,j} .$$

Equation (11) implies that investments in R&D must bring the same expected returns as the investment in an alternative asset with the constant interest rate r. Rearranging (11), together with the profit equation (8) and the values $p_{j,\tau_l^{max}}$ and $x_{j,\tau_l^{max}}$ then yields the expected value of innovation τ:

$$(12) \quad J_{\tau,t} = \sum_{j=f,h} \frac{\sigma_{j,h}}{\gamma} A_{j,\tau_l^{max}} \left[\frac{c}{\alpha} + \left(\frac{1}{\alpha} - 1 \right) \gamma\omega_{j,\tau} \right] \frac{L_{M,j,\tau}}{r + \sum_{j=h,f} \sigma_{h,j}\varepsilon_j L_{R,j}} .$$

One can see that the expected return from domestic R&D is low if foreign competitors are strong in terms of market access $\sigma_{h,f}$, productivity ε_f or pure scale $L_{R,f}$. On the other hand, foreign demand for the intermediate good leads to a higher expected income from domestic R&D. The relative effect of openness, namely of $\sigma_{h,f}$, $\sigma_{f,h}$ on the returns from domestic R&D depends on whether the competition or demand effect dominates. If $\sigma_{h,f}$ is variable, the home country can partly control the profitability of domestic R&D as long as the foreign country does not respond counteractively. It is also evident that technological progress increases the value of an innovation over time because $A_{j,\tau^{max}}$ occurs in equation (12). Hence, equilibrium growth means that all relevant values in manufacturing and R&D increase at the rate of technological progress.

4.2.4 Labor Reallocation and Unemployment

In the previous sections, we have modeled a manufacturing sector, which experiences a decline in relative productivity once a new technological innovation occurs. Now we show how this leads to labor reallocation, continuous job creation and job destruction. A technological innovation makes room for a new firm in manufacturing which creates new employment opportunities. In contrast, the rest of manufacturing reduces labor demand due to its decline in relative productivity. The decrease in existing employment and the parallel increase of new employment opportunities make it necessary to relocate workers. In general, this process is not frictionless. However, we will ignore frictions such as time consuming search, and assume that only skilled labor yields a productive match with the new technological innovation and, hence, is able to fill the new job vacancies. These skills are formed through learning-by-using during work in manufacturing. The reallocation of labor is accompanied by unemployment if skilled labor is in short supply because this means that job destruction exceeds the number of newly filled vacancies.

4.2.4.1 Technological obsolescence and job destruction

Firms in manufacturing are of different age and each firm is endowed with a particular productivity level A_τ. The technological age corresponds to the range between τ_I^{min} and τ_I^{max}, which relate to different productivity levels running from minimum relative productivity $a_{\tau_I^{min}} = A_{\tau_I^{min}} / A_{\tau_I^{max}}$ up to a maximum of $a_{\tau_I^{max}} = 1$. We define the minimum level $A_{\tau_I^{min}}$ as the one that corresponds to zero profits of production, i.e. $\pi_{M,\tau} = 0$. In other words, firms with a level above $A_{\tau_I^{min}}$ generate profits which are used to cover implementation costs, but no firm produces with a level below $A_{\tau_I^{min}}$ as it would imply selling the final good at a loss. The firms receive revenues $A_\tau x_{\tau,j}^\alpha$ and they have to pay overhead costs δ_τ and variable costs $(c_\tau + \gamma x_I)x_{\tau,I}$. In any firm except from the one with $A_{\tau_I^{max}}$, variable costs consist of the price of the intermediate good (equal to its marginal costs of production $p_\tau = c_\tau$), and complementary wage costs. We then find that zero profits correspond to a minimum productivity level of

$$(13) \quad A_{\tau_I^{min}} = \left(\frac{\delta_\tau}{1-\alpha}\right)^{1-\alpha}\left(\frac{c_\tau + \gamma w_I}{\alpha}\right)^\alpha.$$

A firm receives constant revenues over time but wages increase at the rate of technological progress. This means that revenues exceed expenditure in the beginning but profits decline due to the subsequent rise in labor costs.

Therefore, there exists a maximum wage w_τ^{max} that a firm with technology A_τ is able to pay. This wage corresponds to $\pi_{M,\tau} = 0$ and is:

$$(14) \quad w_\tau^{max} = A_\tau^{\frac{1}{\alpha}} \frac{\alpha}{\gamma} \left(\frac{\delta_\tau}{1-\alpha} \right)^{\frac{\alpha-1}{\alpha}} - \frac{c_\tau}{\gamma}.$$

Technological innovations drive the rise in the wage rate and firms cease production when the wage exceeds w_τ^{max}. Let Γ denote the number of innovations it takes to increase the wage to w_τ^{max}. For vintage τ, started with a technology adjusted wage rate $\overline{\omega} = w_{\tau,i} / A_\tau$, the maximum wage is given by $w_\tau^{max} / A_\tau = \overline{\omega} e^{\lambda\Gamma}$. This implies that a firm survives the following number of innovations:

$$(15) \quad \Gamma = \frac{\ln\left(\dfrac{w_\tau^{max}}{A_\tau} \right) - \ln \overline{\omega}}{\lambda}.$$

The rate of technological obsolescence is high if the technology span Γ is small. In this case few innovations are enough to increase wages to maximum and, correspondingly, to reduce relative productivity to its minimum level.

Γ also affects job destruction. The firm with the lowest productivity τ_i^{min} disappears with the arrival of a new τ_i^{max} and dismisses all employees at that date. Recall from the description of the manufacturing sector that labor demand according to (6) is $L_{M,\tau} = \gamma \left[\alpha a_{\tau,A} / (c_\tau + \gamma w_i) \right]^{1/(1-\alpha)}$. The wage of τ_i^{min} is equal to w_τ^{max}. This implies that vintage τ_i^{min} employs the following number of workers:

$$(16) \quad L_{M,\tau_i^{min}} = \gamma \left(\frac{\alpha}{c_{\tau}^{min} + \gamma\overline{\omega} e^{\lambda\Gamma}} \right)^{\frac{1}{1-\alpha}}.$$

Hence, the subsequent job destruction is equal to $L_{M,\tau_i^{min}}$. One can see that a high rate of technological obsolescence in terms of a small Γ results in large-scale job destruction. Firms disappear in spite of their relatively high productivity, which implies that many workers were employed at the date of the firm's closure.

It is not only market exits that cause job destruction. Gradual technological obsolescence also causes unemployment. We can see from the equation of $L_{M,\tau}$ that labor demand is a function of relative productivity a_τ, which declines over time. Only a share φ of workers remains employed in the firm with technology τ once the next innovation reduces relative productivity from a_τ to a_τ / λ. Hence, labor demand $L_{M,\tau}(a_\tau/\lambda)$ divided by the previous demand $L_{M,\tau}(a_\tau)$ yields:

$$(17) \quad \varphi = \left(\frac{c + w_{\tau,l}}{c + \lambda w_{\tau,l}} \right)^{\frac{1}{1-\alpha}} .$$

Consequently, as soon as the next innovation emerges, a share $(1 - \varphi)$ of the current number of manufacturing workers loses their jobs due to gradual technological obsolescence.

The total extent of job destruction is the result of the gradual and the final technological obsolescence $L_{M,\tau_l^{\min}} + (1 - \varphi)L_M$ jobs. With u as the unemployment rate the total employment in manufacturing can be written as $L_M = (1 - u)L - L_R$. As technological innovations emerge with a probability $\sum_{j=h,f} \sigma_{h,j} \varepsilon_j L_{R,j}$, the average flow into unemployment is:

$$(18) \quad U^+ = \sum_{j=h,f} \sigma_{h,j} \varepsilon_j L_{R,j} \quad \{(1 - \varphi)[(1 - u)L_h - L_{R,h}] + L_{M,\tau_l^{\min}}\}$$

4.2.4.2 Job creation

The emergence of a new firm in the manufacturing sector creates new jobs. However, the new jobs relate to the innovative technology, for which employees must be sufficiently skilled to fulfill the new job requirements. From this it follows that some vacancies may remain unfilled if skilled labor is in short supply.

The firm with $\tau_l^{\max}$ aims to employ workers in order to start production. It follows from the input demand and monopolistic profit-maximization[6] that the corresponding number of vacancies is equal to $L_{M,\tau_l^{\max}} = \gamma(\alpha^2 / \gamma \omega_{j,\tau_l^{\max}} + c)^{1-\alpha}$.

This is the demand for skilled labor. We define skills as the ability to apply the innovative technologies. Skills are formed in a stochastic process of learning-by-using in manufacturing firms. Let $\mu < 1$ denote the probability to acquire the relevant skills. The total number of skilled workers therefore is $D = \mu L_M$.

Job creation is unrestricted as long as $L_{M,\tau_l^{\max}} \leq D$ and is limited through skill shortages otherwise. Hence, the number of new job-worker matches is the minimum of either the number of vacancies or the supply of skilled labor. While the share of skilled workers is constant and equal to μ, the total number of skilled workers increases with the employment level in manufacturing. Hence, the labor allocation between the R&D and manufacturing sectors has an effect on whether skill shortages restrict job creation or not.

4.2.4.3 Equilibrium labor reallocation and unemployment

Workers move between the firms and from unemployment to employment in manufacturing firms except from those firms with $\tau_i^{\max}$. Unemployed workers are also excluded from entering the R&D sector. Vacancies are filled with skilled workers previously employed in other firms. The jobs left by the upgraded workers can then be filled by the non-skilled unemployed.

Job destruction and job creation generate flows in the labor market which must be of equal size in equilibrium. The search for labor to fill a vacancy is restricted by the necessity to find a skilled worker. The optimal outcome is when vacancies and skilled workers are abundant. On this condition perfect labor reallocation occurs: all workers, who are recently dismissed from their jobs, immediately reenter new employments. However, vacancies remain partly unfilled in the case of a shortage of skilled workers. This holds true and unemployment occurs if skill formation is not very efficient so that:

$$(19) \quad \mu < \sum_{j=h,f} \sigma_j \varepsilon_j L_{R,j} \left(1 - \varphi + \frac{L_{M,\tau^{\min}}}{L_{M,h}} \right) \quad => \quad u > 0 .$$

Unemployment is the mechanism to even out limited job creation and job destruction. We set $U^- = D$ and solve for the number of unemployed, to get the equilibrium employment level:

$$(20) \quad (1-u)L = L_R + \frac{1}{1-\varphi} \left[\frac{\mu L_{M,h}}{\sum_{j=h,f} \sigma_j \varepsilon_j L_{R,j}} - L_{M,\tau^{\min}} \right] .$$

Extensive labor reallocation (due to low φ) and a high innovation rate are indicators for high job destruction, which tends to reduce employment. Furthermore, job creation is low and employment is low if skill formation is weak in terms of a low μ. Finally, a high impact from foreign R&D tends to reduce employment if it accelerates job destruction via technological obsolescence while leaving job creation and skill formation unchanged.

4.2.5 The Equilibrium

Labor can be allocated freely between R&D and the firm in manufacturing that uses the leading technology level.[7] As long as income differentials between the two sectors exist, workers move to the better income alternative. Furthermore, labor reallocation causes flows out of and into unemployment. Equilibrium requires constant flows in the labor market in such a way that the intersectoral labor allocation and unemployment are fixed. The two conditions for a steady state are the following: no-arbitrage between the sectors, and flow equilibrium in the reallocation of labor between job creation and job destruction.[8]

Researchers who develop an innovative technology $\tau + 1$ expect the discounted value of $J_{\tau+1}$ from being the innovator. However, undertaking research efforts is successful only at unit time probability $\varepsilon_h < 1$. As an alternative, they could move to manufacturing and earn the current wage rate w_t. Hence, no-arbitrage between working in R&D and manufacturing requires $w_t = \varepsilon_h J_{\tau+1}$. Substituting $J_{\tau+1}$ by (12) and some rearranging yields the no-arbitrage equation:[9]

$$(21) \ \text{AE:} \quad L_{R,h} = \sum_{j=h,f} L_{M,j} \frac{\mu\lambda}{\gamma} \left(\frac{1}{\alpha} - 1\right) \frac{\sigma_{j,h} A_{j,\tau^{\max}}}{\omega_h A_{h,\tau^{\max}}} \left(\gamma\omega_j + c\right)$$

$$- \frac{r}{\varepsilon_h} - \sigma_{h,f} L_{R,f} \frac{\varepsilon_f}{\varepsilon_h},$$

where AE is the equilibrium condition for intersectoral labor allocation. Economic integration affects AE twofold, henceforth denoted as the demand effect and the competition effect. On the one hand, foreign manufacturing $L_{M,f}$ increases the overall demand for intermediate goods. This adds to the profits in the domestic R&D sector and tends to increase its employment level. On the other hand, a negative effect on $L_{R,h}$ comes from foreign research competitors threatening the profits of domestic incumbents. The demand effect is large if the value of $\sigma_{f,h}$ is high, whereas the competition effect is large if the value of $\sigma_{h,f}$ is high.

The unemployment level is constant over time if job creation is equal to job destruction as given by equation (20). Rearranging together with $L=uL+L_R-L_M$ yields:

$$(22) \ \text{EE:} \quad L_{R,h} = \frac{\mu}{\varepsilon_h} \left[\frac{L_{M,h}}{(1-\varphi)L_{M,h} + L_{M,\tau^{\min}}} \right] - \sigma_{f,h} \frac{\varepsilon_f}{\varepsilon_h} L_{R,f}.$$

Skill shortages (μ is low) and many foreign technological innovations allow only for a small equilibrium employment in the domestic R&D sector. Economic integration means that technological change along with its accompanying job destruction can be imported. Consequently, equilibrium labor allocation requires domestic R&D activity to be weak.

Figure 4.1 gives a graphical illustration of the equilibrium. The AE curve and the EE curve represent the equilibrium conditions. The locus of AE slopes upwards. This indicates that high employment in manufacturing corresponds to a high demand for intermediate goods and high profits in R&D. Consequently L_R increases with L_M. The locus of EE also slopes upwards. The reason for this is that the level of employment in manufacturing $L_{M,h}$ reflects the amount of skill formation. A higher number of skilled workers enable more labor reallocation caused by R&D activities, without leading to higher unemployment. The intersection points Q and Q' show equilibrium labor allocation and determine $L_{M,h}$ and $L_{R,h}$. In the case of a shortage of skilled labor, EE limits total employment, otherwise the identity $L=uL+L_R\_L_M$ is the relevant restriction.

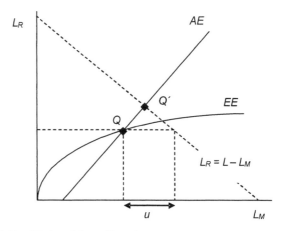

Figure 4.1 Equilibrium labor allocation

4.3 THE EFFECTS OF REGIONAL TECHNOLOGY TRADE

In brief, one could summarize the effects of the enlargement of an integration bloc and the resulting regional technology trade as follows: job destruction rises due to the demand effect and imported technological innovations, but there is also more competition from abroad if trade barriers get reduced, i.e., if $\sigma_{h,f}$ and $\sigma_{f,h}$ increase. However, it is ambiguous how employment and growth change.

Job destruction depends on the rate of technological obsolescence. Technologies developed in a neighboring country increase the rate of obsolescence, so regional trade in technologies is associated with job destruction. However, more job destruction is irrelevant for the employment level as long as skill shortages according to equation (19) do not restrict job creation.

The effects of cross-border technology exchange on domestic research activities are twofold according to the demand effect and the competition effect. The demand effect tends to dominate the competition effect, so the revenues for domestic R&D units will increase as long as there are many foreign manufacturing firms demanding domestic technologies. The opposite holds true if foreign R&D is more productive and therefore introduces many technological innovations. See Appendix for a derivation of these results.

These trade effects tend to change the labor allocation between manufacturing and R&D at home and abroad. Economic integration is allocation neutral, i.e., the labor allocation remains the same only if the demand and competition effects completely offset each other. The expected returns to R&D do not change in this case. Allocation neutrality refers to a no arbitrage condition – see equation (21) – which does not depend on $\sigma_{j,j}$. This is true only if economic integration takes place between structurally identical countries with equal productivity levels and an identical labor force (see Appendix). Otherwise, the employment level and/or domestic R&D output will change.

The import and export of technological innovations involve two effects on employment. The direct effect is that job destruction grows as the availability of technological innovations increases and the rate of technological obsolescence in manufacturing rises. This results in unemployment in the case of skill shortages. Moreover, non-neutral economic integration is another source of variations in employment. The corresponding reallocation of labor towards or away from R&D diminishes or intensifies job destruction. One outcome could be that economic integration is R&D-biased which means that the demand effect dominates the competition effect. Technology formation then gains compared to skill formation, which has a negative side effect on employment when skill shortages worsen. However, a bias towards manufacturing could increase employment.

The effect of economic integration on growth is also not clear-cut. Technological progress and growth may increase even if employment decreases. This is because of the positive scale effect which comes from the growing availability of new technologies, which amplify the productivity levels of domestic manufacturing firms. However, rising skill shortages and lower employment levels in both domestic sectors can work against the scale effect. The import of technological innovations may not compensate for the loss of domestic R&D output, which will lead to declining overall growth.

Negotiations often result in symmetric removals of trade barriers. But it may not be fair and optimal to agree on identical degrees of openness if countries differ in their economic structure. In that case, equal openness does not necessarily mean equal effects on growth in both economies. Equal effects and clear positive results arise only in the case of the integration of identical economies, i.e., in the case of allocation neutrality. In combination with an abundance of skilled workers, we find that economic integration has identical positive effects on growth at home and abroad because integrated economies can share their R&D outcomes. However, technologically backward economies may lose from integration. Equal changes in trade barriers but differences in the economic structure imply that economic integration is biased towards R&D in the technologically advanced economy and towards manufacturing in the less advanced economy. The positive effect of integration on growth is strengthened in the country with the R&D - bias, but less domestic research reduces the positive effects of integration in the economy with the bias towards manufacturing.

The analysis becomes more complex in the case of skill shortages. In that case scale effects, the bias towards R&D or manufacturing, and variations in employment may work in different directions concerning growth and the employment level. While only one country may lose from integration as long as skilled labor is abundant, more trade in technologies can affect both economies in a negative way if skilled labor is in short supply. However, the countries could then agree on asymmetric economic integration instead of an equal removal of trade barriers. The following example shows how asymmetric integration may allow both countries to gain from more liberal exchanges of technology.

We consider two countries that agree on economic integration, where one is somewhat more technologically advanced than the other. However, the technologically advanced economy has a shortage of skilled labor and the continuous labor reallocation produces workers who cannot be reemployed. Economic integration is R&D - biased for the already advanced economy. In contrast to this, labor in the backward economy will reallocate towards manufacturing as a consequence of an increased importation of new technology. In contrast to the standard case without skill shortages, R&D activities will also be slowed in the advanced country, because the R&D-bias makes employment in manufacturing less attractive. This further displaces skill formation in manufacturing, such that the increased shortage of skilled labor weakens workers' employability. Employment in R&D also shrinks because there is now less employment in manufacturing, less demand for intermediate goods and thus lower profits in the R&D sector. As a result, the rate of technological innovation decreases. Moreover, the R&D output in the backward economy falls further because integration is biased towards manufacturing in this case. Hence, the overall R&D output and growth is lower after economic integration, such that both economies are disadvantaged by the removal of trade barriers.

However, asymmetric economic integration improves the results in terms of growth and employment for both countries. We assume that $\partial \sigma_{h,f} = 0$ and $\partial \sigma_{h,f} > 0$, which means that the advanced economy removes trade barriers while the backward economy still protects its market of technologies. The backward economy benefits from economic integration because its weak R&D sector can expect extra profits from foreign demand without facing higher competition. Accordingly, labor in the backward economy reallocates towards R&D in contrast to the case of symmetric integration. However, the advanced economy also benefits from economic integration. The inverse bias now leads to a reallocation of labor towards manufacturing. This effect would reduce technological progress and growth if there was full employment. However, now it is an advantage to replace R&D by manufacturing because this improves skill formation. Labor reallocation becomes more efficient, and more formerly unemployed workers also find new jobs. Since total employment increases, the level of employment in R&D rises as well. The number of technological innovations increases not only in the backward but also in the advanced economy. Asymmetric integration produces overall benefits, whereas in both countries growth and employment decline in the case of symmetric integration.

Figure 4.2 gives a graphical illustration of the previous example. The intersection of the AE curve with the EE curve in A_1 and A_2 represent the equilibrium labor allocation before integration. Symmetric integration then leads to a counter-clockwise shift of AE in the advanced economy and a clockwise shift in the backward economy. Furthermore, the EE curve shifts downward in both countries as job destruction accelerates. Consequently, the new equilibrium is B_1 and B_2.

The importance of both R&D sectors declines with negative effects on total growth. Furthermore, unemployment in the advanced economy increases. However, asymmetric integration leads to a completely different outcome. The R&D sector in the backward economy grows because the domestic market remains protected while the export of technological innovations becomes easier. This technology flow, inverse to the usual case, results in more technological progress in the backward economy and enables the advanced economy to reduce its skill shortages. Equilibria in C_1 and C_2 reveal that both economies can increase the weight of R&D and the advanced economy can also reduce unemployment.

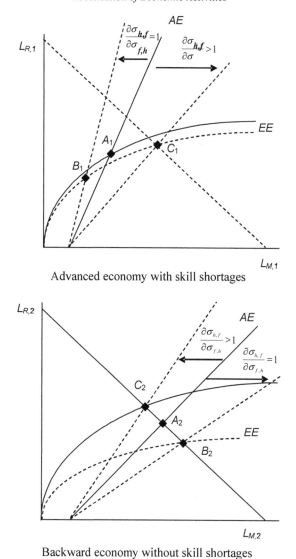

Figure 4.2 *An example of symmetric and asymmetric integration*

4.4 CONCLUSIONS

We have presented a model of endogenous growth with cross-border technology exchange and continuous labor reallocation due to technological obsolescence. The specifications considered a manufacturing sector in which new technological vintages emerge and old ones disappear. The substitution of technologies results in the closure of older firms and the emergence of new firms associated, respectively, with job destruction and job creation. Under the assumption that only skilled labor can be immediately reemployed, skill shortages restrict job creation and cause unemployment. Economic integration increases the availability of innovative technologies but it also accelerates their obsolescence. This includes a higher rate of job destruction as a side-effect of more cross-border technology exchange.

One main result of the model is that the effects of economic integration on growth and employment are ambiguous. If economic integration has opposing biases, which is towards R&D in one country and towards manufacturing in the other one, benefits and drawbacks of integration can be unequally distributed. While we have a win-win or win-lose situation as long as skilled labor is abundant, cross-border technology exchange can have adverse effects on both economies in the case of skill shortages. An example would be that a backward economy and an advanced one with skill shortages agree on the identical removal of trade barriers against technologies. In that case, deeper economic integration would reduce the rate of technological innovation in both countries and unemployment would rise in the advanced economy. However, asymmetric economic integration can be optimal under these circumstances. The one-way import of technological innovations increases employment because skill shortages reduce if only the advanced economy opens its market for foreign technologies, allowing the rates of technological progress and growth to increase in both economies.

One lesson from the model could be that the integration of structurally different countries – such as Mexico into NAFTA, or Romania, Bulgaria and maybe Turkey into the EU – can eventually generate more benefits for all parties involved if the technologically advanced economies open their markets but do not demand an equivalent openness by the new member states. Asymmetric economic integration allows more rapid development in the poorer economies but might also have positive effects on the employment of low-skilled labor in the advanced economies.

APPENDIX

Demand effect

$$\frac{\partial L_{R.h}}{\partial \sigma_{f.h}} = \frac{L_{M.f}}{\gamma(1+\eta)} \lambda \left(\frac{1}{\alpha} - 1\right) \frac{A_{f.\tau^{\max}}}{\omega_h A_{h.\tau^{\max}}} (\gamma\omega_h + c)$$

Competition effect

$$\frac{\partial L_{R.h}}{\partial \sigma_{h.f}} = -L_{R.f} \frac{\varepsilon_f}{\varepsilon_h}$$

Allocation neutrality is defined as $\partial L_{R.h} / \partial \sigma_{h.f} = \partial L_{R.h} / \partial \sigma_{f.h}$. If two countries are structurally identical $(A_{h.\tau^{\max}} = A_{f.\tau^{\max}}, \varepsilon_h = \varepsilon_f, \beta_h = \beta_f)$ this implies:

$$L_{R.f} = \frac{L_{M.f}}{\gamma(1+\eta)} \lambda \left(\frac{1}{\alpha} - 1\right) \frac{(\gamma\omega + c)}{\omega}.$$

This means that the demand effect cancels out the competition effect if the foreign country has the identical AE condition (ignoring a small effect from the exogenous constant minimum employment in manufacturing).

NOTES

1. See Walz (1997) for a survey on the dynamic effects of economic integration.
2. However, Bretschger (1999) shows that regional knowledge spillovers can also reduce growth if changes in relative prices result in a reduction in human capital accumulation.
3. The analysis of technological change in a matching model of unemployment goes back to Pissarides (2000) and Aghion and Howitt (1994). In a more micro-level approach, Mortensen and Pissarides (1998) show on which condition technological progress results in more labor reallocation in combination with an increase in unemployment.
4. Dinopoulos and Segerstrom (1999) give another example for advantages of asymmetric economic integration. They show that growth can be higher if varying tariffs support temporary backward R&D industries.
5. Growth rates and therefore technology levels can diverge between the two economies. For simplicity, we assume that an innovation always introduces the λ-times higher productivity level independent of the current level of $A_{\tau^{\max}.j}$. This guarantees a mutual technology exchange where both countries benefit from foreign R&D.
6. See the description of the intermediate good production in section 4.2.3.
7. However, we ignore international labor mobility as legal restrictions on labor mobility also exist in many integration blocks (e.g. concerning Mexicans and East-Europeans in NAFTA and EU).

8. The analysis in this section considers the home country, but the same analysis can be undertaken for the foreign country.
9. Forward looking R&D firms consider the skill shortages which restrict the demand for their intermediate good. Hence, the market is μL_M instead of $L_{M,\tau^{max}}$.

REFERENCES

Aghion, P. and P. Howitt (1992), 'A Model of Growth through Creative Destruction', *Econometrica*, **60**, pp. 323-351.

Aghion, P. and P. Howitt (1994), 'Growth and Unemployment', *Review of Economic Studies*, **61**, pp. 477-494.

Audretsch, D.B. and M.P. Feldman (1996), 'R&D Spillovers and the Geography of Innovation and Production', *American Economic review*, **86**, pp. 630-640.

Bretschger, L. (1997), 'International Trade, Knowledge Diffusion, and Growth', *International Trade Journal*, **9**, pp. 327-348.

Bretschger, L. (1999), 'Knowledge Diffusion and the Development of Regions', *Annals of Regional Science*, **33** (3) pp. 251-268.

Davis, D.R. (1998), 'Does European Unemployment Prop Up American Wages? National Labor Markets and Global Trade', *American Economic Review*, **88**, pp. 478-495.

Dinopoulos, E. and P.S. Segerstrom (1999), 'The Dynamic Effects of Contingent Tariffs', *Journal of International Economics*, **47**, pp. 191-222.

Feenstra, R. (1996), 'Trade and Uneven Growth', *Journal of Development Economics*, **49**, pp. 229-256.

Grossman, G.M. and E. Helpman (1990), 'Comparative Advantage and Long-Run Growth', *American Economic Review*, **80**, pp. 796-815.

Holod, D. and R.R. Reed (2004), 'Regional Spillovers, Economic Growth, and the Effects of Economic Integration', *Economic Letters*, **85**, pp. 35-42.

Jaffe, A.B., M. Trajtenberg, M. and R. Henderson (1993), 'Geographic Localization of Knowledge Spillovers as Evidenced by Patent Citations', *The Quarterly Journal of Economics*, **108**, pp. 577-598.

Keller, W. (2002), 'Trade and the Transmission of Technology', *Journal of Economic Growth*, **7**, pp. 5-24.

Mortensen, D. and C.A. Pissarides (1998), 'Technological Progress, Job Creation, and Job Destruction', *Review of Economic Dynamics*, **1** (4), pp. 733-753.

Pissarides, C. A. (2000), *Equilibrium Unemployment Theory*, Cambridge: MIT Press.

Rivera-Batiz, L. and P. Romer (1991), 'Economic Integration and Endogenous Growth', *Quarterly Journal of Economics*, **106**, pp. 531-555.

Rivera-Batiz, L. and D. Xie (1993), 'Integrating Among Unequals', *Regional Sciences and Urban Economics*, **23**, pp. 337-354.

Şener, F. (2001), 'Schumpeterian Unemployment, Trade and Wages', *Journal of International Economics*, **54**, pp. 119-148.

Walz, U. (1997), 'Dynamic Effects of Economic Integration, A Survey', *Open Economies Review*, **8**, pp. 309-326.

5. Intra-Industry Trade and Technological Spillovers: The Case of Belgian Manufacturing[1]

Filip Abraham and Jan van Hove

5.1 INTRODUCTION

Empirical evidence shows economic integration leads to intra-industry trade. Both global and country-specific studies point to a dominant role of intra-industry trade in the international trade pattern. Recent studies conclude that intra-industry trade is mainly driven by differences in factor endowments and technology. Especially small open advanced economies are characterised by high levels of intra-industry trade. At the same time they are most likely to benefit from international technological spillovers. This chapter therefore studies the impact of such technological spillovers, apart from domestic technological innovation, on the trade structure of the small open economy of Belgium.

Intra-industry trade can be divided into horizontal intra-industry trade and vertical intra-industry trade. Horizontal intra-industry trade refers to trade in different varieties (Krugman 1980, 1981, 1995), while vertical intra-industry trade refers to trade in products of different quality (Falvey 1981; Falvey and Kierzkowski 1987; Flam and Helpman 1987). This distinction between horizontal and vertical intra-industry trade is important for the validity of empirical studies. The results of early studies, focusing on total intra-industry trade only, are often mi._.⅃ ᵃˢ they are ·influenced by the different determinants of horizontal and vertical intra-industry trade. Most empirical studies investigate the impact of (Heckscher-Ohlin) factor endowment differences (Tharakan 1984; Balassa and Bauwens 1987, 1988; Greenaway et al. 1994, 1995; Greenaway and Torstensson 1997), mostly proxied by income differences. In particular, horizontal intra-industry trade appears to be driven by factor endowment differences, whereas technological differences determine the level of vertical intra-industry trade (Brülhart and Hine 1999; Blanes and Martin 2000). According to Torstensson (1991, 1996), however, factor proportion differences matter for vertical intra-industry trade as well, since high capital-labour ratios improve the relative quality of exports.

We extend the existing literature on the determinants of intra-industry trade by a more detailed analysis of the impact of technology. According to Davis' (1995) theoretical work, technological differences may be a sufficient reason for intra-industry trade, whereas older studies generally find that such differences are only sufficient if combined with economies of scale. Recent theoretical studies confirm the important role of cross-country technological differences (Balboni 2006; Kikuchi et al. 2006), and of cross-sector technological differences and international technological spillovers (Abraham and Van Hove 2006). From these models it appears that technological differences and international spillovers are able to explain the level of vertical intra-industry trade.

This chapter makes a contribution to the empirical literature on the determinants of intra-industry trade. It is original in two ways. First, we distinguish between input and output measures of technology. Most studies stick to one general technology indicator. Second, we incorporate technological spillovers in the analysis. Especially small open economies are not only influenced by domestic innovation, but also by spillovers from the international community. A variety of empirical studies supports this view. In their very influential work Coe and Helpman (1995) find that total factor productivity in small open countries is strongly stimulated by foreign R&D efforts. Openness to trade stimulates these international technology spillovers (Keller 2002). This trade channel will be taken into account in this chapter.

Our empirical study focuses on Belgium. This country is an interesting case given the country's openness to international trade. We use detailed panel data in this paper. We analyse the trade structure of Belgian manufacturing at a detailed sectoral level (24 sectors) for the period 1993-2000. Total trade is split up into bilateral trade to 26 countries, including the OECD partners with some exceptions, European Free Trade Association (EFTA) and some Central-European countries. We perform this analysis by distinguishing between horizontal and vertical intra-industry trade. Vertical intra-industry trade is further split up into high-quality and low-quality. Our research questions can be summarized in four main hypotheses:

- Hypothesis 1: Is it income similarity or technological differences that determine intra-industry trade?
- Hypothesis 2: Does technology affect trade with respect to variety or quality?
- Hypothesis 3: Does technology lead to exports of high-quality products?
- Hypothesis 4: Do technological spillovers influence the trade structure?

We find that technological innovation and spillovers are important determinants for high-quality vertical intra-industry trade. Horizontal and low-quality vertical intra-industry trade are mainly influenced by income, and hence factor endowments. The results clearly depend, however, on the choice of the technology indicators used. This finding raises questions about the robustness of the impact of technology on trade as claimed by previous studies.

The remainder of this chapter is structured as follows. The empirical methodology and data are discussed in section 5.2. In section 5.3 we provide evidence about the importance of intra-industry trade in Belgian manufacturing across sectors and across trading partners. We also give a brief overview of the innovativeness of different sectors of Belgian manufacturing compared to the situation in the main Belgian trading partners. In section 5.4 we discuss the results from estimating the empirical model. Some conclusions are formulated in section 5.5.

5.2 METHODOLOGY AND DATA

5.2.1 Empirical Model

In order to identify the determinants of each kind of intra-industry trade, we estimate the following empirical model for bilateral trade between Belgium and its main trading partners.

$$(1) \quad \begin{aligned} GL_{ikt}^{Z} &= \alpha + \beta_1 IS_{kt} + \beta_2 \ln(DIST_k) + \beta_3 \ln(EMPL_{kt}) \\ &+ \beta_4 \ln(RTP_{ikt}) + \beta_5 \ln(GTS_{ikt}) + \mu_{ikt} \end{aligned}$$

where:

GL_{ikt}^{Z}	=	Grubel-Lloyd index, with Z denoting Total IIT, Horizontal IIT, High-quality Vertical IIT and Low-quality Vertical IIT respectively
IS_{kt}	=	Income Similarity between Belgium and its trading partner k at time t
$DIST_k$	=	Distance between Belgium and its trading partner k
$EMPL_{ik}$	=	Sectoral Employment in trading partner relative to Belgian sectoral employment (average over time)
GTS_{ikt}	=	Relative Technological Performance: Innovation by trading partners relative to Belgian innovation (several indicators: see below)

GTS_{ikt} =   Global Technological Spillovers (see below)

μ_{ikt} =   Error term

α =   Constant term

This model is the reduced form of an extensive model developed in Abraham and Van Hove (2006). We estimate model (1) separately for total intra-industry trade (TIIT), horizontal intra-industry trade (HIIT), low-quality vertical intra-industry trade (VIITlow) and high-quality vertical intra-industry trade (VIIThigh). For each kind of intra-industry trade we compute the Grubel and Lloyd (1975) index (GL index) as follows:

$$(2) \quad GL_{ikt} = \left(\frac{\sum_{j \in i}(X_j + M_j) - \sum_{j \in i}|X_j - M_j|}{\sum_{j \in i}(X_j + M_j)} \right) *100$$

This GL index is equal to the share of intra-industry trade in total trade between Belgium and country k in year t in industry i. We use detailed sectoral trade flows in order to compute this index. The final outcome is an aggregate of all intra-industry flows in sub-sectors j that all belong to industry i. X_j and M_j respectively denote exports and imports in sub-sector j, belonging to sector i. Both intra-industry trade and total trade are aggregated at each industry level in order to compute this GL index. GL takes values between 0 and 100, where the former indicates complete inter-industry trade and the latter complete intra-industry trade.

5.2.2 Splitting up Intra-Industry Trade

After computing total intra-industry trade we fine-tune our analysis. Similar to most recent studies we follow Abd-el-Rahman (1986, 1991) and Greenaway et al. (1994) and split up total intra-industry trade based on relative unit values of sectoral exports and imports. Using this methodology we compute the relative unit values (UV) of bilateral export over bilateral imports as

$$(3) \quad \frac{UV_{jikt}^{EX}}{UV_{jikt}^{IM}}$$

This 'price ratio' is interpreted as an indicator of quality. If export and import prices at a very detailed level, namely at sub-sector j belonging to industry *i*, are almost equal, than this reflects similar quality of differentiated products. In this case we consider the total amount of intra-industry trade in this sector as horizontal intra-industry trade, based on two-way trade in different varieties of the same good. In the other case, namely that these unit values differ by 15 percent or more from each other, we call it vertical intra-industry trade.

We take a step further by defining high-quality versus low-quality vertical intra-industry trade. This distinction is relevant as the role of technology may be very different in both cases. High-quality (low-quality) vertical intra-industry trade is defined as intra-industry trade where Belgium exchanges high-quality (low-quality) products for low-quality (high-quality) products made by its bilateral trading partner within the same industry. The price ratio can be used to determine high and low quality as well. If the price ratio is larger than 1+0.15, then Belgian export products are priced at least 15 percent higher than Belgian imports in the same subsector.[2] As we assume that prices reflect quality, we call this vertical intra-industry trade high-quality. So in our definition we always take the Belgian (domestic) perspective. We speak about low-quality vertical intra-industry trade once Belgian export prices are at least 15 percent lower than the import prices. Once we have determined the kind of trade at each sub-sector *j*, we aggregate all computed horizontal, vertical high-quality and vertical low-quality intra-industry trade at each industry level. We express each kind of intra-industry trade as a percentage of total sectoral trade.

5.2.3 Overview of Independent Variables

In our empirical model we study the determinants of total, horizontal and vertical intra-industry trade. We test for the importance of technological performance and technological spillovers, apart from other determinants that have been studied in the literature. We do not stick to a partial analysis of the role of technology, only as this might cause measurement errors as argued by Leamer and Levinsohn (1995). For convenience as well as to investigate the heterogeneous impact on the different dependent variables, we use the same set of independent variables for each kind of intra-industry trade. We are mainly concerned about the role of technological innovation and spillovers, versus factor endowments, as determinants of (different categories of) intra-industry trade.

Most independent variables are constructed in order to compare the trading partner's performance with the situation in Belgium. An increase in the variables corresponds to a relative improvement in the performance by the trading partners. Hence a positive (negative) sign in the regression results means that relatively good performance abroad has a positive (negative) effect on intra-industry trade.

5.2.3.1 Income similarity and endowments

Similarity in income or endowments is traditionally considered as the main determinant of intra-industry trade. We use the following measure of income similarity:

$$(4) \quad \left(1 - \frac{\left|GDPperCap_{partner} - GDPperCap_{Belgium}\right|}{GDPperCap_{partner} + GDPperCap_{Belgium}}\right) * 100$$

where *GDPperCap* denotes gross domestic product per capita. This index ranges between 0 and 100. While 0 corresponds to very different countries, 100 indicates countries with identical GDP per capita.[3] This index is also a proxy for relative endowment differences, as gross domestic product per capita is often used as an instrument for capital-labour ratios.

5.2.3.2 Scale

Another traditional argument for the explanation of intra-industry trade is the scale of the sector (Helpman 1981). Countries tend to specialise in the production of one good in order to benefit from increasing returns to scale (Harrigan 1991). The resulting specialisation pattern between countries causes intra-industry trade, as larger sectors typically benefit most from increasing returns to scale.

In order to test the necessity of scale effects at the sectoral level, we add a variable measuring sectoral employment by the partner country relative to Belgian employment. If we find a positive relationship, then a larger partner in that sector leads to more intra-industry trade. Due to data limitations we take an average over time for this measure.

5.2.3.3 Geographical distance and trade barriers

Distance, like in the gravity model, can be interpreted as transportation and transaction costs. One typically assumes a positive relationship between geographical distance and the degree of trade barriers. If distance matters for bilateral trade flows, then it also affects the importance of intra-industry trade (Bergstrand and Egger 2006). Therefore we add the distance between Brussels and the capital cities of the trading partners as a variable in our model. The barriers to trade may cause substitution, by domestic firms, of foreign production. Such substitution is most likely in similar or related sectors. Hence intra-industry trade will drop. The latter finding is very robust in the literature (for an overview and discussion, see Amiti and Venables 2001).

5.2.3.4 Technological innovation

We define several measures of technological innovation. A distinction is made between technology-output and technology-input measures. For each indicator, we define technology as the technological performance of the trading partner relative to Belgium.

For the technology-input measure we use the relative performance of the trading partner to Belgium in terms of two alternative indicators: R&D expenditures and value added per worker. We take an average over time for both (because of data limitations). Yearly USPTO (United States Patent and Trademark Office) patent data are used as an indicator of technological output performance. We calculate the ratio of the number of patents granted in the US market (fractional data) to companies from the trading partner to the number of patents granted in the US market to Belgian companies. However as this latter measure is undoubtedly influenced by country size, we scale this variable by dividing the denominator and the numerator of this ratio by the total number of US patents granted to the trading partners and Belgium respectively.

5.2.3.5 Technology spillovers

In order to investigate the impact of technological spillovers, we compute a weighted technology measure. We do this by adding up all patents granted in the US to each trading partner under observation. We refer to this variable as global technology spillovers, recognising the role of trade as a transmission channel for technological diffusion (e.g. Keller 2002; Acharya and Keller 2007). 'Global' simply refers to all countries in our sample, which contains all major innovating countries in the world. We use the relative import share in total Belgian imports as weights. Hence, we have a measure of intra-sectoral technological spillover-effects. We expect to find a positive effect on intra-industry trade, in particular on vertical high-quality intra-industry trade. Our expectations are supported by the positive effect of international innovation on productivity and growth in small open economies.

5.2.4 Data and Econometrics

All trade data are taken from the OECD Trade and Commodity Statistics. We use SITC rev.3 (5-digits) as classification for the sub-sectors j. By using these detailed data, we handle the criticism of sectoral aggregation bias. We calculate the indices and convert them to the ISIC rev.3 (2-digit) classification. All other data are also collected or converted to ISIC rev.3.

Data for value added, production, employment and R&D expenditures are taken from OECD databases (STAN database and SSIS for missing values, ANBERD and OFFBERD for missing values). Sectoral patent data are from USPTO (conversion from USSIC).[4] The GDP and population data are taken from IMF – Financial Statistics.

We use data for eight years (1993-2000) for 26 trading partners of Belgium: OECD-countries (except Luxembourg, Iceland and New Zealand), EFTA-countries and Poland, Hungary, Slovak Republic and Czech Republic. The selection of the period was limited by data availability and compatibility.[5] The ISIC-classification contains 24 manufacturing sectors. There are of course missing values in our dataset. Therefore estimation results are not based on a fully balanced and complete dataset.

We opt for using panel data to investigate the impact of technology on intra-industry trade, as Hummels and Levinsohn (1995) show that the determinants of intra-industry trade are not always stable over time. Greenaway and Torstensson (1997) call the use of panel data one of the most promising extensions of empirical analysis in intra-industry trade. Since we use data for a relatively short period of time (eight years), we focus in our analysis on the cross-sectional and cross-country variation. For this kind of analysis, the between-effects estimator (BE estimator, regression on the group means) is preferred. By using the BE estimator, we measure the impact of cross-country cross-sectional variation in, for example, the technology indicators on the level of intra-industry trade.[6] We also report OLS estimates, simply for comparison.

5.3 STYLISED FACTS ABOUT BELGIAN TRADE AND TECHNOLOGY

Belgium is a small open economy at the heart of Western Europe. In this section we first describe the innovativeness of the Belgian economy. We do this by comparing technological performance in Belgium and the other countries in our data for the 24 manufacturing sectors under study. Second, we examine the importance of intra-industry trade in total Belgian trade. Then we do this for each of 24 manufacturing sectors. Additionally we compare Belgian intra-industry trade bilaterally with the 26 countries mentioned above.

5.3.1 The Relative Innovativeness of the Belgian Economy

In Table 5.1 we compare technological innovation in manufacturing in Belgium with its 26 trading partners.

Analogous to the econometric methodology, we define technology both by output and input variables. Sectoral Technology Intensity is measured as the ratio of the sectoral number of patents (respectively business R&D expenditures) over the total number of manufacturing patents (respectively business R&D expenditures). We calculate one figure for all trading partners jointly (including Belgium) and compare this to the Belgian sectoral technology intensity.

Table 5.1 Sectoral technology intensity of Belgium and its main trading partners (average 1993-2000)

Sector	Sector Name	Technology Output (a)			Technology Input (b)		
		Partners	Belgium	Compare	Partners	Belgium	Compare
15	Food	1.36	2.08	BEL high	0.85	3.15	BEL high
16	Tobacco	0.00	0.00	IDEM	0.04	0.05	BEL high
17	Textiles	1.55	2.39	BEL high	0.23	1.42	BEL high
18	Wearing Apparel	0.56	0.64	BEL high	0.12	0.07	BEL low
19	Leather	0.93	1.40	BEL high	0.03	0.08	BEL high
20	Wood	0.15	0.24	BEL high	0.18	0.07	BEL low
21	Paper	0.00	0.00	IDEM	0.19	0.41	BEL high
22	Printing	0.90	0.57	BEL low	0.04	0.71	BEL high
23	Energy	0.98	1.29	BEL high	1.09	2.89	BEL high
24	Chemistry	10.04	23.57	BEL high	8.53	23.41	BEL high
2423	Pharmacy	5.21	8.53	BEL high	9.56	18.91	BEL high
25	Rubber	2.29	4.16	BEL high	1.88	2.89	BEL high
26	Minerals	2.60	2.88	BEL high	1.15	2.27	BEL high
271+2731	Iron and Steel	0.57	0.29	BEL low	1.12	3.15	BEL high
272+2732	Non-Ferrous Metals	0.72	0.69	BEL low	0.76	1.32	BEL high
28	Metal Products	4.95	3.26	BEL low	1.38	1.67	BEL high
29	Machinery	16.85	13.73	BEL low	7.34	6.43	BEL low
30	Office	6.65	3.19	BEL low	7.71	0.27	BEL low
31	Electrical Machinery	11.42	6.42	BEL low	5.75	4.33	BEL low
32	Communication	9.29	4.87	BEL low	16.83	17.91	BEL high
33	Medical, Precision	14.23	13.00	BEL low	7.66	2.31	BEL low
34	Motor Vehicles	2.76	1.44	BEL low	14.39	3.39	BEL low
35	Other Transport	3.47	2.52	BEL low	8.70	1.81	BEL low
36	Furniture	2.35	2.57	BEL high	0.75	1.03	BEL high

Notes:
(a) Technology Output is measured as the share of the sectoral number of patents granted (fractional) in total manufacturing, in all in-sample countries jointly in the US market (source: USPTO)
(b) Technology Input is measured as the share of sectoral Business R&D expenditures in total manufacturing in all in-sample countries jointly (source: OECD, STAN)

From Table 5.1 we learn that a ranking of technology intensity of sectors depends on the technology measure (input/output) used. If we focus on technology output, *Machinery, Medical and Precision Instruments, Electrical Machinery* and *Chemicals* represent the highest shares in the total number of patents granted to manufacturing sectors. We find the highest R&D expenditures in *Communication, Motor Vehicles, Pharmaceuticals, Other Transport* and *Chemicals*. In general, Belgium has a similar technology intensity pattern as its trading partners. Nevertheless some interesting deviations appear:

Belgium does not perform well in high-tech sectors, generally speaking. Notable exceptions are *Chemicals* and *Pharmaceuticals*. This can be explained by some large and important Belgian companies active in these sectors.

Generally speaking too, Belgium performs relatively well in low-tech sectors, both in terms of R&D expenditure and in terms of patent grants. Striking examples are *Food, Textiles* and *Energy*.

Also striking are the relatively large R&D expenditures in the *Metal Sector (Iron and Steel, Non-Ferrous Metals, Metal Products)*. This clearly contrasts the low performance in terms of patent grants.

5.3.2 The Structure of Belgian Sectoral and Bilateral Trade

We now turn to the measures of intra-industry trade, as defined in section 5.2. We first look at the sectoral variation in intra-industry trade. Next we give an overview of the geographical variation in intra-industry trade.

We compute the GL index for total Belgian trade (world trade) for 24 manufacturing sectors. Table 5.2 shows our findings for total intra-industry trade (TIIT). We also compute separate GL values for horizontal (HIIT) and vertical intra-industry trade (VIIT) based on the price ratio defined in (3). The sum of both adds up to the GL value of TIIT. Vertical intra-industry trade is further decomposed into high-quality and low-quality vertical intra-industry trade (VIIThigh and VIITlow). Again, the sum of both adds up to the GL value of VIIT.

Table 5.2 shows that in all Belgian manufacturing sectors total intra-industry trade (TIIT) exceeds 50 percent of total trade (exports plus imports). More interestingly is the composition of intra-industry trade. In terms of the number of sectors vertical intra-industry trade dominates horizontal intra-industry trade. By contrast, in some important sectors (for Belgium) like *Motor Vehicles* and *Iron and Steel* horizontal intra-industry trade dominates. When we compare high and low quality vertical intra-industry trade (respectively, VIIThigh and VIITlow), high quality exceeds low quality except for *Food and Printing*. This sectoral variation encourages us to include sectoral characteristics, in particular sectoral technology indicators, in the empirical model.

Table 5.2   Relative share of total, horizontal and vertical intra-industry trade in total Belgian trade (world, average 1993-2000)

Sector	Sector Name	TIIT	HIIT	VIIT	VIIT high	VIIT low
36	Furniture	82.63	11.93	70.70	54.63	16.07
30	Office	81.67	33.60	48.07	31.23	16.84
18	Wearing Apparel	78.41	35.08	43.33	38.88	4.45
33	Medical, Precision Instruments	76.27	32.78	43.49	30.65	12.84
2423	Pharmaceuticals	75.54	27.29	48.25	36.91	11.34
32	Communication	74.95	15.96	58.99	49.43	9.56
25	Rubber	74.14	28.98	45.16	34.05	11.11
22	Printing	73.19	16.46	56.74	15.92	40.81
19	Leather	70.10	8.30	61.80	50.83	10.97
21	Paper	70.10	47.96	22.14	13.89	8.25
28	Metal Products	68.88	23.16	45.72	28.36	17.36
29	Machinery	68.74	19.50	49.23	35.03	14.20
31	Electr. Machinery	66.46	21.57	44.90	37.59	7.31
24	Chemicals	65.94	29.79	36.15	22.57	13.59
20	Wood	65.05	34.96	30.10	22.04	8.05
35	Other Transport	64.51	12.86	51.65	40.01	11.63
34	Motor Vehicles	63.95	50.53	13.42	12.54	0.88
16	Tobacco	63.82	21.79	42.03	34.43	7.60
15	Food	60.66	29.28	31.37	14.95	16.42
17	Textiles	59.99	22.94	37.05	28.66	8.38
26	Minerals	59.12	19.79	39.33	24.13	15.20
271+2731	Iron and Steel	52.76	37.32	15.44	10.35	5.09
272+2732	Non-Ferrous Metals	52.70	34.93	17.76	14.98	2.79
23	Energy	51.12	34.12	17.00	13.72	3.28

Source: own computations based on OECD, International Trade Statistics + conversion to ISIC rev.3.

Apart from examining the sectoral variation of intra-industry trade, we also look at the geographical variation. Table 5.3 shows intra-industry calculations similar to Table 5.2, but this time for all countries under study separately. The intra-industry trade in each sector has been added up and weighted by its share in total manufacturing trade (exports plus imports). The final two columns give respectively the ratio of HIIT over VIIT and VIIThigh over VIITlow.

Table 5.3   The bilateral Belgian trade structure (sector-weighted, average 1993-2000)

	TIIT	HIIT	VIIT	VIIT high	VIIT low	HIIT/ VIIT	VIIThigh/ VIITlow
Norway	5.97	1.72	4.25	1.94	2.31	40.49	83.64
Australia	6.00	0.37	5.63	1.50	4.13	6.54	36.25
Mexico	7.13	0.70	6.43	4.49	1.94	10.96	231.08
Korea	7.87	1.00	6.87	5.42	1.45	14.63	374.18
Turkey	8.08	1.99	6.09	4.95	1.15	32.64	431.36
Canada	8.39	0.90	7.49	3.67	3.81	12.08	96.22
Greece	9.86	1.63	8.23	4.41	3.82	19.86	115.58
Finland	12.61	3.06	9.55	6.06	3.49	32.08	173.88
Hungary	14.39	2.19	12.19	7.80	4.39	17.99	177.69
Ireland	15.88	3.84	12.04	4.40	7.63	31.94	57.70
Slovak Republic	16.96	4.94	12.01	5.76	6.25	41.12	92.16
Poland	18.58	6.33	12.26	6.81	5.45	51.63	124.86
Japan	19.25	1.61	17.64	13.55	4.09	9.15	330.79
Portugal	20.76	5.38	15.38	8.23	7.16	34.97	115.00
Czech Republic	22.56	5.91	16.65	11.77	4.88	35.52	241.30
Austria	23.61	5.10	18.52	8.00	10.51	27.52	76.13
Denmark	25.19	5.35	19.84	9.62	10.22	26.97	94.09
Sweden	25.83	4.72	21.11	7.70	13.41	22.37	57.40
Spain	31.78	12.03	19.75	12.69	7.07	60.88	179.45
US	33.25	5.13	28.13	19.78	8.35	18.23	236.84
Switzerland	33.76	8.82	24.94	12.43	12.51	35.35	99.35
Italy	35.54	9.15	26.40	18.08	8.32	34.64	217.35
UK	39.85	9.90	29.95	20.38	9.56	33.07	213.13
Germany	50.94	14.83	36.11	14.96	21.15	41.08	70.74
France	51.60	18.59	33.01	14.30	18.71	56.32	76.42
Netherlands	52.61	17.14	35.48	17.84	17.63	48.30	101.16
World	61.21	27.12	34.09	24.62	9.47	79.57	259.99

Source: own computations based on OECD, International Trade Statistics.

Total intra-industry trade is highest for Belgium's main trading partners, i.e., the neighbouring countries of Western Europe. In addition, for all trading partners vertical intra-industry trade exceeds intra-industry trade. Vertical intra-industry trade seems relatively more important for very distant trading partners. The picture for the relative importance of high-quality vertical intra-industry trade is very heterogeneous. Generally speaking, evidence of geographical variation justifies the inclusion of country-characteristics and distance into the econometric model.

Finally note that the computed levels for GL in Table 5.3 are relatively low compared to other studies. They reject the general view that a small open economy like Belgium is characterised by high levels of intra-industry trade. However, these lower values are a direct result of our large geographical (and sectoral) disaggregation.[7] This structure of trade is typical of a small economy with a high openness to trade in several industries and with multiple trading partners. By using this approach we tackle the criticism on the GL index that intra-industry trade is merely the result of statistical aggregation.

5.4 EMPIRICAL RESULTS

5.4.1 Determinants of Total Intra-Industry Trade

First, the empirical results are presented in Table 5.4. Our main *a priori* expectations are confirmed for total intra-industry trade. The model explains 50-60 percent of the variation in the data. The F-test rejects the hypothesis that all coefficients are jointly equal to zero. Most estimated coefficients are significantly different from zero.

Total intra-industry trade is positively influenced by income similarity. A one percent decrease in income differences between trading partners results in a 0.19 percent increase in intra-industry trade. This effect is small, but very significant. Geographical distance has a large and very significant negative effect on total intra-industry trade. To the contrary, relative scale has a strong positive effect. Relatively high employment in a sector abroad causes more intra-industry trade.

The impact of relative technological performance depends on which indicator we consider. Relative performance in terms of technological output (patents) has a significantly negative impact on total intra-industry trade, but the t-statistic is rather large (in absolute value). Hence, intra-industry trade decreases in the event that the trading partner is granted more patents within the sector in the US market than in Belgium. The opposite is true if we look at relative R&D expenditures. Relatively high R&D expenditures abroad increase total intra-industry trade. The indicator based on value added per worker is insignificant. Perhaps surprisingly, global technological spillovers have a positive and significant impact on total intra-industry trade.

Table 5.4   Regression results for total intra-industry trade

Total IIT
OLS

	(A.1)			(A.2)			(A.3)		
Constant	coef.	s.e.	t	coef.	s.e.	t	coef.	s.e.	t
Income Similarity	0.19	0.01	16.09 *	0.17	0.01	11.84 *	0.13	0.02	6.32 *
Distance	−8.19	0.23	−35.24 *	−8.16	0.23	−35.00 *	−9.80	0.28	−34.5 *
Scale - Employment (av.)	4.56	0.16	27.89 *	4.38	0.16	27.30 *	2.77	0.35	7.91 *
Relative Number of Patents	−0.44	0.25	−1.78 ***						
Global Tech Spillovers	1.34	0.16	8.44 *	1.27	0.15	8.20 *	1.73	0.20	8.85 *
Relative VA/worker (av.)				0.03	0.45	0.07			
Relative R&D Expenditures (av.)							1.72	0.29	5.88 *
Constant	39.10	2.38	16.44 *	41.90	2.49	16.82 *	56.27	3.58	15.73 *
R² adj.	0.43			0.42			0.50		
F	475.29			474.03			414.63		

Panel Between-Effects	(B.1)			(B.2)			(B.3)		
	coef.	s.e.	t	coef.	s.e.	t	coef.	s.e.	t
Income Similarity	0.19	0.03	6.90 *	0.15	0.04	4.01 *	0.14	0.05	2.63 *
Distance	−8.18	0.56	−14.65 *	−8.21	0.56	−14.66 *	−9.75	0.70	−13.94 *
Scale - Employment (av.)	4.56	0.39	11.72 *	4.38	0.38	11.44 *	2.83	0.86	3.28 *
Relative Number of Patents	−0.87	0.76	−1.15						
Global Tech Spillovers	1.31	0.38	3.47 *	1.25	0.37	3.34 *	1.72	0.48	3.57 *
Relative VA/worker (av.)				0.83	1.29	0.64			
Relative R&D Expenditures (av.)							1.67	0.72	2.32 *
Constant	39.15	5.66	6.91 *	43.82	6.32	6.94 *	55.14	9.01	6.12 *
R² between	0.51			0.50			0.58		
F	85.08			83.18			69.56		

Note: *, **, *** indicate significance at the 1, 5 and 10 percent level respectively.

Given these findings, our answer to the research question formulated as hypothesis 1 is as follows: total intra-industry trade is positively affected by income similarity between trading partners. The effects of technology and technological spillovers are mixed and somewhat surprising. However, these findings should be interpreted with caution since they may hide different determinants for horizontal and vertical intra-industry trade separately.

Table 5.5   Regression results for horizontal intra-industry trade

Horizontal IIT
OLS

	(A.1)				(A.2)				(A.3)			
	coef.	s.e.	t		coef.	s.e.	t		coef.	s.e.	t	
Income Similarity	0.05	0.01	6.28	*	0.04	0.01	4.21	*	0.03	0.01	2.53	**
Distance	−2.03	0.15	−13.70	*	−1.98	0.15	−13.31	*	−2.38	0.19	−12.25	*
Scale - Employment (av.)	0.62	0.10	5.99	*	0.57	0.10	5.55	*	0.14	0.24	0.58	*
Relative Number of Patents	−0.06	0.16	−0.38									
Global Tech Spillovers	−0.14	0.10	−1.38		−0.11	0.10	−1.14		−0.23	0.13	−1.7	***
Relative VA/worker (av.)					0.20	0.28	0.72					
Relative R&D Expenditures (av.)									0.53	0.20	2.64	*
Constant	14.16	1.52	9.35	*	14.71	1.59	9.25	*	18.81	2.45	7.68	*
R² adj.	0.08				0.08				0.10			
F	59.57				56.24				47.12			

Panel Between-Effects

	(B.1)				(B.2)				(B.3)			
	coef.	s.e.	t		coef.	s.e.	t		coef.	s.e.	t	
Income Similarity	0.04	0.01	3.62	*	0.04	0.01	2.70	*	0.04	0.02	1.61	
Distance	−2.10	0.22	−9.64	*	−1.98	0.21	−9.22	*	−2.38	0.30	−8.02	*
Scale - Employment (av.)	0.62	0.15	4.07	*	0.57	0.15	3.88	*	0.14	0.37	0.39	
Relative Number of Patents	0.41	0.30	1.38									
Global Tech Spillovers	−0.16	0.15	−1.10		−0.10	0.14	−0.72		−0.24	0.20	−1.17	
Relative VA/worker (av.)					0.20	0.49	0.40					
Relative R&D Expenditures (av.)									0.53	0.30	1.73	***
Constant	15.55	5.66	6.91	*	14.52	2.42	6.01	*	18.82	3.82	4.92	*
R² between	0.26				0.25				0.29			
F	28.62				27.66				20.62			

*Note: *, **, *** indicate significance at the 1, 5 and 10 percent level respectively.*

Only these separate results can be interpreted in the light of the theoretical underpinnings of intra-industry trade models. It is hard to interpret the finding from total intra-industry trade in a meaningful way as this total measure is a combination of two-way trade flows driven by both different characteristics and different quality. Therefore we continue by consecutively discussing the determinants of horizontal and vertical intra-industry trade.

5.4.2 Determinants of Horizontal Intra-Industry Trade

Compared to the findings for total intra-industry trade, the estimated coefficients for horizontal intra-industry trade are smaller and several of them are insignificant. Income similarity still has a significantly positive impact on horizontal intra-industry trade, as theoretically predicted. Although the coefficient is significant and it has the expected sign, the size of the coefficient is rather small. Distance and scale maintain their significant respectively negative and positive impact on horizontal intra-industry trade, but again the significance and the size of the coefficient have decreased compared to the case of total intra-industry trade.

Clearly, the impact of technological performance and spillovers is very limited in the case of horizontal intra-industry trade. As a partial answer to hypothesis 2, we do not find a significant impact on horizontal intra-industry trade, except for a small positive impact of relative R&D expenditures.

5.4.3 Determinants of Vertical Intra-industry Trade

The results for low-quality vertical intra-industry trade are very similar to the results for horizontal intra-industry trade. Income similarity, distance and scale are most important. Technological differences and spillovers have no significant impact at all.

The findings for low-quality vertical intra-industry trade are completely different from the results for high-quality vertical intra-industry trade. Income similarity is no longer statistically significant. In model A.3 the effect becomes even significantly negative (at the 5 percent level). The negative relation between distance and intra-industry trade holds regardless of the kind of intra-industry trade. Scale still has a positive and mostly significant effect on high-quality vertical intra-industry trade.

Most interestingly, technological differences and spillovers play a major role as determinants of high-quality vertical intra-industry trade. Hence the answer to our research hypotheses put forward is clear: innovation and the international spread of knowledge affect two-way trade in products differentiated by quality, in particular the highest quality segment, whereas the impact on products differentiated by other characteristics is much weaker.

Table 5.6 Regression Results for Low-Quality Vertical Intra-Industry Trade

Low-Quality Vertical IIT
OLS

	(A.1)				(A.2)			(A.3)		
	coef.	s.e.	t		coef.	s.e.	t	coef.	s.e.	t
Income Similarity	0.07	0.01	6.62	*	0.05	0.01	3.95 *	0.07	0.02	4.24 *
Distance	−2.33	0.21	−10.99	*	−2.40	0.21	−11.23 *	−2.29	0.24	−9.35 *
Scale - Employment (av.)	0.99	0.15	6.63	*	0.96	0.15	6.54 *	1.37	0.30	4.54 *
Relative Number of Patents	0.16	0.22	0.71							
Global Tech Spillovers	−0.24	0.14	−1.65***		−0.20	0.14	−1.44	0.13	0.17	0.80
Relative VA/worker (av.)					0.98	0.41	2.41 *			
(av.)								−0.35	0.25	−1.38
Constant	18.40	2.17	8.47	*	20.71	2.28	9.09 *	14.74	3.09	4.78 *
R² adj.	0.07				0.07			0.08		
F	47.21				50.48			36.73		

Panel Between-Effects

	(B.1)				(B.2)			(B.3)			
	coef.	s.e.	t		coef.	s.e.	t	coef.	s.e.	t	
Income Similarity	0.08	0.02	4.83	*	0.05	0.02	2.15 *	0.08	0.03	2.68	*
Distance	−2.25	0.36	−6.29	*	−2.38	0.36	−6.63 *	−2.23	0.42	−5.29	*
Scale - Employment (av.)	1.00	0.25	4.02	*	0.96	0.25	3.90 *	1.44	0.52	2.77	*
Relative Number of Patents	−0.24	0.49	−0.49								
Global Tech Spillovers	−0.12	0.4	−0.48		−0.17	0.24	−0.70	0.16	0.29	0.53	
Relative VA/worker (av.)					1.10	0.83	1.33				
(av.)								−0.41	0.43	−0.95	
Constant	15.91	3.63	4.39	*	20.39	4.06	5.03 *	13.29	5.44	2.44	**
R² between	0.18				0.18			0.20			
F	18.32				18.31			12.78			

*Note: *, **, *** indicate significance at the 1, 5 and 10 percent level respectively.*

However also for high-quality vertical intra-industry trade, the impact of bilateral relative innovative performance again depends on the indicators used. On the one hand, looking at patents, high-quality vertical intra-industry trade is reduced if Belgium's trading partner outperforms Belgium, due to a competition effect. Innovative foreign companies hamper Belgian high-quality bilateral exports. On the other hand, using relative R&D expenditures, it appears that higher innovation efforts abroad increase two-way trade. In that case Belgium exports high-quality products in exchange for similar low-quality products. These two opposite findings seem a contradiction at first glance. Hence one could call this evidence for a lack of robustness in the results. Nevertheless, these disparate findings can be reconciled. Especially during the course of new product or process development, companies learn from international contacts, in particular from the imports of similar high-tech goods. This corresponds to the positive coefficient for relative R&D

expenditures. However, once this product or process development is successful (and results in a new patent), cross-border expansion by the innovating firm increases competition. Imports are no longer needed as technology is updated. Finally note that the relative value added per worker is never significant.

Table 5.7   Regression results for high-quality vertical intra-industry trade

High-Quality Vertical IIT
OLS

	(A.1) coef.	s.e.	t		(A.2) coef.	s.e.	t		(A.3) coef.	s.e.	t	
Income Similarity	0.01	0.01	0.87		−0.01	0.02	−0.75		−0.05	0.02	−2.15	**
Distance	−1.79	0.24	−7.40	*	−1.86	0.25	−7.48	*	−2.67	0.30	−8.89	*
Scale - Employment (av.)	1.92	0.17	11.32	*	1.83	0.17	10.72	*	0.48	0.37	1.29	
Relative Number of Patents	−0.56	0.26	−2.18	**								
Global Tech Spillovers	1.41	0.16	8.57	*	1.26	0.16	7.64	*	1.62	0.21	7.82	*
Relative VA/worker (av.)					0.05	0.47	0.11					
Relative R&D Expenditures (av.)									1.30	0.31	4.21	*
Constant	7.05	2.47	2.85	*	10.82	2.65	4.08	*	19.67	3.79	5.19	*
R² adj.	0.07				0.06				0.09			
F	48.09				42.06				43.21			

Panel Between-Effects

	(B.1) coef.	s.e.	t		(B.2) coef.	s.e.	t		(B.3) coef.	s.e.	t	
Income Similarity	0.03	0.02	1.49		0.02	0.02	0.77		−0.04	0.03	−1.28	
Distance	−1.76	0.36	−4.91	*	−1.74	0.36	−4.84	*	−2.67	0.46	−5.80	*
Scale - Employment (av.)	1.94	0.25	7.76	*	1.83	0.24	7.46	*	0.51	0.57	0.90	
Relative Number of Patents	−0.93	0.49	−1.90	* **								
Global Tech Spillovers	1.57	0.24	6.48	*	1.40	0.24	5.89	*	1.83	0.32	5.76	*
Relative VA/worker (av.)					−1.02	0.82	−1.24					
Relative R&D Expenditures (av.)									1.26	0.47	2.65	*
Constant	4.73	3.63	1.30		6.51	4.04	1.61		18.39	5.94	3.09	*
R² between	0.23				0.21				0.29			
F	24.61				22.18				20.01			

Note: *, **, *** indicate significance at the 1, 5 and 10 percent level respectively.

Next to domestic innovation, global technological spillovers clearly have a large, positive and significant impact on high-quality vertical intra-industry trade. This confirms our hypothesis that a small open economy like Belgium benefits from the successful research efforts undertaken by its trading partners, which leads to an increase in Belgian exports of high-quality products in exchange for imports of low-quality products. This positive spillover effect is moreover not affected by the choice of relative (domestic) innovation indicators.

5.5 CONCLUSION

We started this chapter by establishing hypotheses regarding the determinants of intra-industry trade. Since a small open economy, like Belgium, is particularly influenced by events in the international economy, we examine the link between two well-known phenomena. On the one hand, small open economies are characterised by high levels of intra-industry trade. On the other hand, in order to remain competitive, continued technological innovation takes place by all players in the world. Even if a small economy chooses a policy that is directly focusing on substantial investments in R&D and innovation, it will at all times be confronted with large trading partners who have a much more influential position in international innovation. However, as technology has some characteristics of a public good, technological spillovers may compensate for the disadvantages of a smaller size.

This chapter investigated the role of technological innovation and technological spillovers in shaping the trade structure of a small open economy, using the example of Belgium. Theoretical models predict a positive effect of domestic technological innovation and technological spillovers on the importance of (vertical) intra-industry trade (hypothesis 2 and 3). Also technological spillovers increase the relative importance of high-quality vertical intra-industry trade in the trade pattern of a small open economy, pointing to a positive effect of international knowledge diffusion on the quality of Belgian exported products (hypothesis 4). Our empirical study confirmed these predictions. The role of technology becomes clearer if investigated for all kinds of intra-industry trade separately. We confirm the theoretical prediction that relative technological performance matters more for high-quality vertical intra-industry trade than for horizontal intra-industry trade.

In addition, we tested the hypothesis that relative factor endowments are a crucial determinant of intra-industry trade (hypothesis 1). We find that this is indeed the case, but mainly for horizontal intra-industry trade, and also for low-quality vertical intra-industry trade. But endowments do not explain everything. We find that trade barriers hamper all kinds of intra-industry trade and that relative production scale is relevant, especially for vertical intra-industry trade.

This research is among the first attempts to analyse the impact of technological spillovers, apart from technological innovation, on intra-industry trade. Many interesting extensions are possible. In particular the channels through which these spillovers are beneficial for the economy could be further explored in both theoretical and empirical research. Moreover, more detailed analysis is needed to investigate the impact of technological innovation and spillovers at the sectoral level.

NOTES

1. Acknowledgements: This paper was prepared for the 7th INFER Annual Conference 2005 in London. We gratefully acknowledge financial support by FWO-Flanders (Research Grant G.0241.02). We benefited from comments on earlier versions of this paper, as well as from interesting discussions. In particular, we like to thank Alan Deardorff, Juan Carlos Hallak, Isao Kamata, Siwook Lee, Ellen Brock and José de Sousa, as well as participants at the EIIE-Conference in Ljubljana (June 2004), the Applied Micro Seminar at the University of Michigan, Ann Arbor (November 2004), the International Economics Workshop at the University of Leuven (April 2005) and the European Trade Study Group Conference in Dublin (September 2005).
2. Following the literature, we alternatively used 25 percent. Although the choice of this cut-off level is arbitrary, it does not influence our results to a large extent. For an extensive discussion on the measurement of quality in intra-industry trade, we refer to Azhar and Elliott (2006).
3. This index resembles the GL index. As interpretation in terms of percentages is straightforward, we do not use the logarithmic form of this variable in the regressions. We take a logarithmic transformation of the other independent variables, but not of the dependent variable. Hence we estimate a so-called 'level-log-model'.
4. Conversion details and newly created conversion tables are available on request.
5. More technical details are available upon request.
6. By doing so, we accede to the findings of Menon and Dixon (1996), who formally prove that the interpretation of GL indices over time may be misleading. An increase in the GL index merely indicates a higher share of intra-industry trade in total trade. Growth of inter-industry trade possibly exceeds growth of intra-industry trade. Under particular conditions, inter-industry trade might have grown relative to intra-industry trade. As Brülhart (2002) argues, it is justified to use the GL index as long as one is interested in a comparison of the pattern of trade at different points in time. Deriving dynamic or adjustment conclusions based on the GL evolution, however, is not an adequate methodology. Consequently, the BE estimator should be taken instead of, for example, a random-effects or fixed-effects estimator. Moreover, the fixed-effects estimator cannot be used easily in the model as some of our independent variables do not change over time (like, e.g., distance). Hence, multicollinearity problems would arise, if we estimate the coefficients by a fixed-effects estimator.
7. A formal proof is available upon request.

REFERENCES

Abd-el-Rahman, K.S. (1986), 'Réexamen de la Définition et de la Mesure des Echanges Croisés de Produits Similaires entre les Nations', *Revue économique*, **37** (1), pp. 89-115.

Abd-el-Rahman, K.S. (1991), 'Firms' Competitive and National Comparative Advantages as Joint Determinants of Trade Composition', *Weltwirtschaftliches Archiv*, **127** (1), pp. 83-97.

Abraham, F. and J. Van Hove (2006), *Intra-Industry Trade, Innovation and Technological Spillovers: A Theoretical Approach*, mimeo.

Acharya, R.C. and W. Keller (2007), *Technology Transfer through Imports*, Centre for Economic Policy Research Discussion Paper No. 6296, London.

Amiti, M. and A.J. Venables (2001), 'The Geography of Intra-industry Trade', in Lloyd P.J. and H.-H. Lee (eds), *Frontiers of Research in Intra-industry Trade*, Basingstoke: Palgrave Macmillan, pp. 87-106.

Azhar, A.K.M. and R.J.R. Elliott (2006), 'On the Measurement of Product Quality in Intra-Industry Trade', *Review of World Economics*, **142** (3), pp. 476-495.

Balassa, B. and L. Bauwens (1987), 'Intra-Industry Specialisation in a Multi-Country and Multi-Industry Framework', *Economic Journal*, **97** (388), pp. 923-939.

Balassa, B. and L. Bauwens (1988), *Changing Trade Patterns in Manufactured Goods*, Amsterdam: North Holland.

Balboni, A. (2006), 'Cross-Country Technological Differences as a Determinant of Vertical Intra-Industry Trade: A Theoretical Model', *Economie Internationale*, **106** (2), pp. 25-55.

Bergstrand, J.H. and P. Egger (2006), 'Trade Costs and Intra-Industry Trade', *Review of World Economics*, **142** (3), pp. 433-458.

Blanes, J.V. and C. Martin (2000), 'The Nature and Causes of Intra-industry Trade: Back to the Comparative Advantage Explanation? The Case of Spain', *Weltwirtschaftliches Archiv*, **136** (3), pp. 423-441.

Brülhart, M. and R.C. Hine (1999), *Intra-Industry Trade and Adjustment: The European Experience*, Basingstoke: Palgrave Macmillan.

Brülhart, M. (2002), 'Marginal Intra-Industry Trade: Towards a Measure of Non-Disruptive Trade Expansion', in: Peter J. Lloyd and H.-H. Lee (eds), *Frontiers of Research in Intra-industry Trade*, Basingstoke: Palgrave Macmillan, pp. 109-130.

Coe, D.T. and E. Helpman (1995), 'International R&D Spillovers', *European Economic Review*, **39** (5), pp. 859-887.

Davis, D.R. (1995), 'Intra-industry Trade: A Heckscher-Ohlin-Ricardo Approach', *Journal of International Economics*, **39** (3-4), pp. 201-226.

Falvey, R.E. (1981), 'Commercial Policy and Intra-industry Trade', *Journal of International Economics*, **11** (4), pp. 495-511.

Falvey, R.E. and H. Kierzkowski (1987), 'Product Quality, Intra-Industry Trade and (Im)Perfect Competition', in H. Kierzkowski (ed.), *Protection and Competition in International Trade: Essays in Honour of W.M. Corden*, Oxford: Blackwell.

Flam, Harry and E. Helpman (1987), 'Vertical Product Differentiation and North-South Trade', *American Economic Review*, **77** (5), pp. 810-822.

Greenaway, D. and J. Torstensson (1997), 'Back to the Future: Taking Stock on Intra-Industry Trade', *Weltwirtschaftliches Archiv*, **133** (2), pp. 249-269.

Greenaway, D., R.C. Hine and C. Milner (1994), 'Country-Specific Factors and the Pattern of Horizontal and Vertical Intra-industry Trade in the UK', *Weltwirtschaftliches Archiv*, **130** (1), pp. 77-100.

Greenaway, D., R.C. Hine and C. Milner (1995), 'Vertical and Horizontal Intra-Industry Trade: a Cross-Industry Analysis for the United Kingdom' *Economic Journal*, **105** (433), pp. 1505-1518.

Grubel, H.G. and P. Lloyd (1975), *Intra-industry Trade: The Theory and Measurement of International Trade in Differentiated Products*, London: Macmillan.

Harrigan, J. (1991), *Scale Economies and the Volume of Trade*, mimeo, University of Pittsburgh.

Helpman, E. (1981), 'International Trade in the Presence of Product Differentiation, Economies of Scale, and Monopolistic Competition', *Journal of International Economics*, **1** (3), pp. 305-340.

Hummels, D. and J. Levinsohn (1995), 'Monopolistic Competition and International Trade: Reconsidering the Evidence', *Quarterly Journal of Economics*, **110** (3), pp. 799-836.

Keller, W. (2002), 'Trade and the Transmission of Technology', *Journal of Economic Growth*, **7** (1),pp. 5-24.

Kikuchi, T., K. Shimomura and Z. Dao-Zhi (2006), 'On the Emergence of Intra-industry Trade', *Journal of Economics*, **87** (1), pp. 15-28.

Krugman, P.R. (1980), 'Scale Economies, Product Differentiation, and the Pattern of Trade', *American Economic Review*, **70** (5), pp. 950-959.

Krugman, P.R. (1981), 'Intra-industry Specialization and the Gains from Trade', *Journal of Political Economy*, **89** (5) pp. 959-973.

Krugman, P.R. (1995), 'Increasing Returns, Imperfect Competition and the Positive Theory of International Trade', in G.M. Grossman and K. Rogoff (eds), *Handbook of International Economics*, vol. 3, Amsterdam: North Holland, pp. 1243-1277.

Leamer, E.E. and J. Levinsohn (1995), 'International Trade Theory: The Evidence', in G. Grossman and K. Rogoff (eds), *Handbook of International Economics*, vol. 3, Amsterdam: North-Holland, pp. 1339-1394.

Menon, J. and P.B. Dixon (1996), 'How Important is Intra-Industry Trade in Trade Growth? ', *Open Economies Review*, **7** (2), pp. 161-175.

Tharakan, P.K.M. (1984), 'Intra-Industry Trade between the Industrial Countries and the Developing World', *European Economic Review*, **26** (1-2), pp. 213-227.

Torstensson, J. (1991), 'Quality Differentiation and Factor Proportions in International Trade: An Empirical Test of the Swedish Case', *Weltwirtschaftliches Archiv*, **127** (1), pp. 183-194.

Torstensson, J. (1996), 'Can Factor Proportions Explain Vertical Intra-Industry Trade?', *Applied Economics Letters*, **3** (12), pp. 307-310.

6. Industrial Clusters and Transaction Cost

Hailin Sun and Luoping Sun

6.1 INTRODUCTION

Over the last decade, increased attention has been given to the nature of industrial clusters and regional development. Industrial activities tend to be concentrated in certain districts, which are indispensable to regional growth, especially with respect to how local competitiveness may transcend historical restrictions. The striking examples include China's electronic manufacturers of Zhujiang Delta, the rag trade of Yangtze Delta, and industrial districts in European countries, in which many similar groups of small independent firms, connected through horizontal and vertical intra-group relationships, make a significant contribution to the country's export mix. According to Marshall, geographic proximity offers to local firms a variety of external economic benefits, such as flows of knowledge, a specialized local labour pool and extensive local provision of non-traded inputs. However, a dearth of appropriate formal methods led neo-classical analysts and researchers (Krugman 1991a and 1991b, Venables 1996) to rely heavily on the principle of increasing returns to scale, which drives firms and workers to congregate in order to take advantage of increased factor rewards. Other approaches descended from Porter (1990) consider location as an important aspect of constructing optimal relationships between firms, customers and suppliers. In the institutional economic literature, there has been a rethinking of transaction cost arguments, such that vertical integration is now considered to be based on an entrepreneurial choice between mediating production through external market processes or through hierarchical organization.

To summarize an extensive literature, we believe the efficiency of industrial clusters stems in the first place from their ability to reduce transaction costs. From the perspective of both suppliers and customers, agglomerations of firms increase opportunities for stable contractual arrangements with other upstream or downstream firms, and thus provide the involved parties with better information on baseline prices and other factors.

We stress that the expected transaction costs associated with the processes of planning, negotiating and executing decisions depend on the extent to which one market contract is superior to other potential contracts rather than on expected profit gain. Transaction costs are thus not isolated from market structure, but instead arise from poorly defined property rights that are substantially reduced in industrial clusters.

In this chapter, the industry is modelled according to Hotelling's (1929) spatial setting, with open entry and in which all final goods at either of two locations are supplied through a network of K types of intermediate goods production. We might observe an intermediate goods production network clustering at any location because individual profit-seeking firms make contracts that divide the expected economic surplus with downstream and upstream firms. By reformulating transaction costs as poorly defined property rights derived from bilateral bargains between buyers and sellers of intermediate goods, the model shows that agglomerations increase opportunities for exchange and thus reduce transaction costs. In our model, clustering is treated as an investment in ongoing interaction, so the realization of either dual or single locations within a cluster involve equilibria of capital movements associated with spatial planning decisions by profit-maximizing firms. The model reveals that, if the capital share of a potential new cluster is smaller than some critical value, then an existing cluster has an advantage of lower transaction costs due to scale effects, so preventing formation of new clusters.

Our model is based on several approaches. In Marshall's (1920) analysis of the advantages of industrial districts, the agglomeration of industry mediates flows of knowledge and information, and thus improves the utilization of locally specialized labour and the local provision of industry-specific inputs (Krugman 1991a). The key assumptions are constant returns to scale at the firm level and the presence of external economies for the whole industrial district, such that competitive advantages are achieved through local specialization and cooperation rather than from individually identified businesses. Porter (1990) developed this theory further by attributing these competitive advantages to four interlinked aspects: firm strategy, structure and rivalry; demand conditions; related supporting industries; and specialized factors. According to Porter, industrial clustering enhances the interaction among corporations and improves competitiveness for the entire industry by expanding the vertical and horizontal division of labour and by strengthening competition and innovation. Although Porter's work captured the importance of identifying clusters, it devoted little attention either to any formal cluster analysis or to any empirical application of this approach.

In economic geography, hierarchical spatial cluster patterns arise in response to the uneven balance of scale economies with transport costs (Krugman 1991a and 1991b). Two important models of this so-called new economic geography (NEG) are home market effect models (HME) and the core-periphery models (CP) (Ottaviano and Thisse 2004). While the first one leads to a concentration of imperfectly competitive sectors in larger markets, the CP models explain, either assuming mobility of labour or taking account vertical linkages (Venables 1996), the appearance of a core-periphery pattern of the economy. That means that after a temporary shock to market size due to circular causation all firms of the modern sector agglomerate in one region, i.e., as the core. However, the NEG models, which are mainly based on the Dixit and Stiglitz (1977) monopolistic competition setting, makes two technical simplifications: a representative consumer is assumed for all or most types of goods, and a large number of firms is assumed to assure a competitive market. Other economists have introduced labour specialization advantages into the model of spatial concentration (Venables 1996). However, the model presented here implicitly assumes that downstream firms use all or most upstream products as input, which may not be the case for all production network clusters.

Within the transaction cost literature, the issue of using external market transactions vs. internal hierarchical organization is seen as the essential determinant of the degree of vertical integration (Williamson 1971). Recently, as a critique of neo-classical economics, social-network models have shown that trust-based interpersonal relationships can lead firms in a social network to undertake risky co-operation and to act uniformly as a group in accord with common norms (Gordon and McCann 2000). Italy's economic experience with variegated and multi-modal development demonstrates another way for a modern economy to gain competitive advantage through productive efficiencies. Though lacking a unified formula or methods, these approaches suggest alternative means for introducing social integration into economic research.

The focus of these various approaches includes external and internal scale economies, strategic linkages, locational optimization of transaction cost problems, market organization and social integration. Our discussion, which incorporates many of these elements, is organized as follows. Section 6.2 presents our framework, in which a bi-location production network involves strategic intra-location linkages at the intermediate goods level, along with consumer cost minimization and inter-locational spatial planning. Section 6.3 addresses the transaction costs for a typical contract between suppliers and customers on a certain type of intermediate good. Section 6.4 classifies the spatial patterns of clusters on the basis of a stability analysis, in which the equilibrium may either be dual- or single-cluster, depending on the levels of market efficiency, transportation costs, productivity and purchasing power. Section 6.5 summarizes the significance of transaction costs and market structures in regard to evolving institutional and innovation policies.

6.2 THE BASIC FRAMEWORK

Consider an economy of a linear region of length L, along which homogeneous consumers are uniformly distributed with density $1/L$ along this interval. Consumers can purchase similar final goods from either extreme ($i = 1, 2$). There are N similar ($N > K$) small firms each of which chooses one location and produces one type of intermediate good.

Intermediate Good Production Network: All final goods are supplied through a network of K types[1] of intermediate goods. Borrowing from input-output analysis, the supply network and production functions are represented in a $K \times K$ matrix Ω,[2] where the kk'-th ($k, k' = 1, ..., K$) entry $\Omega_{kk'} = 1$ if type k' uses type k as an input and $\Omega_{kk'} = 0$ if not.[3] The production technology varies across each of these K types. Then, taking the total amount of final good as a numeraire for any type of intermediate good, we assume that producers have a technology that transforms one mixed unit of input into one mixed unit of output.

Suppose that N_1 firms choose location 1 and N_2 choose location 2 ($N_1 + N_2 = N$). Also assume that firms are distributed among K types according to the demand for that type,[4] such that a firm can buy one type of input from only one supplier of that type.[5] Now suppose that transport costs are sufficiently high to prevent the formation of any inter-location markets for intermediate goods.

Market Share: Assume that the prices of final goods at the two locations do not differ greatly, such that the market clears. A consumer buys final products from the location where he/she pays least for a unit of final good.

Location Choice: The absence of inter-firm loyalty among consumers means that locational choices are based solely on prices and profits. The existence of multi-concentrated or single locations within a cluster district therefore represent equilibria of capital movements in response to spatial planning by profit-maximizing firms. In other words, each firm's spatial choice is interpreted as capital placement driven by profit differences.

6.3 TRANSACTION COST ANALYSIS: BILATERAL VERTICAL STRATEGY

Type k intermediate good is always produced by type k firms of number N^S_k and used in $\sum^k_{k'=1} \Omega_{k,k'}$ types of intermediate goods production, each with number $N^B_{k'}$. Consider the following situation, in which a buyer and a seller negotiate over q units of intermediate goods. Suppose the unit production cost for a seller is c, while the value for a buyer is v.

Assumption 1: *There exists* $v > c$.[6]
It is presumed that all co-operative forms are profit-driven in a competitive environment. Here, all firms have the same knowledge about the products produced and used, as well as about the size of the surplus, and they only care about the outcome of the negotiation in terms of their own profit share, without regard to the process by which agreements are reached.[7] Contract Agreement: Any agreement a in the possible agreement set A is expected to divide surplus S according to some proportion, z for the buyer and $(1 - z)$ for the seller. Given any particular expected agreement a in A, the profit set Π of all possible surplus combinations is:

$$\Pi = \{[zS, (1 - z) S] \mid S = (v - c) \times q, a \in A \}$$

Market Agreement: If two firms fail to reach agreement, they shall search for other contracts with an expected surplus that must also cover an expected search cost. Assume that both the buyer and the seller also expect there exists some market agreement price p.

Assumption 2: *i) There exists* p *with* $c < p < v$.[8]
         ii) Both players expect the market agreement price to be p.
Suppose that firms can always make an agreement with those with whom they had formerly failed to reach an agreement. Since the number of firms in the market increases the chances of a new offer, the search cost will be in inverse proportion to the number of potential buyers or sellers. Formally, the search costs for a buyer of type k' and seller of type k are,

(1) $C_B = \alpha / N^S_k$
       $C_S = \alpha / N^B_{k'}$

where the exogenously given search coefficient α – as a variable reflecting the technology and degree of market organization and social integration – can be estimated through an empirical investigation of productive processes, formal and informal interfirm contacts, and particular market structures. This coefficient reflects both the difficulty of the information search and the chances of failure in making a possibly profitable contract that matches products with appropriate inputs.

If we denote the disagreement point as $d = (d_B, d_S)$ where d_B and d_S reflect the reservation levels of profit for buyers and sellers, respectively, then we have:

$$(2) \quad d_B = (v-p)q - C_B \qquad d_S = (p-c)q - C_S$$

Assume also that transaction costs, which include the costs of planning, negotiation, execution and supervision, do not affect product valuations so do not change the expected distribution of any surplus. The technical restrictions on the profit set of all possible combinations of division – therefore indirectly on A, d, and the firms' preferences – are thus satisfied.[9]

A Nash (1950) bargaining solution can be used here to suggest the likely division of expected surplus, if we treat the players in this game as realistic and rational. The bargaining solution is obtained from solving the following maximization problem:

$$(3) \quad \max_{0 \leq z \leq 1} [zS - d_B] \times [(1-z)S - d_S]$$
$$\text{s.t. } zS \geq d_B, \ (1-z)S \geq d_S.$$

Proposition 1: *Under Assumption 1 and 2, there exists an equilibrium where the players equally divide the surplus, which is also the sum of the search costs.*

Proof: The equilibrium solution can be easily obtained as follows:

$$(4) \quad z^* S = d_B + \frac{1}{2}(S - d_B - d_S) = d_B + \frac{1}{2}(\alpha / N_k^S + \alpha / N_{k'}^B)$$

$$(1 - z^*)S = d_S + \frac{1}{2}(S - d_B - d_S)$$

$$= d_B + \frac{1}{2}(\alpha / N_k^S + \alpha / N_{k'}^B)$$

Here the incomplete contract, the open entry condition and the flexible bargaining process all determine firms' profit distribution from a contract. Intuitively, the disagreement profit is the opportunity cost and therefore the base or reservation price of accepting a contract. The opportunity cost subtracted from the surplus gives the pure bargaining profit

$(S - d_B - d_S) = (\alpha / N_k^S + \alpha / N_{k'}^B)$ on which firms will negotiate. Not surprisingly, the pure bargaining profit is also the sum of the search costs for a potential new contract due to the fact that by signing the contract, both buyers and sellers save future expenditure on additional search. Given their symmetric knowledge, a bargaining solution means that the available surplus will be more or less symmetrically distributed between agents. This division of surplus, however, represents only a firm's expectation prior to negotiation; it does not define how this process is actually implemented.

Assumption 3: *Realized transaction cost* c^T *is in certain proportion to the surplus.*

Naturally, the higher the bargaining profit or potential search cost, the greater will be firms' investment in time, energy and money in the contracting process. The new institutional economics procedure is to formulate transaction costs as a proportion of revenue. However, transaction costs are not unrelated to issues of market structure. Here transaction costs are considered in accord with the old Chinese saying that "negotiation is only over poorly-defined property rights." Formally, the transaction cost for a type k seller and a type k' buyer depends crucially on market structure:

$$(5) \quad c^T = \theta(\alpha / N_k^S + \alpha / N_{k'}^B)$$

$$\theta \in (0, \frac{1}{2}), \ (\alpha / N_k^S + \alpha / N_{k'}^B) \leq S.$$

From both buyers' and sellers' perspectives, agglomeration increases the opportunities for exchange and reduces transaction costs. The total transaction cost of a type k firm consists in the associated costs of both selling and buying.

There are $N_i \sum_{k'=1}^{K} \Omega_{kk'} / \sum_{k=1}^{K} \sum_{k'=1}^{K} \Omega_{kk'}$ similar firms in type k. Therefore, at any location i, the total transaction cost of all contracts is,

$$(6) \quad C_i^T = \sum_{k=1}^{K} N_i \frac{\sum_{k'=1}^{K} \Omega_{kk'}}{\sum_{k=1}^{K} \sum_{k'=1}^{K} \Omega_{kk'}} \left\{ \theta \sum_{k'=1}^{K} \Omega_{kk'} \left[\alpha / \left(N_i \frac{\sum_{k'=1}^{K} \Omega_{kk'}}{\sum_{k=1}^{K} \sum_{k'=1}^{K} \Omega_{kk'}} \right) \right. \right.$$

$$+ \alpha / \left(N_i \frac{\sum_{\kappa'=1}^{K} \Omega_{k'\kappa}}{\sum_{\tau=1}^{K} \sum_{\kappa=1}^{K} \Omega_{\tau\kappa}} \right)$$

$$\left. + \theta \sum_{k'=1}^{K} \Omega_{kk'} \left[\alpha / \left(N_i \frac{\sum_{\kappa'=1}^{K} \Omega_{k'\kappa}}{\sum_{\tau=1}^{K} \sum_{\kappa=1}^{K} \Omega_{\tau\kappa}} \right) + \alpha / \left(N_i \frac{\sum_{k'=1}^{K} \Omega_{kk'}}{\sum_{k=1}^{K} \sum_{k'=1}^{K} \Omega_{kk'}} \right) \right] \right\} \equiv C$$

6.4 SPATIAL PATTERNS OF INDUSTRIAL CLUSTERS

Assumption 4: *i) Production cost of any final good at either location*
$c_i^P = c^P$, i = *1,2.*

ii) Transportation cost is linear, with t *of unit length*

iii) Production of final goods Q_i *is in proportion to the number of firms* N_i; *i.e.,* Q_i = g N_i, *g > 0,* i = *1, 2.*

iv) Purchasing power of unit length is s.

Proposition 2: *Under assumption 4,*

i) There exists a symmetric equilibrium, with $N_1 = N_2$

ii) There exist two asymmetric equilibria,
if tgN(sL − 2C) > 4.

iii) The symmetric equilibrium is stable,
if tgN(sL − 2C) > 4.

iv) The asymmetric equilibrium is unstable.

Proof: The producer cost of one unit of final good at location *i* is

(7) $c_i = c^P + C_i^T / Q_i = c^P + C / Q_i$, i = 1, 2

where Q_i denotes the amount of final good at location *i*.
A consumer who is indifferent between the two is located at *y*, which is given by equating the payments for one unit of final product; i.e.,

(8) $C_1 + ty + \pi_1 = c_2 + t(L - y) + \pi_2$

where π_i is producer profit per final good.

In a steady state, $\pi_1 = \pi_2$ is satisfied with $xN = N_1$ firms at location 1 and $(1 - x)N = N_2$ firms at location 2. So producer profits are:

(9) $\pi_1 = \dfrac{sy}{Q_1} - c_1$; $\pi_2 = \dfrac{s(L - y)}{Q_2} - c_2$

Hence the necessary condition for steady state can be derived from (7) and (9),

(10) $\dfrac{sy}{x} - \dfrac{C}{x} = \dfrac{s(L - y)}{1 - x} - \dfrac{C}{1 - x}$

From (7) and (8), we have the equation about market share as:

(11) $\dfrac{C}{gxN} + ty = \dfrac{C}{g(1-x)N} + t(L-y)$

From (7) and (8), we have:

(12) $y = \dfrac{L}{2} + \dfrac{C}{2tgN} \dfrac{2x-1}{x(1-x)} - \dfrac{D}{2t}$

From (9) and (12), we acquire the profit difference function $D = \pi_1 - \pi_2$ as follows:

(13) $D = \dfrac{sC}{gN} \times \dfrac{2x-1}{2tgNx(1-x)+s} \times \left[\dfrac{1}{x(1-x)} + \dfrac{tgN(2C-sL)}{sC} \right]$

$\equiv \sigma \times f_1(x) \times f_2(x)$

where $\sigma > 0$.

A steady state requires $D = 0$. So, the solutions are:
(1) a symmetric solution where $x = 1/2$ with $f_1(1/2) = 0$ and
(2) asymmetric solutions $x \in (0, 1)$ and $x \neq 1/2$ with $f_2(x) = 0$, if $tgN(sL - 2C) > 4sC$

Suppose there is a temporary shock that makes an amount of capital flow from location 2 to 1, i.e., $x > 0$. A stable solution requires $dD/dx < 0$.

The asymmetric solutions are unstable. From $f_2(x) = 0$ and $0 < x < 1$, we have:

(14) $tgN(sL - 2C) > 4sC$

Denote the two asymmetric solutions as x_1 and x_2. We can prove that:

(15) $\left. \dfrac{dD}{dx} \right|_{x=x_1,x_2} = \sigma \times f_1 \times \left. \dfrac{2x-1}{x^2(1-x)^2} \right|_{x=x_1,x_2} > 0$

The symmetric solutions are stable. When $x = 1/2$,

(16) $\left. \dfrac{dD}{dx} \right|_{x=1/2} = \dfrac{2B}{2tgNx(1-x)+s} \times f_2 \Big|_{x=1/2}$

The sign of the above lies on $f_2(1/2)$, and it is not hard to show that $f_2(1/2) < 0$ if and only if (14) is satisfied, which guarantees the existence of asymmetric solutions.

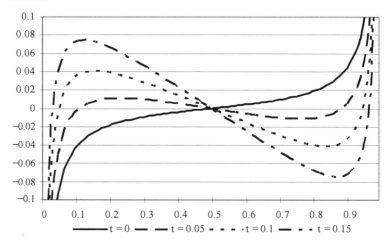

Figure 6.1 Profit difference function (related to transportation cost)

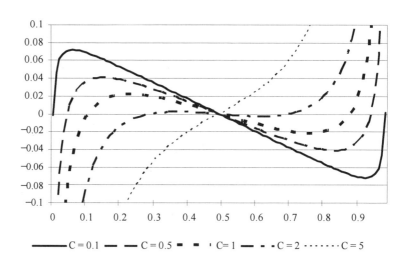

Figure 6.2 Profit difference function (related to transaction cost)

Figure 6.1 shows the calculated profit difference functions relating to different levels of transportation cost, for $N = s = 100$, $g = L = 1$, $A = 0.1$ and $t = 0.1, 0.05, 0.01, 0$. The figure tells a simple story which offers an intuitive version of the stability of the solutions given above. As the transportation costs decrease, the dual-location outcome becomes less stable and so industrial activities will more likely concentrate at single location. When transportation costs are zero, there would be only one core area in the industry.

Figure 6.2 shows calculated profit difference functions relating to different levels of transaction cost, for $N = s = 100$, $g = L = 1$, $t = 0.1$ and $C = 0.1, 0.5, 1, 2, 5$. When the transaction cost is potentially large, the dual-location outcome is less stable and industrial activities would tend to concentrate at single location. While all the firms cluster at one location, the effect of transaction cost reduction is maximized.

Remark 1: Stability
Symmetric Bilateral Clusters
If the condition for an asymmetric solution is satisfied, making the symmetric solution stable, industry tends to agglomerate at two locations and equally share the market. However, these conditions are not sufficient to guarantee dual clustering. The formation of clusters is a dynamic process and a certain scale has to be reached in order to form a new cluster in a market with an existing cluster. The critical scale can be derived from the model, given by two solutions, x_1 and x_2, by solving $f_2(x) = 0$, which is also the condition for the existence of an asymmetric solution. Assume that a cluster already exists at location 2, which covers the market. If the capital share of a potential new cluster at location 1 is smaller than x_1, the existing cluster enjoys the advantage of a lower cost resulting from scale effects, which limit the potential market share of a new cluster.

This critical scale limit depends on equation (14), and it increases in relation to factors affecting transaction costs: (1) the percentage of profit that firms are willing to invest in the bargaining process θ; and (2) the inefficiency of the organization of the market α. This critical scale limit decreases with factors related to the non-competitiveness of the market: (1) the unit transportation cost s; (2) productivity g; (3) the distance of locations L; and (4) purchasing power s. This limit also decreases with the total number of firms N.

The higher the return of a project is, the more funds firms are willing to invest in multi-targeted negotiations. Multi-centred clusters are less likely if an industry is in some way irreducible, such as with significant internal economies of scale. With more efficient markets or strong interpersonal producer relationships, second clusters become more likely.

In a market with distant potential production locations, high transport costs, high potential productivity and ample purchasing power, competitive pressures might not be sufficient to prevent the formulation of additional clusters.

The effect of the number of potential firms is more difficult to assess. On one hand, the existence of more firms lessens the expected bargaining profit, which might reduce transaction costs, but on the other hand, the existence of additional firms also intensifies the degree of market competition. In our model, the first effect dominates the second.

Exclusive Single Cluster

If the condition for the existence of an asymmetric solution is not satisfied and thus the symmetric solution is unstable, industry tends to agglomerate at a single location with exclusivity. Here, equation (14) is not satisfied and $f_2(1/2) > 0$. From equation (14), the factors that cause the exclusivity are the same as the factors that drive up the critical scale. Meanwhile, from $f_2(1/2) > 0$, it follows that critical scale reaches its peak as $x_1 = x_2 = 1/2$ and beyond this value, a dual-existence is not possible.

Remark 2: Comparison with NEG models

Home Market Effect

The HME, which appears when the larger region hosts a disproportionately large share of capital, can be derived from equation (10), which can also be written as:

$$(17) \quad sL(x - y/L) = C(2x - 1)$$

From the above equation, $x > 1/2$ implies $x > y/L$, which means the capital share is greater than the market share.

Core-Peripheral Structure

The case of a single cluster returns a similar result as CP, but with more realistic assumptions.

6.5 CONCLUDING REMARKS AND EXTENSIONS

Recently, an increasing interest in spatial industrial concentration has led to diverse analytical approaches ranging from economic geography and business relations to institutional and sociological economics. This chapter presents a model developed from the classical tradition that owes much as well to the new institutional economics. Our model also draws from location theory, input-output analysis, firm theory and social network models, which seem quite complementary and suggest that local transaction costs and the intensity of competition shape the pattern of industrial clusters. By reframing transaction costs as poorly-defined property rights and assuming the clustering to occur along a historical path, this model concludes that the main advantage of industrial clustering lies in the reduction of transaction costs, such that the pattern of clusters depends upon a critical scale affected by the levels of market efficiency, transportation cost, productivity and purchasing power.

There are many potential extensions of this approach. At present, the monopolistic competition network has not been adequately explored, but this void can be filled through an investigation of inter-agent transaction costs and their structural effects. The approach may also clarify how businesses manage themselves, and may contribute to a better understanding of firms' choice between market contracts and hierarchical organization. Empirical work should focus on linkages and strategies within intermediate production networks, and on the impact of innovation on the structure of production and economic organization. The input-output matrix can be extended to consider dynamic changes in its components.

The competitive advantage of industrial clusters has a paradoxical character. Many of the industrial choices between integrated operations and external contracts depend on a firm's routine interactions. Clustering is a combination of prior capital investment and ongoing relations between interacting firms. In response to institutional change, transaction costs shift, affecting property rights and other arrangements in an evolutionary process of change and growth. These uncertainties, in turn, may undermine firms' incentives for risk-taking and innovation. Consequently, there may be a need for local government to invest in the promotion of industrial clusters, innovative activities, new organizational forms and associational economies, in order to transcend scale restrictions and thus promote economic growth.

NOTES

1. And as long as K is big enough, the existence of the final goods market shall not affect the producers' strategy in the intermediate good markets.
2. Type k' intermediate good is produced by using $\sum_{k=1}^{K} \Omega_{kk'}$ types as inputs.
3. Here, the diagonal elements could not be 1 under the assumption that no intermediate good can be used as input for its own production process.
4. So there are $N_i \sum_{k'=1}^{K} \Omega_{kk'} / \sum_{k=1}^{K} \sum_{k'=1}^{K} \Omega_{kk'}$ firms producing type k intermediate goods at location i.
   In the type k intermediate good market at location i, $N_k^S \equiv N_i \sum_{k=1}^{K} \sum_{k'=1}^{K} \Omega_{kk'}$ firms of type k sell products to $N_k^B \equiv N_i \sum_{k'=1}^{K} \Omega_{k'k} / \sum_{r=1}^{K} \sum_{k'=1}^{K} \Omega_{rk'}$ firms of type k'.

5. So, a representative type k firm may purchase from $\sum_{k'=1}^{K} \Omega_{k'k}$ firms, transforms that product, and sells to $\sum_{k=1}^{K} \Omega_{kk'}$ firms.
6. It can be indicated in the later formula, that the internal monopoly profit is in fact equal to the sum of the opportunity costs for the buyer and the seller for signing a contract, and is therefore the total searching cost for a potential new contract.
7. That is to say, the producers' attitude toward the bargain will be completely determined by the potential and actual profit to him or her from a successful bargain relative to that from a bargaining failure. The bargaining can be over either the price or the share proportions, where only the resulting profits are of concern.
8. As long as depreciation exists, there is at least one p strictly between c and v.
9. (a) Π is closed, bounded and convex: closed as A is closed; bounded as all elements in A yield a finite profit to each producer; convex as always possible for producers to achieve an outcome in A by an agreed randomization rule.
    (b) $d \in \Pi$: The firms can agree to give themselves what they would get if there was no agreement i.e. they can agree to disagree.
    (c) There exists an element of Π such that both buyers and sellers get more profit than disagreement profit: This ensures that the bargain is interesting.

REFERENCES

Dixit, A. and J. Stiglitz (1977), 'Monopolistic competition and optimum product diversity', *American Economic Review*, **67** (3), pp. 297-308.

Gordon, I. and P. McCann (2000), 'Industrial clusters: complexes, agglomeration and/or social networks?', in *Urban Studies*, **37** (3), pp. 513-532.

Hotelling, H. (1929), 'Stability in Competition', *Economic Journal*, **39** (153), pp. 41-57.

Krugman, P. (1991a), *Geography and Trade*, Cambridge MA.

Krugman, P. (1991b),'Increasing returns and economic geography', *Journal of Political Economy*, **99** (3), pp. 483-499.

Marshall, A. (1920), *Industrial and Trade*, Macmillan: London.

Nash, J. (1950), 'The bargaining problem', *Econometrica*, **18** (2), pp. 155-162.

Ottaviano, G. and J.-F. Thisse (2004), 'Agglomeration and economic geography', in J.V. Henderson and J.-F. Thisse (eds), *Handbook of Regional and Urban Economics, Volume 4, Cities and Geography*, North Holland: Amsterdam, pp. 2563-2608.

Porter, M. (1990), *The Competitive Advantage of Nations*, New York: The Free Press.

Venables, A. (1996), 'Equilibrium locations of vertically linked industries', *International Economic Review*, **37** (2), pp. 341-359.

Williamson, O. (1971), 'The vertical integration of production: market failure considerations', *American Economic Review*, **61** (2), pp. 112-123.

7. Fiscal Design and the Location of Economic Activity[1]

Ulrike Stierle-von Schütz

7.1 INTRODUCTION

Since the initial work of Tiebout (1956) and Oates (1972), there has been, both in the economic literature and in political practice, a wide interest in the optimal division of providing public services between different government levels. Especially for countries in transition and developing countries, the decision on whether to centralize or decentralize governmental tasks in order to promote economic and social development is an important issue. Also in developed countries, changes in the vertical structure of governments could be observed over the last few decades (OECD 2002). Although there is evidence of increasing decentralization in a majority of OECD countries, a unique pattern of favouring the one or the other structure does not seem to occur (Stegarescu 2005). At the same time, increasing integration, particularly the creation of the Single Market in the European Union, which facilitates the movement of labour and capital, has led to reflections on changing production structures in countries and regions. Here, a fear of over-specialized regions, unable to cope with asymmetric shocks, may emerge. But the analysis of direction and determinants of regional specialization is still an open debate in the theoretical and empirical literature. Additionally, the possible role of the public sector in influencing the process of spatially changing production structures is increasingly becoming a crucial part of this discussion (Baldwin et al. 2003; Brakman et al. 2002; Brülhart and Trionfetti 2004).

This chapter aims at linking these two topics by asking whether the autonomy of a region in deciding about revenue and expenditure might influence its level of specialization and, thus, its potential capacity for shock absorption. The analysis is organized as follows: section 7.2 summarizes recent theoretical and empirical work on decentralization and specialization and offers some hypotheses for the empirical analysis in section 7.3. Results are presented in section 7.4, and the chapter ends with conclusions and prospects for future research.

7.2. THEORETICAL AND EMPIRICAL INSIDES

In the following analysis theoretical and empirical considerations will be explored in order to elaborate testable hypotheses for the above-mentioned research question.

Before starting to investigate the effects of decentralization on economic performance and on determinants of specialization, it is important to ascertain whether the public sector is able to shape the production structure. In the theoretical and the empirical literature, there exist different positions. While results of the proponents will be discussed in 7.2.1, opponents, such as Davis and Weinstein (2002, 2004) and Brakman et al. (2004), point out in their empirical analyses that even large temporary shocks like the Allied bombing of Japanese and German cities in World War II, did not have any effect on the growth paths of these cities and, more importantly, did not even change the urban industrial structure of the Japanese cities. The implications for the effectiveness of regional policy are far reaching, since, following Davis and Weinstein (2004), policy makers may not be able to choose between multiple equilibria and select with temporary interventions the one which is convenient for long-term regional development. However, the Allied bombing failed to destroy the social and transport infrastructures and the specific human capital that may have served as an important basis for reconstruction.[2] In the case of the West German cities, the Federal Government aimed at rebuilding them to their pre-war levels and provided specific grants to cities and private persons in order to stimulate the re-construction of houses and buildings (Brakman et al. 2004). These arguments may thus limit the rather pessimistic views that exist on policy actions and effects of changing institutions.

7.2.1 Decentralization and Economic Performance

There is a large debate in economics and political science[3] on the advantages and weaknesses of decentralization and, thus, about its impact on economic performance. Table 7.1 summarizes briefly the main arguments on this subject:

Table 7.1   Arguments supporting and challenging the effects of fiscal decentralization

Gains from decentralization	Arguments against decentralization
+ *diversification hypothesis*: increased efficiency due to better information on residents' needs	− *inequities and the need for a centralized redistribution policy*
+ *Leviathan restraint hypothesis*: intense competition between local governments reduces the size of governments	− *macroeconomic stabilization*: counter-cyclical actions and co-ordination of local governments are difficult to manage
+ *productivity enhancement hypothesis*: incentives for political and product innovations ('laboratory federalism') as well as a better quality of public services due to autonomy and accountability of the local government	− presence of *inter-jurisdictional spillovers*
	− exploiting *economies of scale* in production and administration of public goods
+ *specialization of functions*: efficiency gains may arise through specialization of representatives in any one tier dealing with specific activities	− *quality of governments*: central governments may attract higher qualified people, lobbying and corruption activities may be less controlled on the local level
+ *high per capita income*: fixed costs of maintaining a decentralized system may only be affordable at a higher stage of economic development and thus countries with high per capita income are more likely to be decentralised	− *small size of the country/population*: preferences can be assumed to be rather homogenous and decentralization may not offer additional advantages[4]
	− *scarcity of good local taxes* meaning taxes and fees relying on the benefits received principle represent only a minor share of total taxes levied
+ *high degree of urbanization*: economies of scale are more likely to occur at a lower government level if the population is concentrated	− *low per capita income level*: see Gains
	− *low degree of urbanization*: see Gains

Source: Thießen (2003), OECD (2002), Feld et al. (2005), own compilation.

Given this range of possible positive and negative effects of fiscal decentralization, empirical testing was needed. Currently cross country studies and single country studies analyse the impact of fiscal decentralization on economic performance by focussing on economic growth, capital formation and total factor productivity growth. However, these analyses come to very diverse results.[5] This fact might be mainly due to different measures of decentralization, since the commonly used one provided by the IMF's Government Finance Statistics (GFS) – the subnational share of total government expenditure or the subnational share of total government revenue – does not capture the fiscal autonomy that the subnational units possess to decide about expenditure (including different grant schemes) and revenue (taxes, tax bases, fees etc.) (Ebel and Yilmaz 2002). In order to include these missing aspects, the OECD started to create new measures of fiscal decentralization (OECD 1999) for 18 OECD countries. Stegarescu (2005) extends this data set to 23 countries and covers the period between 1970 to 2001. Further details will be given in the Data section, since these data will be used in the empirical analysis.

7.2.2 Determinants of Regional Specialization

The theoretical literature provides very different explanations for the emergence of regional specialization. Following traditional trade theory, comparative advantages will mainly lead to the specialization of those regions which open their borders. In neoclassical theories, political institutions are not taken into account and regional policy activities tend to disturb market forces. 'New theories' allowing for imperfect competition and economies of scale provide a rich set of possible explanations leading to specialization/agglomeration but also to dispersed and multiple equilibria. Especially recent theoretical models of the New Economic Geography (NEG) in the tradition of Krugman (1991) have tried to analyse the role of public sector interventions in shaping the spatial production structure and influencing break and sustain points. Up to now, the analysis has focused mainly on the impact of policy instruments, such as taxes and tax competition (Anderson and Forslid 2003; Baldwin and Krugman 2004), government spending (Brakman et al. 2002; Brülhart and Trionfetti 2004) and specific regional policy measures such as the providing of infrastructure, or the relocation of government agencies or similar institutions to peripheral regions or subsidies (Baldwin et al. 2003; Forslid 2004; Dupont and Martin 2006).

Regarding taxes and tax competition, the models demonstrate that, in the course of integration with an emerging centre-periphery structure, production factors in the core will benefit from an agglomeration rent which can be taxed by the region without losing the mobile production factors. Extending this model by government expenditure and thus taking the relations of taxes and spending into account, Brakman et al. (2002) show that increased public spending entering into the firms' production functions can stimulate agglomeration, since location becomes more attractive for production factors operating under localized economies of scale. Moreover, governments are able to change the equilibrium, i.e., from agglomerating to spreading forces, depending on the relative size or efficiency of public goods production and distribution. Brülhart and Trionfetti (2004) regard public procurement from the demand side and show theoretically and empirically that a region with a large home-biased public procurement will specialize in high-demand goods produced in a monopolistically competitive sector ('pull effect'). The emergence of the so-called spread effect is a second result of home-biased public procurement, meaning that, due to public spending, agglomeration forces may be offset. Theoretical results of the impact of public infrastructure investment on the production structure depend on the presence of localized spillovers and the policy objectives, since here, the trade-off between equity and efficiency becomes predominant (Baldwin et al. 2003). In their empirical study, Combes and Lafourcade (2001) confirm for French regions the positive relationship between decreasing transport cost and regional specialization and concentration.

Empirical studies focussing on policy activities and specialization are very scarce for the time being, but there are a few econometric studies providing insight on the sources of the specialization process as such. Stirböck (2004) identifies several determinants of regional specialization in capital investment and employment coming from different theories such as neoclassical trade theory, polarisation theory and NEG. Another approach has been chosen by Kalemli-Ozcan et al. (2003) who focus on the positive impact of risk sharing on specialization patterns.

Theoretical and empirical work on determinants of specialization, especially the role of public activities and institutions, is still in an early stage. As far as the author knows, there are no studies on regional specialization which take the fiscal design of the nation state encompassing the regions into account.

7.2.3 Hypotheses

In the following part, hypotheses for the empirical analysis coming from the theoretical and empirical considerations above will be summarized.

i) Decentralization
   The measures of decentralization capture revenue and expenditure autonomy. Since higher specialization is, in general, related to a higher

exposure of economic risk, autonomous regions may try to insure against possible shocks by diversifying the local production structure. On the other hand, if there is a mechanism of the central government to regulate these risks via redistribution schemes among regions, local levels need not cover the risk themselves and may focus instead on attracting specific industries in order to tax agglomeration rents. Another possible explanation for a positive relationship between decentralization and specialization may be deducted from the NEG models mentioned above. Since local governments would take advantage of greater autonomy to provide specific public goods, they may be able to attract mobile production factors, which could promote a process of agglomeration and intensify specialization. Following Brakman et al. (2002), this can only be possible if the public sector works efficiently. As shown by Baldwin and Krugman (2002) the subnational unit benefits from these developments by levying taxes on agglomeration rents.

ii) Exogenous variables from New Economic Geography models

The NEG models point to several determinants of location decisions, which should be considered. Market size, population density and the location or market access of a region are important factors in these models.

The market access argument is linked to market demand and influenced by distance and quality of transport and/or quality of infrastructure. Since, in general, core regions are closer to market demand and trading partners, i.e., they have better market access they would rather attract industrial sectors and market services and thus industries with economies of scale. Firms in peripheral regions have to bear higher transport costs in order to reach large markets and trading partners. As a result, the periphery may specialize in economic activities which rely heavily on factor endowments (agricultural territory, touristic services etc.) or which have to be provided by the public sector (health, education, government agencies etc.).

The intuition behind market size and population density might lead in the same direction, as monopolistically competitive sectors prefer a location near large markets with short distances in order to minimize transport costs and to have a diversified labour market. Considering the last argument from the perspective of mobile workers, they may also want to insure against shocks and will choose a location with a rather diversified production structure. A positive relationship between population density and regional specialization could be a sign of cumulative agglomeration tendencies in the centre.6 On the other hand, the overall effect is not clear, since congestion costs and other diseconomies of scale may arise and drive firms out of the centre as a densely populated area.

iii) Other influencing variables

The size of a region might also influence the degree of regional specialization. It is likely that larger regions will be less specialized, since their population and physical characteristics are rather heterogeneous (Kalemli-Ozcan et al. 2003: 907).

Since the magnitude of the decentralization measure may also be influenced by economic fluctuations, control variables such as unemployment rates, have to be included in the empirical analysis to capture effects of business cycle. The attractiveness of a region may also depend on research activities, and thus patents, as an indicator of research intensity should be taken into account.

7.3 EMPIRICAL ANALYSIS

7.3.1 Data

In the following, two important indicators of interest – the specialization and decentralization indicators – and their data sources will be described. All other data descriptions are given in the appendix.

In order to analyse the described determinants of specialization, we use a panel of 13 EU Member States at NUTS2 level (and thus 200 regions).[7] The NUTS2 regions are defined by administrative conditions and might not measure economic regions. This problem refers to the well known 'modifiable area unit problem' MAUP (Brülhart and Traeger 2005). Finding the appropriate economic regions for the analysis is often an arbitrary task and depends on the analysed variables and sectors. The advantage of administrative units is data availability and, especially, the NUTS2 regions seem to be the right spatial units when focussing on regional policy implications or on regional structural programmes.

The analysis is based on several data sources. This is, first, due to the fact that none of the possible sources was able to provide a complete and reliable data set and, consequently, several gaps had to be filled. However, the starting point was the regional database (REGIO) of Eurostat.[8]

The basic economic variable for constructing the degree of regional specialization in production structure is the gross value added (GVA). As far as possible, the data set is compiled according to the European System of National Accounts ESA95 including 17 sectors following NACE Rev. 1.[9] The rather short time period of investigation (1995-2001) is due to the introduction of the new European System of National Accounts (ESA) in 1995, which fundamentally changed the sectoral disaggregation.

As the data for fishing (sector B) are, for most regions, not separately available, we took the aggregate figure for agriculture and fishing (A + B). Consequently, two sub-sectors (A + B as well as mining and quarrying (C)) are included for the primary sector. The breakdown into branches of the secondary sector is rather limited in ESA95, as only three sub-sectors are available (i.e. manufacturing (D), electricity, gas, water supply (E) and construction (F)). On the other hand, ESA95 reflects the increased importance of services. The breakdown of the tertiary sector into ten branches (i.e. G to P[10]) including retail services, tourism, financial intermediation and real estate as well as public services, is now more detailed than it was before, when the data were based on ESA79.[11] The author is conscious of the limitation of this rather broad sectoral breakdown because it is questionable as to whether the statistical classification is fine enough, since it might hide heterogeneous developments in specific sub-sectors or not be able to show the economic dependence of some regions on specific sub-sectors. This is rather the case here since, for example, manufacturing is not disaggregated. However, this data set allows for a more comprehensive overview of the overall economic activity rather than focussing on manufacturing, which represents on average only 27 percent of production in the incumbent EU Member States, in contrast with 70 percent for services. Moreover, although their tradability is limited, services are increasingly part of international production chains, as becomes clear for example from foreign direct investment (FDI) data.[12] Consequently, limiting an analysis of specialization to manufacturing, as is frequently the case, leaves aside the main part of local and also international economic transactions.

Instead of using employment data we draw on GVA since employment data show some limitations for our purpose:

- differences in labour productivity within and between regions have to be accounted for,
- employment definitions still vary from country to country,
- flexible employment schemes, which are becoming increasingly important, make international comparisons difficult and
- statistical employment data is influenced more directly by public policy because of, for example, labour protection laws, etc. (Aiginger and Leitner 2002: 12).

However, GVA data also have disadvantages such as the need to convert them into one currency. Possible misalignments of exchange rates are one major disadvantage of operating with GVA data (Brülhart and Traeger 2005).[13]

In the empirical literature various indicators are used for analysing the sectoral specialization of regions and regional concentration of sectors. All indicators have their advantages and shortcomings.[14] In order to obtain results that can be easily compared to other studies and compared between each other, we chose one indicator that is commonly used.

Specialization in relative terms should reveal how much the production structure in one *region* differs from the average of a given set of regions. For this analysis of relative regional specialization the *dissimilarity index D* has been used. This indicator is one of the most commonly applied indicators for regional specialization, used e.g. by Krugman (1991):

$$(1) \quad D_j = \frac{100}{2} \sum_{i=1}^{1} \left| x_{ij} - x_{ij} \right|$$

For each branch i in a region j, the absolute values of the differences of sectoral shares in GVA between region j and the average of all regions of the nation state[15] (X_{ij}) are added up. In contrast to Krugman, we divide the result by 2 and multiply it by 100, so the index will take the value zero when no specialization can be observed, i.e. the production structure does not differ from the average of all regions included, and it will take the value 100 if full specialization exists.

The dissimilarity index offers the advantage that it is, in comparison to others, easily interpretable. It has also been applied already in several other empirical studies, so that the results can be compared to the findings of these studies. Moreover, outliers do not influence the values as much as is the case with other indicators.

As already stated in section 7.2.1, a data set compiled by Stegarescu (2005) is the basis of the decentralization indicators. He distinguishes between tax revenue decentralization and revenue decentralization, including non-tax revenue[16] (e.g. user fees, capital revenue etc.). Following his argumentation, measures of fiscal autonomy have to take into account 'legislative competencies in order to determine the tax base and tax rate, the attribution of the tax receipts, and tax administration' (Stegarescu 2005). The OECD scheme of tax autonomy (OECD 1999) has been used to provide a classification of taxes (Table 7.2). While local governments have total or significant control over their taxes with regard to cases a - c and d.1 - d.2, they only have very limited or no tax autonomy in all the other cases.

Table 7.2   Classification of sub-national taxes sorted by decreasing order of control

a	sub-central government (SCG) sets tax rate and tax base
b	SCG sets tax rate only
c	SCG sets tax base only
d	tax sharing arrangements
d.1	SCG determines revenue split
d.2	revenue split can only be changed with consent of SCG
d.3	revenue split fixed in legislation, may unilaterally be changed by central government
d.4	revenue split determined by central government as part of the annual budget process,
e	central government sets rate and base of SCG tax.

Source: OECD (1999: 11).

Three indicators capture three different degrees of tax revenue decentralization. In order to construct the indicators, the above classified taxes have to be added up and this sum has to be weighted by the tax revenue of general government (GG):

$$D\_tax1 = \frac{SCG\ a-c}{GG\ total\ tax\ revenue}$$

$$D\_tax2 = \frac{SCG\ a-c+d.1-d.2}{GG\ total\ tax\ revenue}$$

$$D\_tax3 = \frac{SCG\ a-e}{GG\ total\ tax\ revenue}$$

Data and indicators are used on a yearly basis and are analysed for the time period 1995 - 2001.

7.3.2 Investigation Approach

Following the working hypotheses derived in section 7.2.3, the empirical investigation tries to work out if fiscal decentralization may be one determinant of regional production specialization, taking into account other possible factors influencing the regional production structure.

The analysis is carried out by using a pooled cross-section time series model with time-specific fixed effects. These results will be compared with a two-way fixed-effects model including time and country fixed effects. While pooled regressions mostly exhibit the problem of unobserved heterogeneity and thus a bias in the estimators, fixed-effects models account for all time-invariant unobserved or not-quantifiable country-specific factors. Herewith the problem of time-constant heterogeneity can be solved. However, difficulties with the latter techniques arise if time-invariant effects play a role (such as the decentralization variable and the peripherality index here) or if the assumption of strict exogeneity is violated. Pluemper and Troeger (2007) developed a vector decomposition procedure allowing for the estimation of time-invariant variables in an augmented fixed-effects approach. The model will be estimated in three stages: First, a fixed-effects model without the time-invariant variables will be run. In the second stage, the unit-effects vector is decomposed in one part, which is explained by the time-invariant variable and an error term (η). The last stage re-estimates the first stage with a pooled OLS analysis, but now includes the time-invariant variables and the obtained error term obtained from stage 2. This method is especially useful for this analysis, since the decentralization variable, which we are most interested in, is only changing gradually over time, as can be seen in Figure 7.1.

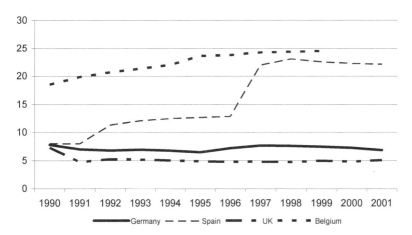

Source: Own computation after Stegarescu (2005).

Figure 7.1 Decentralization   indicator   dtax1,   1990-2001   for   different countries

In addition, the peripherality indicator capturing the distance of a region from the core can now be included in the fixed-effects model.

Formally, the basic equation takes the following form:

$$D_j = b_0 + b_1 dtax_j + b_2 transf_j + b_3 efficiency_j + b_4 rgdp_j + b_5 density_j + b_6 perind_j + b_7 size_j + b_8 patents_j + b_9 unemp_j + \varepsilon_j$$

D_j represents the dissimilarity index D, as described above in region j.[17] $Dtax_j$ indicates the tax decentralization variable in region j. Since changes in institutions (here, the federal structure) do not lead to an immediate reaction of sectoral change, the variable has been included with a three-year lag.[18] One has to note that this variable has been computed on a national basis. Considering the derived hypotheses it is not ultimately clear in which direction the decentralization variable will influence the specialization patterns of a region.

In order to capture the intranational insuring aspect, the variable $Transf_j$, standing for transfers to sub-national units from other levels of government (% of total sub-national revenues and grants), has been included in the analysis. If this variable shows a positive sign, one could infer that these transfers are used as insurance against economic risk which rises with production specialization.

As Brakman et al. (2004) demonstrate, the capacity of regions influencing agglomeration tendencies hinges on the efficiency of the public sector. Unfortunately, there are no efficiency indicators available at the regional level. Thus we use the Bertelsmann Success Index ($Efficiency_j$) (Hafemann and van Suntum 2004), which indicates the performance of the national economy.

Determinants coming from the NEG models are considered in the variables $RGDP_j$, $Density_j$ and $Perind_j$. The regional gross domestic product (RGDP), measured as the GDP per capita can serve as an indicator of demand capacity, whether population density and the peripherality index[19] representing market access of a region can represent indicators for the attractiveness of a region for mobile firms and workers. The same also applies for the regional research intensity captured by the variable $Patents_j$.

The variable $Size_j$ controls for the size of the region computed as log-population.

In order to control for business cycle fluctuations, we included the regional unemployment rate $Unemp_j$.

The robustness of the results will be checked by using a distinct variable for the efficiency indicator – the Bertelsmann Activity Index[20] – and by applying different concepts of decentralization. Firstly, this can be done by looking at the expenditure side of decentralization. Expenditure decentralization (*ExpDez*) is measured by sub-national expenditure as a percentage of total expenditure. As Stegarescu (2005) points out, the analysis of revenue decentralization may also be broadened by including almost all sources of public revenue such as user charges, operational surplus or capital revenue and not only taxes. Thus, the variable *drev1* is analysed.

7.4 RESULTS

In Table 7.3, first results for the pooled OLS estimations are presented. The overall performance of the estimation is relatively good in explaining 29 to 35 percent of changing specialization patterns in this short time period.

Table 7.3 Influence of fiscal variables and regional indicators on specialization patterns, 1995-2001; Pooled OLS estimations with time fixed effects

	(1)	(2)	(3)	(4)	(5)
dtax1		−0.072		−0.071	
		(6.25)***		(5.24)***	
dtax2			−0.014		−0.009
			(1.72)*		(0.52)
transf				−0.011	−0.007
				(1.28)	(0.44)
suc	−0.011	−0.023	−0.020	−0.018	−0.011
	(0.74)	(1.57)	(1.24)	(1.07)	(0.60)
rgdp	−0.131	−0.077	−0.115	−0.105	−0.135
	(4.31)***	(2.44)**	(3.57)***	(2.61)***	(3.30)***
perind	−0.014	−0.016	−0.013	−0.015	−0.011
	(6.89)***	(7.87)***	(6.05)***	(6.44)***	(4.01)***
density	0.003	0.002	0.003	0.002	0.003
	(14.61)***	(13.36)***	(14.47)***	(12.07)***	(12.39)***
size	−3.587	−3.591	−3.614	−3.474	−3.385
	(19.51)***	(19.44)***	(19.43)***	(13.59)***	(12.68)***
unemp	0.081	0.085	0.075	0.069	0.062
	(3.09)***	(3.37)***	(2.92)***	(2.57)**	(2.05)**
patents	0.003	0.003	0.003	0.003	0.003
	(7.36)***	(6.67)***	(7.50)***	(5.53)***	(5.82)***
Constant	39.962	41.051	40.900	40.840	38.964
	(19.64)***	(19.91)***	(18.89)***	(14.41)***	(10.84)***
Observations	1398	1398	1398	1110	1110
R-squared	0.34	0.35	0.34	0.30	0.29

Note: Robust *t*-statistics in parentheses; * significant at 10%; ** at 5%; *** at 1%.

The negative sign of the decentralization variables shows that tax autonomy might be linked with decreasing regional specialization, i.e., the more sub-national units are allowed to influence their tax revenues (tax rate and tax base as well as joint taxation), the more they tend to have a diversified production structure.[21] This result remains stable when transfers are included (column 4 and 5) although these do not have a significant impact on the specialization indicator.

The effect of efficiency (*Suc*) does not seem to be very important or does not capture the desired efficiency level, since the coefficients are very low and not significant.

Regarding the NEG variables, the regional GDP per capita is negatively related to specialization independently from the autonomous degree of tax revenue. This is rather surprising, since it would mean that regions with a diverse production structure would have a higher regional GDP per capita and not those regions profiting from specialization rents.

While population density slightly encourages a specialized production structure, the peripherality index shows that regions in the core are rather less specialized in relation to peripheral regions. Also, regions with a higher research intensity (patent output) seem to be more specialized.

The advantages of the vector decomposition model of Pluemper and Troeger (2007) become obvious when estimating the same models with the augmented fixed-effects model (Table 7.4), since the time-invariant peripherality index can now be included in the panel analysis and the small variation of the decentralization indicator be taken into account.

The negative impact of higher autonomy of the sub-national unit on regional specialization remains and shows even higher coefficients. Thus, regions which are allowed to decide on tax rate and tax base are insuring themselves through decentralizing the production structure during the observed time period. Interestingly now the variable *transfers* is significantly and positively related to specialization and, the insurance argument of decentralized regions holds, i.e. the coefficient of the decentralization variable is positively related to the specialization indicator (column 9). This might indicate that interregional transfers do not completely fulfil their insurance function.

The efficiency indicator *suc* points to the fact that successful regions in terms of the Bertelsman Success Index have a rather specialized production structure.

Further, the size of demand in a region (measured as GDP per capita), peripherality and patent activities, all have a positive impact on regional specialization. Regions with higher market demand show a tendency to be more specialized. The positive influence of R&D activities on specialization could be explained by local knowledge spillovers or local knowledge networks. Since the effect is not always significant and quite small, this effect should not be overemphasized. Also data quality at this regional level shows some limitations.

Table 7.4   Influence of fiscal variables and regional indicators on specialization patterns, 1995-2001, fixed-effects models with vector decomposition (time and region fixed effects)

	(6)	(7)	(8)	(9)	(10)
dtax1		−0.125		−0.085	
		(7.08)***		(8.50)***	
dtax2			−0.054		−0.035
			(3.09)***		(3.54)***
transf				0.008	0.004
				(4.84)***	(0.20)
suc	0.062	0.048	0.035	0.110	0.108
	(3.51)***	(23.94)***	(17.46)***	(47.50)***	(47.23)***
rgdp	0.063	0.056	0.050	0.060	0.053
	(10.66)***	(9.17)***	(2.72)***	(2.57)**	(2.29)**
perind	0.007	0.006	0.014	0.015	0.022
	(14.29)***	(20.34)***	(26.90)***	(26.10)***	(34.23)***
size	−1.711	−1.763	−1.789	−0.790	−0.753
	(45.97)***	(47.47)***	(48.16)***	(16.70)***	(15.92)***
density	−0.007	−0.007	−0.007	−0.009	−0.009
	(15.85)***	(2.44)**	(0.22)	(2.68)***	(0.24)
unemp	−0.031	−0.023	−0.018	−0.019	−0.006
	(6.16)***	(0.74)	(3.55)***	(0.51)	(1.03)
patents	0.001	0.001	0.001	0.001	0.001
	(0.39)	(2.41)**	(0.28)	(1.81)*	(0.31)
Residuals	1.000	1.000	1.000	1.000	1.000
	(171.3)***	(169.4)***	(171.8)***	(150.8)***	(153.2)***
Constant	19.633	22.719	23.076	8.631	8.232
	(48.14)***	(63.92)***	(55.58)***	(19.55)***	(13.34)***
Obser-vations	1398	1398	1398	1110	1110

Note: *t*-statistics in parentheses,* significant at 10%; ** significant at 5%; *** significant at 1%.

Densely populated regions seem to be less specialized; consequently one could conclude that congestion costs might lead to a rather diversified production structure. This might contradict the result that regions in the centre are more specialized than in peripheral regions. Since both coefficients have only small effects on the specialization indicator, it is not possible to detect strong polarization tendencies in this analysis.

The results of the robustness tests can be found in the appendix, Table 7.A.5. Considering expenditure decentralization, the results suggest a positive relationship between decentralization and specialization. Thus one might infer that, if a region has a relatively high expenditure rate relative to the national level, it attracts specific sectors, resulting in a more specialized production structure. However, one has to be very careful with these proposals, since the expenditure variable does not reflect regional autonomy on spending; it only covers the level of sub-national expenditure. Thus further analysis should be based on differentiated expenditure indicators.

An extension of the analysis of public revenue decentralization by including non-tax revenues, the relationship between the decentralization variable and regional specialization remains stable. As shown in Table 7.A.5, columns 4 and 5, the variable *drev1* has a significantly negative impact on specialization, even if transfers are included.

7.5 CONCLUSIONS

Summing up this empirical exercise regarding the influences of different vertical government structures on specialization patterns, we have been able to show by using a panel of 13 EUR Member States in the period of 1995-2001 that the organization of government levels has a certain impact on the regional production structure. Rather independent sub-national units, in terms of revenue autonomy, seem to have a diversified production structure. This relationship supports the hypothesis that autonomous regions might try to diversify their production structure in order to insure against adverse shock. Interestingly, if intergovernmental transfers are included in the analysis, this effect reverses, so that transfer schemes have the function of an insurance scheme for regions.

Scope for future research is offered by several aspects:

The variable for expenditure decentralization does not capture regional expenditure autonomy and should be refined, since this measure could give more insight on the impact of public activities on shaping the economic landscape. It would also be interesting to see which sectors are mainly attracted by more or less autonomous regions. Thus, sectoral indicators should be included in the analysis. Also, the measure of public efficiency lacks generality and can only be seen as a rough proxy. It would be very helpful for the analysis to have an index on regional government performance.

The regarded time span is short at the moment, and the small variation in the data could be overcome with a longer time period.

The new Member States of the European Union would be another interesting field of research, since production structure and public organization have been changing over the last few years. Up to now, data problems have made an in-depth analysis difficult.

APPENDIX

Data Sources and Description

Gross value added
- at basic prices
- Eurostat Database REGIO

Table 7.A1 Sectors included according to NACE Rev. 1

	Sector
A_B	Agriculture, hunting, forestry and fishing
C	Mining and quarrying
D	Manufacturing
E	Electricity, gas and water supply
F	Construction
G	Wholesale and retail trade; repair of motor vehicles, motorcycles and personal and household goods
H	Hotels and restaurants
I	Transport, storage and communication
J	Financial intermediation
K	Real estate, renting and business activities
L	Public administration and defence; compulsory social security
M	Education
N	Health and social work
O	Other community, social, personal service activities
P	Private households with employed persons

Table 7.A2 Regional disaggregation

Member State	No. of Regions	Member State	No. of Regions
Austria (AT)	9	Italy (IT)[22]	20
Belgium (BE)	11	Netherlands (NL)	12
Finland (FI)	5	Portugal (PT)[23]	5
France[24] (FR)	22	Spain (ES)[25]	16
Germany (DE)[26]	40	Sweden (SE)	8
Greece (GR)	13	United Kingdom	37
Ireland (IE)	2		

Localisation of Economic Activities

Table 7.A3 Data adjustments

General rules		• Due to data problems, some regions had to be excluded or sub-regions taken together as one region, as explained in Table 7.A2.
		• Negative values or zero values were replaced by a value equal to 1 pro-mille of the reported value for the corresponding region.
		• Missing values in a region in the first or last year were calculated using the corresponding growth rate in the next higher regional aggregate for which data was available.
		• Missing values in the middle of the time span were calculated using linear interpolation.
		• After all adjustments, new sums were calculated before calculating regional or sectoral shares.
Germany	F, I, J	Breakdown of NUTS1 into NUTS2 according to sector specific regional employment shares. Source for employment shares: Bode et al. (2004)
	C, E, G, H	Result of $(C + D + E + F) - (D - F)$ on NUTS 2 level, i.e. $(C + E)$ was split up between these two sectors according to the corresponding shares of the single sectors C and E on NUTS1 level. Similar approach for G and H.
	D	Source: Federal Statistical Office, Germany
	K	Result of $(J + K) - J$
	L, M, N, O, P	Due to a lack of better possibilities, $(L + M + N + O + P)$ on NUTS2 level had to be split up according to the sectoral shares in those EU-13 countries where these data are available
Greece		In 2001, regional breakdown from NUTS1 into NUTS2 according to regional shares in 2000 of the corresponding sector.
United Kingdom	All sectors	Source: Office for National Statistics (ONS), United Kingdom. In 2001, regional breakdown from NUTS1 into NUTS2 according to regional shares in 2000 of the corresponding sector.
	P	Source: Office for National Statistics (ONS), United Kingdom. Regional breakdown from NUTS1 into NUTS2 according to regional shares in all other sectors in the corresponding year.

Regional Gross Domestic Product, Population Density, Patents,
Unemployment
Eurostat Database REGIO

Peripherality Index
This measure has been taken from Schürmann and Talaat (2000). This is an index of the potential or gravity-model type where market size / potential and distances in terms of accessibility are taken into account. High (low) values of the peripherality index indicate a central (peripheral) position of the related region.

Decentralization indicators Dtax_1, Dtax_2, Drev_1, Drev_2
For methodology and sources, see Stegarescu (2005).

Expenditure Decentralization ExpDez
Sub-national expenditures (% of total expenditures).
IMF's Government Finance Statistics (GFS).
Downloadable from the official website of the Worldbank: Decentralization and Sub-national Regional Economics:
http://www1.worldbank.org/publicsector/decentralization/fiscalindicators.htm.

Transfers
Transfers to sub-national from other levels of Government (% of total sub-national revenues and grants).
IMF's Government Finance Statistics (GFS).
Downloadable from the official website of the Worldbank: Decentralization and Sub-national Regional Economics:
http://www1.worldbank.org/publicsector/decentralization/fiscalindicators.htm.

Efficiency
Success Index (Suc) of the Bertelsmann Foundation
Being the core measure for the International Employment and Growth Ranking of the Bertelsmann Foundation, it contains variables of labour market performance and economic growth. Values range from 0 to 120, with higher values indicating better performance.
Activity Index (Act) of the Bertelsmann Foundation
This measure focus on 12 indicators of three areas of activity: 'labour market, government and economy, economy and labour and management" and takes values from 0 to 120, where higher values indicate a better performance.
Both measures are only available on a national basis.
For a summary and the methodological background, see:
http://www.bertelsmann-stiftung.de/de/4303_8886.jsp.

Table 7.A4 Descriptive Statistics of the specialization and decentralization indicators

Variable	Obs.	Mean	Std. Dev.	Min	Max
ksi	1398	12.032	5.462	2.417	34.202
dtax1	1317	11.062	10.069	0.166	47.016
dtax2	1317	22.169	18.475	0.166	50.343
drev1	679	16.221	9.285	5.186	42.875
drev2	679	22.560	15.767	5.186	50.102
expdez	1067	26.943	9.225	10.740	41.860

Table 7.A5 Robustness tests, expenditure and revenue decentralization, 1995-2001, fixed-effects models with vector decomposition (time and region fixed-effects)

	(1)	(2)	(3)	(4)	(5)
dtax1	−0.555				
	(5.6)***				
expdez		0.093	0.141		
		(27.10)***	(33.34)***		
drev1				−0.264	−0.284
				(10.16)***	(29.82)***
transf			0.032		0.009
			(16.46)***		(3.93)***
suc				0.055	0.050
				(16.12)***	(13.30)***
act	0.081	0.201	0.172		
	(21.92)***	(46.86)***	(39.23)***		
rgdp	0.057	0.069	0.058	0.066	0.072
	(2.48)**	(10.13)***	(8.36)***	(9.26)***	(9.39)***
perind	0.006	0.011	0.011	0.012	0.013
	(12.04)***	(21.15)***	(20.51)***	(21.46)***	(23.02)***
size	−1.732	−1.297	−1.402	−1.488	−1.500
	(46.86)***	(29.68)***	(32.31)***	(35.73)***	(33.43)***
density	−0.009	−0.007	−0.006	−0.004	−0.004
	(1.92)*	(95.09)***	(93.74)***	(1.46)	(1.33)
unemp	−0.025	−0.011	−0.010	0.048	0.065
	(0.55)	(1.93)*	(1.61)	(16.55)***	(21.7)***
patents	0.001	0.001	0.002	0.001	0.001
	(1.89)*	(13.68)***	(15.06)***	(2.01)**	(2.76)***
Residuals	1.000	1.000	1.000	1.000	1.000
	(169.18)	(157.58)	(158.30)	(169.06)	(160.78)
	***	***	***	***	***
Observations	1398	1065	1065	677	637

Note: *t*-statistics in parentheses. * significant at 10%; ** significant at 5%; *** significant at 1%.

NOTES

1. The author would like to acknowledge a grant from the German Science Foundation (DFG SPP 1142). The usual disclaimer applies.
2. This argument was mainly forwarded in the comments of F. Robert-Nicoud and the authors admit that point to a certain degree in their paper.
3. For a comprehensive survey see e.g. Thießen (2001: 2-8).
4. However, this rule does not seem to be supported by clear real world experience regarding the heterogeneity of small countries like Belgium or Switzerland (Stegarescu 2005).
5. For a recent survey see Feld et al. (2005: 9-12).
6. This concept has already been stated by the founders of the polarization theory.
7. NUTS refers to Nomenclature of Statistical Territorial Units (NUTS) and is a hierarchical classification of regions in a Member State, where higher numbers indicate a smaller administrative unit (Eurostat 1999).
8. For the adjustments made, see Table 7.A2 in the appendix.
9. Nomenclature des activités économiques dans les Communautés Européennes, see Table 7.A1 in the appendix.
10. Since no data are available for sector Q (exterritorial organizations) it has been left out of the analysis.
11. For a list of the NACE sectors, see Table 7.A1 in the appendix.
12. Services account, on a worldwide scale, for 60 percent of FDI inward stocks as well as for two thirds of inward flows (UNCTAD 2004).
13. Due to data problems, the dissimilarity indicator has only been computed with GVA data. The comparison with employment data is left to future research.
14. For surveys see, for example, Amiti (1997), Krieger-Boden (1999), WIFO (1999), Bode et al. (2004), Brülhart and Traeger (2005), Combes and Overman (2004).
15. This is the reason why one-region countries such as Luxembourg and Denmark had to be left out of this analysis.
16. Due to data problems, this second measure has been left out of the analysis.
17. As pooled data are used, the time index has been taken out of the specification.
18. The lag of three years produced the best results and is used throughout the chapter.
19. High values of this index represent regions in the core; low values regions in the periphery of EU-13.
20. This index focuses on factors describing the sources of performance differences between countries.
21. Since the results for *dtax2* and *dtax3* do not differ substantially, only the results for *dtax2* are reported.
22. As data are not yet sufficiently available for ITd1 (Provincia Autonoma Bolzano-Bozen) and ITd2 (Provincia Autonoma Trento) separately, we have taken them as one region by subtracting ITd3, ITd4 and ITd5 from ITd.
23. PT20 (Região Autónoma dos Açores) and PT30 (Região Autónoma da Madeira) have been excluded.
24. Overseas departments have been excluded.
25. ES63 (Ciudad Autónoma de Ceuta) and ES64 (Ciudad Autónoma de Melilla) as well as ES70 (Canarias) have been excluded.
26. The new division of DE40 (Brandenburg) has not been taken into account, due to several missing data for the sub-regions.

REFERENCES

Anderson F. and R. Forslid (2003), 'Tax competition and economic geography', *Journal of Public Economic Theory*, **5**(2), pp. 279-304.

Aiginger, K. and W. Leitner (2002), 'Regional concentration in the USA and Europe: Who follows whom?', *Weltwirtschaftliches Archiv*, **138**(4), pp. 652-679.

Amiti, M. (1997), *Specialization Patterns in Europe*, CEPR Discussion Paper 363, London.

Baldwin, R.E. and P. Krugman (2002), *Agglomeration, Integration and Tax Harmonization*, CEPR Discussion Paper 2630, London.

Baldwin, R.E. and P. Krugman (2004), 'Agglomeration, integration and tax harmonisation', *European Economic Review*, **48**, pp. 1-23.

Baldwin, R., R. Forslid, P. Martin, G. Ottaviano and F. Robert-Nicoud (2003), *Economic Geography and Public Policy*, Princeton and Oxford.

Bode, E., Ch. Krieger-Boden, F. Siedenburg and R. Soltwedel (2004), *European Integration, Regional Structural Change and Cohesion in Spain*, EURECO Working Paper.

Brakman, S., H. Garretsen and Ch. van Marrewijk (2002), *Locational Competition and Agglomeration: The Role of Government Spending*, CESifo Working Paper 775, Munich.

Brakman, S., H. Garretsen and M. Schramm (2004), 'The strategic bombing of German cities during World War II and its impact on city growth', *Journal of Economic Geography*, **4**, pp. 201-218.

Brülhart, M. and R. Traeger (2005), 'An account of geographic concentration patterns in Europe', *Regional Science and Urban Economics*, **35**(6), pp. 597-624.

Brülhart, M. and F. Trionfetti (2004), 'Public expenditure and international specialisation', *European Economic Review*, **48**(4), pp. 851-881.

Combes, P.-P. and H.G. Overman (2004). 'The spatial distribution of economic activities in the European Union', in: J. V. Henderson and J.-F. Thisse (eds.). *Handbook of Regional and Urban Economics*, **4**, pp. 2845-2909, Cities and Geography, Amsterdam.

Combes, P.-P. and M. Lafourcade (2001), *Transport cost decline and regional inequalities: evidence from France*, CEPR Discussion Paper 2894, London.

Davis, D.R. and D.E. Weinstein (2002), 'Bones, bombs, and breakpoints: The geography of economic activity', *American Economic Review*, **92**(5), pp. 1269-1289.

Davis, D. and D. Weinstein (2004), *A Search for Multiple Equilibria in Urban Industrial Structure*, NBER Working Paper 10252, Cambridge, MA: National Bureau of Economic Research.

Dupont, V. and P. Martin (2006), 'Subsidies to poor regions and inequalities: Some unpleasant arithmetic', *Journal of Economic Geography*, **6**(2), pp. 223-240.

Ebel, R.D. and S. Yilmaz (2002), *On the Measurement and Impact of Decentralization*, Policy Research Working Paper, 2809, Washington.

Eurostat (1999). *Regions – Nomenclature of Territorial Units for Statistics*, NUTS, Luxembourg.

Feld, L.P., T. Baskaran and T. Dede (2005), 'Fiscal Federalism and Economic Growth: Cross-Country Evidence for OECD Countries', unpublished manuscript, University of Heidelberg.

Forslid, R. (2004), *Regional Policy Integration and the Location of Industry in a Multiregion Framework*, Stockholm University Working Papers in Economics.

Hafemann, K. and U. van Suntum (2004), *Internationales Standort-Ranking 2004*, Bertelsmann-Stiftung, Gütersloh.

Kalemli-Ozcan, S., B.E. Sorensen and O. Yosha (2003), 'Risk sharing and industrial specialization: Regional and international evidence', *American Economic Review*, **93**(3), pp. 903-918.

Krieger-Boden, C. (1999), 'Nationale und regionale Spezialisierungsmuster im europäischen Vergleich', *Die Weltwirtschaft*, **2**, pp. 234-254.

Krugman, P. (1991), *Geography and Trade*, Cambridge (MA).

Oates, W. E. (1972), *Fiscal Federalism*, New York etc.

OECD (1999), 'Taxing powers of state and local government', *OECD Tax Policy Studies* 1, Paris.

OECD (2002), 'Fiscal Decentralisation in EU Applicant States and Selected EU Member States', Report Prepared for the Workshop on Decentralisation Trends, Perspective and Issues at the Threshold of EU Enlargement; Denmark October 10-11 2002, Paris.

Pluemper, T. and V.E. Troeger (2007), 'Efficient estimation of time-invariant and rarely changing variables in finite sample panel analyses with unit fixed effects', *Political Analysis,* **15**(4), pp. 124-139.

Schürmann, C. and A. Talaat (2000), *Towards a European Peripherality Index – Final Report*, Report for the DG Regional Policy of the European Commission, Dortmund.

Stegarescu, D. (2005), 'Public sector decentralization: Measurement concepts and recent international trends', *Fiscal Studies* 26, pp. 301-333.

Stirböck, C. (2004), *Comparing Investment and Employment Specialisation Patterns of EU Regions*, ZEW Discussion Paper 04-43.

Thießen, U. (2003), 'Fiscal decentralization and economic growth in high income OECD countries', *Fiscal Studies*, **24**, pp. 237-274.

Tiebout, Ch.M. (1956), 'A pure theory of local expenditures', in *Journal of Political Economy*, **64**, pp. 416-424.

UNCTAD (2004), *World Investment Report 2004 – The Shift Towards Services*, Geneva.

WIFO (Aiginger, K., M. Böheim, K. Gugler, M. Pfaffermayr and Y. Wolfmayr-Schnitzer) (1999), *Specialisation and (Geographic) Concentration of European Manufacturing*, European Commission, DG Enterprise Working Paper 1, Brussels.

PART FOUR

European Regional Policy:
Experiences and Lessons

8. Do Economic Models Tell Us Anything Useful about Cohesion Policy Impacts?

John Bradley and Gerhard Untiedt

8.1 INTRODUCTORY REMARKS

Since 1989, the European Commission has implemented cohesion policies that now absorb over one third of its available annual budgetary resources.[1] These policies are embedded in a sophisticated system of public investment planning that represents a creative partnership between the national governments of the recipient states and the Commission authorities. The magnitude of the financial resources devoted to implementing EU Cohesion Policy demands that detailed and searching evaluations of the likely policy outcomes be carried out.

The challenge of evaluating the impacts of Cohesion Policy programmes lies in the extreme complexity of the public policy instruments being used, in terms of individual projects, wider measures, operational programmes and the entire investment package taken as a whole. The goal of Cohesion Policy – to promote accelerated growth and development in lagging EU member states and regions – is ambitious, and draws on economic and other research that is still at an early stage of its evolution. The context within which Cohesion Policy is designed, implemented and evaluated is also complex, and this should serve as a warning against simplistic evaluations and premature judgements. Economic models are used to deal with these complex evaluation challenges and are the subject of this chapter.

The task of this chapter is three-fold. First, we attempt to stand back from the technical aspects of the analysis of Cohesion Policy impacts and identify and describe the logical stages of the whole process starting with the challenge of the European Cohesion Policy, the different steps to be taken to implement the programmes, and finally to discuss evaluation steps in order to isolate specific areas where evaluators may legitimately differ from each other. Second, we examine three recent model-based evaluations of Cohesion Policy impacts that were produced using different models: the (European Commission internal) QUEST II model of DG-ECFIN, the ECOMOD model of EcoMod Network/Free University of Brussels and the COHESION system of HERMIN models of GEFRA/EMDS.[2] These results were recently published as part of the Commission's Fourth Cohesion Report, and have been widely discussed (European Commission, 2007). Third, in light of the radically different policy impact results obtained from these three models, we initiate a discussion of possible explanations for these differences.[3]

8.2 THE LOGIC OF COHESION POLICY ANALYSIS

Rather than plunging immediately into a detailed technical examination of the policy analysis results of the three models, and the properties of the models that may be influencing the different impact conclusions, we suggest that it is first necessary to widen the examination into the context within which Cohesion Policy is formulated, implemented and evaluated. Only then can the use of models be properly interpreted. In section 8.3 we will present the actual model impact results, followed by a technical examination of the reasons why models (and modellers) differ from each other in their approaches to capturing how economies function and respond to these policy shocks.

In an effort to identify the wider taxonomy of Cohesion Policy formation and analysis, we can identify a series of fourteen separate logical steps. These can then be collected into the four main stages involved in the analysis of the impacts of Cohesion Policy, which are the following:

- *Stage 1: The Cohesion Policy challenge (step 1)*
- *Stage 2: Designing Cohesion Policy interventions (steps 2-4)*
- *Stage 3: The methodology of Cohesion Policy impact evaluation (steps 5-10)*
- *Stage 4: The presentation and interpretation of results (steps 11-14)*

The structure and interrelationships of these fourteen steps and four stages we briefly describe in the following section.

8.2.1 Stages and Steps in Cohesion Policy Design and Analysis

Stage 1: The Cohesion Policy challenge

Step 1: *The cohesion challenge*: Before embarking on model-based analysis, we need to explore and understand the main characteristics of the Objective 1-type lagging economies, compared with the 'advanced' or 'mature' EU economies. Prior to the 2004 enlargement that brought in eight new member states that had previously been within the Communist centrally planned system, the lagging states had been the economies of the EU's southern (Greece, Portugal and Spain) and western (Ireland) periphery.[4] Why were they lagging? Could they catch up simply through participating in the integrated Single Market and Monetary Union? What are (if any) the specific barriers to convergence that need an EU policy initiative like Cohesion Policy? How much need we learn before we commit to specific macro-modelling frameworks?

Stage 2: Designing Cohesion Policy interventions
Step 2: *Cohesion Policy guidelines*: This step deals with the role of the development planning process in each recipient state as it prepares to receive and use EU aid. It is a combination of the identification of national priorities and heavily influenced by guidelines issued by the Commission. In each case, one has to examine carefully how each country or region has carried out this task. What techniques (if any) were used to select measures within the investment programmes within the overall policy package? Were formal micro-evaluation techniques applied (e.g., cost-benefit analysis, micro-scoring, etc.)?[5] How good is the local institutional capacity likely to be? How did the authorities proceed with implementation?

Step 3: *Cohesion Policy financial inputs*: This step deals with the formal financial plan, where the ex-ante funding allocations are set out in terms of different administrative categories of public investment. It also reviews how the administrative investment categories are mapped into 'economic' categories of investment, such as physical infrastructure, human resources and direct aid to firms. One needs to identify carefully the main economic categories of investment that are likely to be drivers of faster convergence, since different types of investment will influence an economy in different ways and through different mechanisms. This step tends to be somewhat neglected in past evaluations and evaluation designs.

Step 4: *Economic classification of policy instruments*: This step examines how the investment flows are transformed into stocks of physical infrastructure, human capital and R&D. Although the flow of investment expenditures impact on the demand side of the economy during implementation, it is the improved stocks that actually produce the improved economic performance of the economy, even after the investment flows cease.[6]

Stage 3: Evaluating Cohesion Policy interventions: methodology
Step 5: *Economic theory and public investment*: Recent theoretical advances in trade theory, growth theory and economic geography provide insights that

can be drawn on for the planning and analysis of Cohesion Policy.[7] These theoretical advances tell us something about the role of investment in physical infrastructure, human resources and R&D. In particular, they suggest ways in which these policies could promote growth.

Step 6: *Empirics of investment impacts*: Given the theoretical insights that are provided in the trade, growth and spatial literatures, we can then seek to establish what the international empirical literature tells us about the strength of these drivers. This literature is still at an early stage, and it is easy to become agnostic![8] What is important is to draw lessons from empirical studies that provide guidance as to how these driving forces can be related to model mechanisms and equations that trace through the consequences for changes in sectoral output and productivity.

Step 7: *Why are models needed*: The complexity of Cohesion Policies means that models must be used to evaluate their impacts. Without models, one is unable to isolate the influences of Cohesion Policy from all the other factors that drive a small open economy.[9] In addition, the financial injections are usually so large that there will be macroeconomic consequences that will affect all aspects of the economy, and not just the areas that are directly influenced by the investments (e.g., output and productivity).

Step 8: *What kind of macro model*: One then has to ask the important question of what kind of model is appropriate for the evaluation of Cohesion Policy impacts. This will be influenced by insights into what are the key characteristics of the recipient countries (step 1 above). What kind of paradigm best captures these characteristics and gives an appropriate description of the supported country? What level of sectoral disaggregation is required? We return to this vital step in the next section. But it is important to stress a methodological point here. Economic models are very imperfect representations of the real world. Modern modelling practice has tended to assign high status to frameworks that incorporate complete rational optimising behaviour and perfect foresight.[10] Such models are elegant but may trap policy analysts into interpreting policy impacts on the basis of models that do not represent the realistic behaviour of agents in the real world (Akerlof, 2005 and 2007). The price of realism may be a lack of complete optimising elegance!

Step 9: *Demand versus supply impacts*: It is well known that Cohesion Policy investments have demand impacts during implementation, and supply impacts both during and long after the programmes have terminated. One must be careful to ensure that this distinction is captured in the models. A wide range of other questions also become important. In particular, how are we to handle demand and supply impacts that arise during implementation and after termination? The recipient states sometimes have rather specific characteristics. Given the known characteristics of the recipient states, what could be expected? Total crowding out of private sector activity by the rise in public sector activity? Partial crowding out? Crowding in? Ricardian equivalence? The answers to these questions surely must be heavily influenced by the known facts about the economies being aided.

Step 10: *Sectoral issues in modelling*: A final specific and very important issue arises with the models, and concerns the level of disaggregation of sectoral production. One needs to be aware of how each different model addresses questions of sectoral disaggregation on the production side of the economy (e.g., QUEST, ECOMOD, HERMIN, etc.). Can these differences be subjected to empirical testing? Which approach is more plausible?

Stage 4: Evaluating Cohesion Policy interventions: results
Step 11: *The 'no Cohesion Policy' counterfactual*: The notion of a 'no-Cohesion Policy' baseline in not trivial. In using a macro-model to quantify the impacts of Cohesion Policy shocks, all models must go through the following stages:[11]

a) Project all non-Cohesion Policy (CP) exogenous variables out to the terminal year of the simulation (i.e., world, domestic policy instruments, etc.). For the 2007-2013 Cohesion Policy analysis, this year was taken to be 2020 for all three models.
b) Set all CP instruments to the appropriate counterfactual values (see below).
c) Simulate the model out to 2020.
d) Re-set the Cohesion Policy instruments to the appropriate values.
e) Re-simulate the model to 2020.
f) Compare results obtained from stage (e) to results from stage (c), to evaluate CP impacts.

However, a range of different 'no-Cohesion Policy' counterfactuals are possible. We distinguish three main cases: the 'zero substitution' case; the 'full substitution' case; and the 'partial substitution' case. We explain each below.
(a) The 'zero substitution' case:
Domestic authorities do not substitute with domestic finance, and cancel the entire investment programme (usually selected as the default case). In some cases, the fiscal imbalances in a recipient economy would preclude any

expansions of public investment. However, in other cases the national authorities could step in and fund the Cohesion Policy investment programme purely out of local resources.[12] Of course, in the latter situation, there would be more severe fiscal consequences for the public sector budget balance compared to the case of EU-funded Cohesion Policy.

(b) The 'full substitution' case:
Domestic authorities fully implement original CP investments, but financed entirely out of own resources (see discussion above). This could be a mixture of public funding re-allocation to the kinds of public investments involved in Cohesion Policy, borrowing and tax increases.

(c) The 'partial substitution' case:
Domestic authorities implement only part of the original CP investments, but financed out of their own resources.

Very different implications arise from these counterfactuals. For example, in the 'zero substitution' case, impact analysis would attribute to Cohesion Policy the entire economic benefits of the CP investments, treating the funding as a grant. In the 'full substitution' case, impact analysis in this case would be identical to the 'zero substitution' case, except for the negative impacts (such as higher tax rates, offsetting cuts in expenditure, higher interest rates, exchange rate effects, etc.) of the need to finance domestically. Finally, the 'partial substitution' case is difficult to evaluate. If the cancelled Cohesion Policy investments were genuine barriers to growth, the outcome might fall well below 'full' substitution. If the cancelled investments were poorly designed (high deadweight/crowding out), then this case might be actually better than the case of 'full' substitution.

Step 12: *Policy impacts for a single country:* It is useful to present the empirical results, initially for a single country so that the presentation can refer to country specifics. The analysis should then provide a wide range of information aimed at interpreting the analysis.

a)   Present stylised facts about the country model.
b)   Present the no-Cohesion Policy baseline under different assumptions, e.g., zero substitution and full substitution.
c)   Present sensitivity analysis with respect to important model parameters, e.g., the so-called externality parameters that link changes in stocks of infrastructure, human capital and R&D to changes in sectoral output and productivity. Discuss the consequences in terms of

what micro-scoring might indicate about the 'quality' of the CP planning and implementation.

d)   Design the presentation of the results for a given country in a way that facilitates comparisons with other countries. The concept of a cumulative Cohesion Policy multiplier is particularly useful here (and is explained in the next section).

Step 13: *Policy impacts for many countries:* In a multi-country evaluation, present summary results for all the countries, and explore international differences (within a given model system) as well as national differences (between the three models).

Step 14: *Drawing conclusions.* Discuss what the evaluations tell about the initial structure and characteristics of the economies. Why do the models produce different results? What can be done about it? This is, of course, the most important question of all. But it comes at the end of a list of other issues that also influence the answers. Only when the question of model-based impact comparisons is placed in the above wider context can we isolate and rationally explore these differences.

It is useful to enquire informally into whether there are likely to be strong differences of approach to these steps as between the various modelling groups. To that end, we suggest that the fourteen points can be further subdivided into two distinct groups. In the first, we suggest that there ought to be no strong differences of approach between the three modelling groups. In the second, unfortunately, strong differences of approach can and do legitimately arise.

8.2.2 Areas of Possible Broad Agreement

Within the range of different impact evaluation studies, there are likely to be areas within the above 14 steps where there is broad agreement. The most obvious cases for agreement might be the following:

Step 2: *Cohesion Policy guidelines*: Although there may be differences between the modelling groups with respect to the underlying characterisation of the cohesion challenge (step 1, to which we will revert below), the Cohesion Policy guidelines – as set out by the Commission – have to be accepted. The bottom line is that the modellers are usually asked to evaluate the Commission's policy, and not any alternative or hypothetical policy package.

Step 3: *Cohesion Policy financial inputs*: These public investment policy instrument settings must also be accepted by all modelling groups.

Step 4: *Economic classification of policy instruments*: Only very minor differences of opinion can exist between the three groups concerning how the administrative categories of investment are to be reclassified into economic categories. Most modelling groups adopt a three-way classification into physical infrastructure, human resources and direct aid to firms (of which R&D is a sub-component), although a higher level of disaggregation might be more desirable.

Step 5: *Economic theory and public investment*: Faced with the challenge of analysing Cohesion Policy impacts, all modelling groups dip into new growth theory and economic geography in order to articulate the theoretical roles of physical infrastructure, human capital and R&D in promoting faster growth and catch-up. There is likely to be a lot of common ground here.

Step 7: *Why are models needed*: All modelling groups tend to accept that the role of models is to place the Cohesion Policy interventions in a wider macro context, where macro and other spillover impacts can be examined.

Step 11: *The 'no Cohesion Policy' counterfactual*: There should be little or no differences between modelling groups on the taxonomies of the counterfactuals. However, the counterfactuals are seldom discussed explicitly (see previous material on step 11 above), and there may be differences of opinion as to the most appropriate counterfactual to adopt as a standard.

8.2.3 Areas of Possible Disagreement

Step 1: *The cohesion challenge*: The nature of the cohesion challenge could be regarded as having certain ambiguities. For example, Greece, Portugal and Spain experienced dramatic convergence in the 1960-1980 period, without any trans-European policy interventions. The Baltic States have recently experienced double-digit growth, before any credible role for Cohesion Policy could be asserted. Some authors display an almost ideological distaste for Cohesion Policy, and the book by Herve and Holtzman (1998) is a long catalogue of the potential evils of policy intervention, untroubled by any actual empirical analysis of the situation in individual countries or the conduct of Cohesion Policy. More recent research by the Dutch CPB that failed to find any significant Cohesion Policy impacts was largely based on data that preceded the 1989 expansion of Cohesion Funding and its narrower focus on Objective 1 countries.[13] Although they are largely subliminal, there are probably major differences of interpretation between modelling groups, and these interpretations of the actual situation in the recipient countries and regions may influence the choices of scientific modelling strategies adopted.

Step 6: *Empirics of investment impacts*: It is possible that all modelling groups have a common interpretation of the role of theory in exploring the drivers of growth and catch-up. However, there may be differences between the groups as to the strength of these relationships. Here we are focusing on the immediate relationship between (say) improved physical infrastructure and (say) manufacturing output or manufacturing productivity. We are not referring to the wider macro-economic outcome that is obtained when the immediate relationships are embedded in large-scale models. The literature presents a wide range of options from empirical studies, and is fraught with methodological and conceptual difficulties. However, even if there was agreement on what to take from the rather confused empirical literature, there would still be problems. The structures of the different models often impose differences in the underlying cohesion mechanisms.

Step 8: *What kind of macro model*: The most important difference between the three groups QUEST, ECOMOD and HERMIN probably lies in their choice of the modelling framework. This is not to say that there are any deep, fundamental *paradigmatic* differences between the models. All three draw in varying degrees from recent advances in modelling within the neo-Keynesian and CGE traditions. All three have a significant degree of micro underpinnings and are probably reasonably robust to the so-called Lucas critique.

The origins of QUEST II in the analysis of the economies of the 'old' EU member states may have led to a stance on crowding out that may be appropriate for fiscal policy interventions in developed economies that are attempting to stabilise about given concept of capacity output. However, the carryover of these mechanisms to the relatively less developed new member state economies, many of which are operating at low rates of utilisation of already low rates of capacity, may be problematic or inappropriate. We return to this important point in the next section.

Step 9: *Demand versus supply impacts*: Although the need to distinguish demand (implementation) effects from long-lasting supply (post-implementation) effects is accepted by all groups, the empirical analysis can lead to dramatically different outcomes, mainly due to the issues mentioned in Step 8 above.

Step 10: *Sectoral issues in modelling*: Under this heading we draw attention to the fact that any detailed examination of Cohesion Policy impacts needs to be performed at a level of sectoral disaggregation that permits – at the very least – the separate analysis of manufacturing, market services, agriculture and government. With few exceptions, the main sectoral driver of growth has been manufacturing, or sub-sectors of manufacturing. The rise of market services from a very low base has been a common characteristic of the post-Communist transition of the new EU member states of the CEE area. Also, the agricultural sector has very specific characteristics that may serve to distort Cohesion Policy analysis unless the sector is isolated. For example, it is conceivable that the one sector approach used by QUEST, compared to the modestly disaggregated approach of HERMIN and the highly disaggregated approach of ECOMOD, may distort the comparisons of their results.

Steps 12-14: *Policy impacts*: The dramatically different analyses of Cohesion Policy impacts derived from the three models (QUEST, ECOMOD and HERMIN) are simply the results of all the divergences in modelling that are outlined above.

8.3 THREE MODEL-BASED EVALUATIONS OF COHESION POLICY: 2007-2013

Three model-based ex-ante evaluations of EU Cohesion Policy were commissioned by DG Regional Policy in early 2007, and formed an input to the Fourth Cohesion Report published in May.[14] These evaluations explored the likely impact of the investments funded during the 2007-2013 expenditure programme. A common set of Cohesion Policy financial data was used by all three modelling groups: the QUEST II model of DG ECFIN; the ECOMOD model of EcoMOD Network/Free University of Brussels and the HERMIN models of the COHESION-System developed for the Commission by GEFRA/EMDS.[15]

Although the different models have the potential to examine the impacts of Cohesion Policy on many different aspects of economic performance, the impacts on aggregate GDP and on aggregate employment serve to characterise the key features of the three different evaluations. Such analysis is usually presented in terms of the comparison of a 'with Cohesion Policy' scenario relative to a 'without Cohesion Policy' scenario. This distinction is not without its complications, and there are a range of alternative counterfactuals. Using the terminology set out above, all three models implemented the 'zero' substitution counterfactual.

In the following we present a comparison of the impacts of the 2007-2013 Cohesion Policy programmes taking the case of Poland as an example.[16]

Figure 8.1 shows the percentage increase in the level of GDP in the 'with-CP' case when compared to the baseline 'without-CP' case.

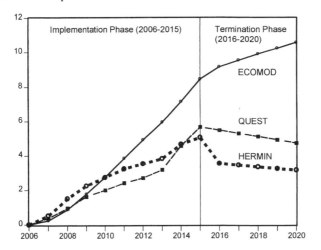

Note: QUEST figures for 2016 to 2019 follow from a linear interpolation.
Source: ECOMOD (2007), DG ECFIN (2007), GEFRA/EMDS (2007).

Figure 8.1 QUEST, ECOMOD and HERMIN – GDP impacts, Poland (percentage deviation from baseline)

In Figure 8.2 we present a comparison of the impacts on the level of total employment. Once again, the graphs show the percentage increase in the level of total employment in the 'with-CP' case when compared to the baseline 'without-CP' case.

The patterns of the impacts on GDP and on employment derived from the three models show significant differences. The ECOMOD analysis shows a rapid build-up of the impact on GDP, to about 8 percent higher than the baseline in the termination year 2015.[17] After termination, the impact on GDP continues to rise, reaching about 10 percent above the baseline by the year 2020. In the cases of QUEST and HERMIN, the GDP impacts indicated by both models during the implementation period 2007-2015 resemble each other, reaching a peak impact of 5.7 percent (QUEST) and 5.1 percent (HERMIN). Thereafter, the HERMIN impacts fall off more than the QUEST impacts, to end at 4.7 percent (QUEST) and 3.2 percent (HERMIN).

The differences between the models in the impacts on total employment are much more dramatic. The ECOMOD impacts follow the same pattern as the impacts on GDP, rising to an increase of 4.7 percent by end 2015, and increasing further to almost 6 percent by 2020 (relative to the 'no-CP' baseline level of total employment).

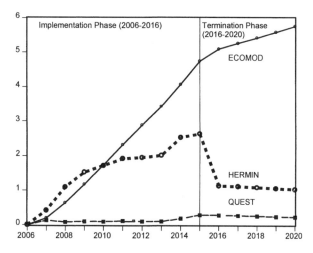

Note: QUEST figures for 2016 to 2019 follow from a linear interpolation.
Source: ECOMOD (2007), DG ECFIN (2007), GEFRA/EMDS (2007).

Figure 8.2   QUEST, ECOMOD and HERMIN – employment impacts, Poland (percentage deviation from baseline)

The QUEST analysis suggests that there will be almost no impact on employment, either during implementation (peaking at 0.3 percent above the baseline) or after termination (reaching 0.2 percent above the baseline by 2020). The HERMIN analysis suggests that there will be fairly strong impacts during implementation, rising to 2.6 percent by 2015, but falling off rapidly after termination and stabilising at a long-term increase of just over 1 percent (relative to the no-CP baseline).

Clearly these three model-based impact studies are pointing in very different directions. ECOMOD suggests that there are likely to be very strong and ever-increasing impacts on GDP and employment associated with the Cohesion Policy investment programmes for the period 2007-2015. These GDP impacts are dramatically larger than those found using either QUEST or HERMIN.

Turning to employment impacts, serious differences now emerge between QUEST and HERMIN, even though both of these models broadly agree on the GDP impacts. The almost insignificant employment impact shown by QUEST (even during the implementation period 2007-2015) is in contrast to the stronger implementation impact shown by HERMIN. But in the case of

HERMIN, the termination of the Cohesion Policy funding after 2015 induces a demand contraction that reduces the longer-term employment increase. In summary, by the year 2020, the increase in employment suggested by ECOMOD is six times bigger than that found using HERMIN and almost thirty times bigger than the QUEST results.

We conclude our presentation of the modelling impact results by showing two figures that are based on the HERMIN analysis.[18] In Figure 8.3 we show the results of impact analysis for Poland in a situation where there are no spillover effects from the improved stocks of physical infrastructure, human capital and R&D.[19] This is an unrealistic and extreme counterfactual, and represents a case of Cohesion Policy investment programmes that was so badly designed and poorly implemented that no enduring benefits arose from the investments.[20] Figure 8.3(a) shows the Cohesion Policy funding injection (as a percentage of GDP), and the GDP impact (expressed as a percentage increase relative to the no-CP baseline). Although there is a modest 'Keynesian' demand-side boost during implementation (2007-2015), there are no enduring benefits.

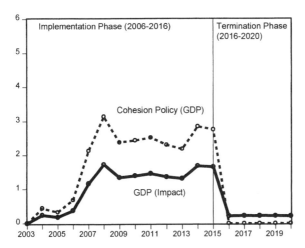

Note: Cohesion Policy (GDP) as a percentage of GDP and GDP (Impact) as percentage deviation from baseline.
Source: Own calculations.

Figure 8.3a   HERMIN: Demand- vs. supply-side effects of Cohesion Policy interventions, zero spillover elasticities, Poland

Figure 8.3(b) shows the case of 'standard' spillover effects on GDP, that were used in the earlier analysis reported in Figure 8.1 above. These spillovers are phased in linearly from the year 2004, and have full effect after five years. As the stocks of physical infrastructure, human capital and R&D build up after 2007, the supply-side benefits take effect, and even after termination, the economy is more productive. In summary, the CP shock is the same in Figures 8.3(a) and (b), but the difference in the impacts on GDP is accounted for by the supply-side spillover effects that are assumed to be absent in 3(a) but are present (in 'standardised' form) in 3(b).

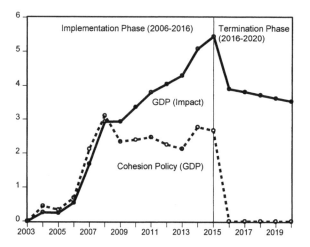

Note: Cohesion Policy (GDP) as a percentage of GDP and GDP (Impact) as percentage deviation from baseline.
Source: Own calculations.

*Figure 8.3b   HERMIN: Demand- vs. supply-side effects of Cohesion Policy
intervention, standard spillover elasticities, Poland*

Finally, in Figure 8.4 we show the so-called cumulative Cohesion Policy multiplier for the HERMIN analysis, in the cases of zero and standard spillover effects. The normal policy multiplier (at time t) is defined as follows:

$$Normal\ policy\ multiplier = \frac{Change\ in\ GDP}{Change\ in\ public\ investment}$$

However, the cumulative policy multiplier (between time t and time $t + n$) is defined as:

$$Cumulative\ CP\ multiplier = \frac{Cumulative\ percentage\ change\ in\ GDP}{Cumulative\ percentage\ share\ of\ CP\ in\ GDP}$$

Figure 8.4 illustrates how the spillover effects from the Cohesion Policy investments generate a return in terms of increased output. When these spillovers are positive (as in a well-designed Cohesion Policy intervention) the cumulative multiplier increases. When the spillover effects are assumed to be zero (as in a very poorly designed investment programme), the cumulative multiplier is flat, and merely captures the Keynesian multiplier effects.

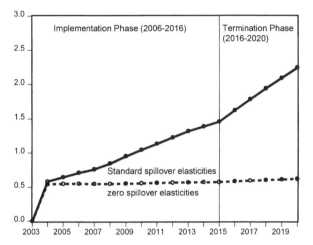

Note: Cumulative Impact defined as: Cumulative GDP (Impact)/ Cumulative Cohesion Policy (GDP).
Source: *Own calculations.*

Figure 8.4 HERMIN: Cumulative multiplier of Cohesion Policy interventions, Poland

8.4 INTERPRETING THE DIFFERENT MODEL-BASED IMPACT ANALYSES

Unfortunately it is only possible to compare and contrast the structure of QUEST and the HERMIN models, since full information on the ECOMOD model was not available at the time of writing. Drawing on comparisons of analysis carried out using QUEST and HERMIN, one is driven to the conclusion that these are based on rather different views of how the economies of the recipient countries behave. These different views have been incorporated into QUEST and HERMIN, both of which operate according to broadly neo-Keynesian rules.

Our diagnosis is that the first key difference between QUEST- and HERMIN-based CP analysis concerns the manner in which spillover or externality effects from the Structural Funds are incorporated into the two models. These were briefly discussed in Steps 5 and 6 above. We now examine this issue in more detail.

8.4.1 Modelling Cohesion Policy Supply-side Spillover Effects

Both QUEST and HERMIN used similar financial data for the Cohesion Policy shock. The demand-side impact mechanisms are handled in a similar way, with elements of expenditure being affected during the programmes implementation phase (i.e., 2007-2015). Of course, both models differ in the modelling of expenditure (private consumption and investment, in particular), but we return to this point later. There are some differences in the manner in which the financial data were transformed into changed stocks of physical infrastructure, human capital and R&D, but these are likely to be minor. The biggest difference is in the manner in which the improved stocks influence sectoral output and productivity in the models.

QUEST is a one-sector model, with modelling only at the level of aggregate private sector output. Improved stocks of infrastructure and human capital feed into capacity output in QUEST, through a Cobb-Douglas (CD) production function that has constant returns to private factor inputs (labour and private capital) and increasing returns to public capital. Consequently, it is mainly through the consequences of capacity utilisation that QUEST reacts on the supply-side. During the implementation phase, capacity utilisation is driven up, as demand impacts outstrip the gradual build-up of new capacity. This generates large crowding-out mechanisms. This may be further increased by assumptions made on the expenditure side of QUEST, and we return to this below.

Production modelling in the HERMIN models of the Cohesion system is on the basis of five sectors: manufacturing, market services, building and construction, agriculture and non-market services (Bradley and Untiedt, 2007). Factor demands in the first three are determined on the basis of cost minimisation (using a CES production function constraint). A simpler approach is used in agriculture, and output in non-market services is policy driven through employment and wages.

For the important manufacturing sector (and also for the service and building and construction sector), HERMIN drew on the SOE modelling research of Bradley and Fitzgerald (1988), and where country (capacity) output is not determined directly by a national production function constraint (as in QUEST). Rather, the national production function appears in the determination of the national technology (via national factor demand equations), and the national output equation originated from a higher level 'global' production function. This approach attempts to capture the essential notion that integrating within the EU Single Market, and particularly the integration of its peripheral and weakest economies, is best handled directly through the internationalisation of production than indirectly, through trade flows.

Consequently, output determination in manufacturing can be directly influenced by improved infrastructure, human capital and R&D, through making the recipient economies more attractive as hosts to inward investment, and strengthening the internal attractiveness of the competitive environment for locally owned firms. The international empirical literature is used to provide plausible values for the externality parameters.

National productivity can also be influenced directly by improved stocks of infrastructure, human capital and R&D, and these effects are incorporated into the national CES production functions. In other words, while the output effects are mainly international in their consequences (affecting the international allocation of production), the productivity effects are local and serve to modify the local production technology.[21]

8.4.2 Other Differences Between QUEST and HERMIN

Another important difference between the QUEST- and HERMIN-based analysis probably lie in the different nature and strength of crowding out mechanisms, through the labour market (Philips curve), through fiscal tightening and through monetary tightening. The analysis presented in the reports made available to the authors does not permit a thorough analysis of these issues, but they need to be examined. For example, the assumption is made in QUEST that *all increases* in productivity are passed on to labour. Consequently, none of the productivity increases caused by Cohesion Policy will have any effect in increasing cost competitiveness in the recipient countries. In HERMIN, on the other hand, empirical analysis suggests that there is a less than full pass-through of productivity changes to wages. This is quite striking in some countries, such as Poland. Where there is significant foreign ownership of firms, this affects the role of productivity pass-through. Our judgement is that the strong crowding-out features of QUEST may not be appropriate to the lagging economies of many of the new member states. In particular, the 'grant' nature of Cohesion Policy funding, with a 'weakened' concept of additionality, may not be reflected in the QUEST analysis.

Another big difference between QUEST and HERMIN is that the former imposes model-consistent expectations, while the latter uses static (or auto-regressive) expectations. What this means is that in QUEST, agents have perfect (model consistent) information about the exact future consequences of cohesion policy impacts and consequences, and can react today in light of tomorrow's impacts. HERMIN makes no such assertion. Rather, it takes a pragmatic view that for the analysis of extremely long-tailed investment policies in rapidly transforming economies, the incorporation of model consistent expectations (MCEs) is probably not justifiable in terms of the context of these economies. Furthermore, if the basic model set-up is inappropriate, the incorporation of MCEs simply compounds the error and increases the possibility of misinterpretation of the policy analysis. MCEs are perhaps more appropriate for the analysis of short-term demand and monetary shocks, where the underlying economic structure is fairly stable and well understood. There is less justification for their use for long-term supply-side shocks administered mainly through public investment in productive infrastructure and human capital, in a situation where the underlying structure is not well understood, and is rapidly changing.

On a more technical issue, in QUEST the degree of liquidity constrained consumption behaviour assumed for the new member state models is 40 percent compared with 30 percent in the OMS.[22] Is there strong empirical evidence that the liquidity constraint in the new member states of the CEE area is so low? With such a low degree of liquidity constraint, and the assumption of MCEs, it is not surprising that there is so much crowding out of employment in the QUEST-based analysis.

Another technical issue concerns the nature of the production technology used in QUEST. It should also be noted that a property of the Cobb-Douglas production function is that all factor inputs are substitutes.[23] In a more generalised production function (e.g., nested CES, Generalised Leontief, etc.), the possibility arises that public and private capital might actually be complements. This CD-based restriction may be a factor in the high crowding out mechanisms that appear to operate within QUEST.

8.5 CONCLUDING REMARKS

It is possible to attempt to pinpoint more accurately those aspects of the QUEST and HERMIN model frameworks that may be at the basis of the dramatic differences in their implications for the analysis of the impacts of Cohesion Policy. We stress that we offer merely initial insights for the purposes of stimulating further discussion. Macro-models are very complex tools, and are intrinsically difficult to compare. And the most active area of design and analysis of Cohesion Policy are currently the former centrally planned states of Eastern Europe, where one has access to time series data only from the mid-1990s.

We conclude with the observation that the impact analysis of Cohesion Policy interventions is very complex and the final results shown to the audience are determined by a series of hidden decisions taken by the modellers which are seldom obvious but determine the outcome. To be able to use and judge the results it is absolutely necessary to be fully transparent concerning the exact set-up of the models. Otherwise, macro-economic Cohesion Policy impact analysis will continue to be an impenetrable 'black box'. The obvious theoretical advantage claimed for macro-models, i.e., to be able to look at Cohesion Policy impacts in a way that takes into account the specific and realistic economic relations within the recipient countries and their linkage to the rest of the world, will not be realised in practice.

NOTES

1. Cohesion policy programmes have been variously called Structural Funds (SF), Cohesion Funds (CF), Community Support Frameworks (CSF), Single Programming Documents (SPD) and National Strategic Reference Frameworks (NSRF). In this chapter we use the term 'Cohesion Policy' (or CP) to refer to all of the above.
2. The documentation of large-scale macro-models sometimes lags behind improvements made to the operational software versions. Basic descriptions of each of the three model systems can be obtained from Roeger and in't Veld (1997), for QUEST II; Bayar (2007) for ECOMOD; and Bradley and Untiedt (2007) for the COHESION System of HERMIN models.
3. The authors carried out analysis based on the COHESION system of HERMIN models. Although they attempt to be dispassionately scientific in their judgements, it would be reasonable to assume that they have certain preferences! However, they try to make any such judgement calls very explicit.
4. The re-unification of Germany brought in the eastern Länder from the early 1990s, but this region was also the recipient of massive internal transfers within Germany. It is difficult to single out the separate role of EU Cohesion Policy.
5. For a review of commonly used micro-evaluation techniques, see Bradley et al. (2006).
6. It should be recalled that EC Cohesion Policy aid is not open-ended. The aid programmes tend to run for periods of from five to seven years, and are renegotiated when the programming period ends.
7. Helpman and Krugman (1985), Lucas (1988), Grossman and Helpman (1991), Romer (1994), Krugman (1995), Fujita et al. (1999), Aghion and Howitt (2005).
8. Aschauer (1989), Bajo-Rubio and Sosvilla-Rivero (1993), Munnell (1993), Acemoglu and Angrist (2000), Schalk and Untiedt (2000), Sianesi and van Reenen (2003), Congressional Budget Office (2005), Romp and de Haan (2007).
9. Monitoring should be clearly distinguished from impact evaluation. Monitoring indicators can be used to show (for example) how much motorway has been constructed, but cannot identify the role of roadway improvements in boosting output and/or productivity.

10. Bayoumi (2004) describes the IMF DSGE model, GEM; Ratto et al. (2005) describe DG-ECFIN's new DSGE implementation of QUEST III.
11. Hanging over step 11 is the spectre of the so-called Lucas critique. However, all three models are based carefully on micro-foundations, albeit in different ways and to different degrees. But we have come a long way from the reduced form, time-series models that Lucas convincingly destroyed in the 1970s!
12. Countries are expected to grow out of the need for EU development aid. For example, the Irish Cohesion Policy funding effectively ended in 2006, having run from 1989 to 2006. But the Irish authorities have continued with a seven-year national programme that is funded purely out of local sources (National Development Plan, 2007).
13. Ederveen et al. (2002). See Bradley (2008) for a critique of the Ederveen et al. work and Rodrik (2005) for a more general critique of using growth regressions to investigate policy interventions.
14. See European Commission (2007), Chapter 2 for the model results.
15. http://ec.europa.eu/regional_policy/sources/docgener/evaluation/rado_en.htm
16. Poland is a useful example, since it absorbs a very significant proportion of total Cohesion Policy funding.
17. Although the Cohesion Policy programme for the seven year period 2007-2013 is being analysed, the so-called 'n + 2' rule is invoked by all three models, so that financial aid terminates at the end of the year 2015. The assumption is also made post-2015 that there is no subsequent Cohesion Policy aid, nor any domestically funded alternative. This is an extreme assumption, but one that was mandated by the Commission in their instructions to the model users.
18. The analysis in Figures 8.3 and 8.4 could easily be replicated for QUEST and ECOMOD, but the authors only have access to the HERMIN software.
19. The spillover (or externality) effects of improved physical infrastructure, human capital and R&D are described in Steps 5 and 6 of Section 8.2 above. All three models incorporate such mechanisms, but differ in the empirical values assumed.
20. In his *General Theory of Employment, Interest and Money*, John Maynard Keynes described how an economy in recession could be stimulated if the government paid for holes to be dug in the ground, and filled in again. An NSRF/NDP with zero spillover impacts would be a bit like this!
21. See Bradley et al. (2004) for further details.
22. In other words, 40 percent of households are assumed to be liquidity constrained, and the remaining 60 percent can be modelled in terms of (forward-looking) permanent income.
23. The assumption is also made in QUEST that the marginal product of public capital stock (K_{pub}) is the same as the marginal product of private capital stock (K_{priv}).

REFERENCES

Acemoglu, D. and J. Angrist (2000), 'How Large are Human Capital Externalities? Evidence from Compulsory Schooling Laws', in B. Bernanke and K. Rogoff (eds), *NBER Macoeconomics Annual 2000*, Cambridge, MA: The MIT Press.
Aghion, P. and P. Howitt (2005), *Appropriate Growth Policy: A Unifying Framework*, available at: http://www.economics.harvard.edu/faculty/aghion/papers.html.
Akerlof, G.E. (ed.) (2005), *Explorations in Pragmatic Economics: Selected Papers of George A. Akerlof (and Co-Authors)*, Oxford and New York: Oxford University Press.
Akerlof, G.E. (2007), 'The missing motivation in macroeconomics', *American Economic Review*, **97** (1), pp. 5-36.

Aschauer, D. (1989), 'Is Public Expenditure Productive?', *Journal of Monetary Economics*, **3**, pp. 177-200.

Bajo-Rubio, O. and S. Sosvilla-Rivero (1993), 'Does public capital affect private sector performance? An analysis of the Spanish case, 1964-1988', *Economic Modelling*, **10** (3), pp. 179-185.

Bayar, A. (2007), *Study on the Impact of Convergence Interventions 2007-2013*, ULB/EcoMOD Working Paper, May.

Bayoumi, T. (2004), *A New International Macroeconomic Model*, IMF Occasional Paper 239, International Monetary Fund, Washington.

Bradley, J. (2008), 'EU Cohesion Policy and the debate on Structural Funds', *International Journal of Public Policy*, forthcoming.

Bradley, J. and J. Fitzgerald. (1988), 'Industrial output and factor input determination in an econometric model of a small open economy', *European Economic Review*, **32** (6), pp. 1227-1241.

Bradley, J. and G. Untiedt (2007), *The COHESION System of Country and Regional HERMIN Models: Description and User Manual*, Report prepared for the European Commission, DG-Regional Policy, Brussels.

Bradley, J., T. Mitze, E. Morgenroth and G. Untiedt (2006), *How can we Know if EU Cohesion Policy is Successful? Integrating micro and macro approaches to the evaluation of Structural Funds*, Muenster, GEFRA Working Paper, available at: http://www.gefra-muenster.org/deutsch/publikationen/abstract.php?pub_id=96.

Bradley, J., G. Petrakos and I. Traistaru (2004), *Integration, Growth and Cohesion in an Enlarged European Union*, New York: Springer.

Congressional Budget Office (2005), *R&D and Productivity Growth*, Congressional Budget Office, The Congress of the United States, June.

Ederveen, S., J. Gorter, R. de Mooij and R. Nahuis (2002), *Funds and Games: The Economics of European Cohesion Policy*, The Hague: CPB Netherlands Bureau for Economic Policy Analysis.

European Commission (2007), *Fourth Progress Report on Economic and Social Cohesion*, Brussels.

Fujita, M., P. Krugman and A.J. Venables (1999), *The Spatial Economy: Cities, Regions, and International Trade*, Cambridge, MA: The MIT Press.

Grossman, G. and E. Helpman (1991), *Innovation and Growth*, Cambridge, MA: The MIT Press.

Helpman, E. and P. Krugman (1985), *Market Structure and Foreign Trade: Increasing Returns, Imperfect Competition and the International Economy*, Cambridge, MA: The MIT Press.

Herve, Y. and R. Holtzmann (1998), *Fiscal Transfers and Economic Convergence in the EU: An Analysis of Absorption Problems and an Evaluation of the Literature*, Baden-Baden: NOMOS Verlagsgesellschaft.

Krugman, P. (1995), *Development, Geography, and Economic Theory*, Cambridge, MA: The MIT Press.

Lucas, R. E. (1988), 'On the mechanics of economic development', *Journal of Monetary Economics*, **22** (1), pp. 3-42.

Munnell, A. (1993), 'An Assessment of Trends in and Economic Impacts of Infrastructure Investment', in OECD (ed), *Infrastructure Policies for the 1990s*, Paris: OECD.

National Development Plan (2007), *Ireland: National Development Plan 2007-2013: Transforming Ireland*, Dublin: Stationery Office.

Ratto, M., W. Roeger, J. in't Veld and R. Girardi (2005), *An Estimated New Keynesian Dynamic Stochastic General Equilibrium Model for the Euro Area*, Brussels: European Commission Directorate-General for Economic and Financial Affairs, European Economy Economic Papers 220.

Rodrik, D. (2005), *Why we Learn Nothing from Regressing Economic Growth on Policies*, Harvard University Working Paper.

Roeger W. and J. in 't Veld (1997), *QUEST II: A Multi Country Business Cycle and Growth Model*, Brussels: European Commission Directorate-General for Economic and Financial Affairs, European Economy Economic Papers 123.

Romer, P. (1994), 'The origins of endogenous growth', *The Journal of Economic Perspectives*, No. 8 (1), pp. 3-22.

Romp, W. and J. de Haan (2007), 'Public capital and economic growth: a critical survey', *Perspektiven der Wirtschaftspolitik*, No. 8 (Special Issue), pp. 6-52.

Schalk, H.J. and G. Untiedt (2000), 'Regional investment incentives in Germany: impacts on factor demand and growth', *The Annals of Regional Science*, **34**, pp. 173-195.

Sianesi, B. and J. van Reenen (2003), 'The returns of education: macroeconomics', *Journal of Economic Surveys*, **17**, pp. 157-200.

9. Conditions for a Contribution by the Structural Funds to Real Convergence of the Recently Acceded Member States

Michael H. Stierle and Anita Halasz*

9.1 INTRODUCTION

EU enlargement poses immense challenges for EU regional policy. This is not only due to the significantly increased disparities within the enlarged EU and the substantially lower per capita income in the Recently Acceded Member States, but also due to these economies being far from homogenous. However, the characteristics of these countries will not be the focus of this chapter, but rather the question of whether – or more precisely under which conditions – EU structural funds can be effective in making a significant contribution to real convergence. Based on theoretical insights and experiences in incumbent Member States, conclusions will be drawn (though not exclusively) for the new Member States.

The role of the Structural Funds is, in essence, to co-finance investments in physical and human capital, using financial means coming mainly from other economies. If public investment has an impact on productivity and growth as well as a leverage rather than a crowding-out effect on private investment, EU cohesion policy can be expected under both the neo-classical and the endogenous growth model to be effectively contributing to growth and employment in the recipient territories, since it adds to physical and human capital stocks and promotes technological progress. However, in view of the very limited budgetary means of EU cohesion policy, representing less than 0.5 percent of the EU-15 GDP, the following conditions will be identified as being important for maximising the impact. First, sound and supportive national policies, including macroeconomic policies, national regional policies and good governance, are an essential precondition for a real impact. Second, the scarce financial means must be concentrated spatially, i.e., on the poorest Member States and regions, and they must be focused on national growth and growth poles rather than on equalising living conditions across the country and on more dispersion of economic activity. Third, the strategic design of Structural Funds programmes must allow for a concentration on those types of expenditures most likely to lead to growth and employment. Before these conditions for maximising the impact of Structural Funds are described, empirical evidence and methods for assessing their contribution to real convergence in Europe will be discussed.

9.2   EVIDENCE OF STRUCTURAL FUNDS IMPACT

Can European Regional Policy contribute to real convergence? Some authors raise strong doubts by criticising Structural Funds as having only a marginal, if any, impact on real convergence in Europe (e.g., Boldrin and Canova 2001; Ederveen and Gorter 2002 or Midelfart 2004). However, in contrast to the impression one might get from the frequently cited studies, with few exceptions (e.g., Ederveen and Gorter 2002) most regressions tend to find a significant positive effect of cohesion support policies on national growth and convergence (e.g., García Solanes and María-Dolores 2002 or Beugelsdijk and Eijffinger 2003). At the regional level, across the EU and in some cases also within countries, most studies identify a positive impact.[1]

Nevertheless, most of these attempts to link national and regional GDPs or productivity growth to cohesion assistance by econometric regressions are plagued with methodological, econometric and data weaknesses. Even if, in principle, regressions might be expected to be an adequate approach for a realistic 'ex-post' assessment, standard growth regressions testing for absolute or conditional ß-convergence cannot, as such, provide any evidence on the impact and effectiveness of the EU cohesion policy. No causality can be inferred from either the presence of or the lack of convergence or from its speed, any of which may result from many economic, social and policy factors other than from the EU assistance. No structural model of such a complex mechanism like growth can be represented by a single equation linking the former to one variable, i.e., the amount of Structural Funds transfers, as was done in Boldrin and Canova (2001), or two variables if initial income per capita is also considered. Moreover, since the beneficiaries of EU cohesion policy are poor economies, the amount of EU assistance works in some regressions as a proxy for the omitted variables, which presumably explains why these economies have below average incomes (de la Fuente 2003). As a result, the estimated coefficient on the volume of aid is negative, while the inclusion of additional variables in the equation, even in a simple form, leads to a positive impact of EU assistance on growth.[2] In other words, imposing an assumption of absolute convergence creates a downward bias on the estimated impact of cohesion support, while it can be significant and positive if convergence is only conditional (which seems to be the consensus view today). In addition, such regressions, when performed at the regional (NUTS II) level, are faced with acute problems of data availability and reliability. Not only is the bulk of cohesion support national or transregional and thus difficult to attribute to regions, but also available statistics are insufficient to control for other factors that can influence growth.

Consequently, results of regression-based impact assessments have to be considered with extreme caution, as not only are they very sensitive to the different methods, time periods and data sets on which they are based, but also in many cases they fail to include sufficient control variables to explain the complex convergence process.

As an alternative method for the assessment of the impact of the EU cohesion policy, macroeconomic model simulations are applied. Modelling has two main advantages: it shows how the policy affects the demand and supply sides of the domestic economy, depending on a wide range of other factors; and it allows for a counterfactual (i.e. without policy) simulation. On the other hand, simulations tend to assume that cohesion support is fully turned into productive public investment, overlooking possible weaknesses in policy delivery. They may thus assess the potential rather than the actual impact of the cohesion policy (Ederveen et al. 2002). At the same time, in model simulations, several positive effects are not reflected, such as strengthening the strategic planning capacity by setting up an integrated development strategy in a multi-annual framework, or introducing or enforcing the monitoring and evaluation culture or financial management and control rules and minimal standards for public procurement.

Two frequently used macroeconomic models are QUEST II and HERMIN, in attempts to assess both (short-term) demand side and (long-term) supply-side effects by comparing the simulation results with and without Structural Funds support. Even though it is difficult to compare the results, as the applied methodologies are heterogeneous, it is interesting to take a look at the simulations (see Table 9.1). Particularly short and partly also long-term growth impacts based on HERMIN tend to exceed the outcomes of QUEST II experiments.[3]

As opposed to HERMIN, in QUEST II, endogenous real interest and exchange rates allow for stronger policy crowding-out effects that reduce the impact of the funds. The risk of crowding out of private or public national investments as highlighted by Ederveen et al. (2002) seems limited. Concerning private investment, in the case of direct business support, public funds may certainly finance investments that would have been carried out anyway. However, Structural Funds mainly co-finance typical public investments that can be reasonably assumed to be complementary to private production factors; these interventions should therefore work rather stimulate private investments by an improvement of the business environment and by reduced transaction costs. In order to avoid a crowding out of national public investments, the principle of additionality has been enshrined in the Structural Funds regulations.[4]

Table 9.1   Ex ante assessment of the impact of cohesion policy, 2007-2013 – difference from baseline in % of GDP

		2007	2008	2009	2010	2011	2012	2013	2014	2015	2020
CZ	HERMIN	1.29	3.41	4.78	5.41	6.06	6.20	6.42	7.95	8.33	3.59
	QUESTII	0.61	0.76	1.25	1.59	1.99	2.32	2.78	3.80	4.58	3.77
HU	HERMIN	0.66	1.79	2.56	2.98	3.42	3.60	3.81	4.67	4.99	2.75
	QUESTII	0.37	1.03	1.76	2.30	2.90	3.37	3.97	5.14	5.99	4.52
PL	HERMIN	0.53	1.51	2.26	2.75	3.25	3.54	3.84	4.66	5.06	3.17
	QUESTII	0.39	0.96	1.64	2.02	2.44	2.71	3.19	4.55	5.65	4.71
SK	HERMIN	0.75	2.01	2.86	3.30	3.74	3.88	4.06	4.92	5.18	2.45
	QUESTII	0.81	1.18	2.02	2.72	3.54	4.28	5.17	6.71	7.92	7.27
EE	HERMIN	1.06	2.86	4.10	4.74	5.36	5.56	5.80	7.05	7.45	3.45
	QUESTII	1.14	0.92	0.84	0.98	1.34	1.69	2.11	2.91	3.47	3.57
LT	HERMIN	1.08	2.89	4.10	4.72	5.33	5.51	5.74	6.95	7.32	3.60
	QUESTII	1.30	1.17	1.07	1.18	1.53	1.85	2.30	3.22	3.80	4.32
LV	HERMIN	1.23	3.33	4.73	5.41	6.07	6.19	6.39	7.96	8.33	2.94
	QUESTII	3.06	1.59	0.68	0.44	0.61	0.79	1.08	1.86	2.27	2.13

Source: European Commission.

Summing up, while the magnitude of the potential impact may vary depending on the model's specifications, the economy's characteristics, the amount of assistance, and the types of public investments targeted, model simulations conclude that cohesion support contributes significantly (HERMIN) or, at least to a moderate extent (QUEST II), to growth and employment at the national or – when analysed – at the regional level. However, there is a range of factors that could hamper the realisation of this potential impact. To what extent this potential is realised therefore depends on various conditions.

9.3   THE ROLE OF NATIONAL POLICIES

Structural Funds cannot bring about a self-supporting growth led by additional private investment if national policies have not achieved sound framework conditions. In this context, the importance of the national economic and political environment has three main aspects: a sound macroeconomic and regulatory framework, national regional policies, and good governance, including administrative capacity.

Empirical studies show that a sound economic-political environment not only increases the growth and employment perspectives of the corresponding country and its regions,[5] but is also crucial for the effectiveness of international support. Drawing on a study by Burnside and Dollar (2000), Ederveen et al. (2002) perform cross-country regressions on the effectiveness of Structural Funds with panel data for 13 EU countries and 7-year periods from 1960 to 1995, based on a standard neo-classical growth model. When they introduce into their regression a proxy variable for openness, the interaction is significantly positive. Similar results are obtained with some variables which serve as proxies for the institutional context, namely a corruption perception index and an index of institutional quality. These results, in line with previous studies on the determinants of long-term growth, tend to confirm that the effectiveness of cohesion policy is highly dependent on the growth orientation of national policies.

When the new Member States have been included for the first time in the *Broad Economic Policy Guidelines* (BEPGs) (European Commission 2004a), needs for progress in the area of sound macro-economic environment in the new Member States have been highlighted. For several countries, it has been suggested that measures allowing wages to better reflect productivity and skill differentials would facilitate the attraction of investment flows into higher unemployment areas. At present, structural reforms covering macroeconomic, microeconomic and labour market policies are being pursued by the Member States in the context of the Lisbon Agenda. The Annual Progress Report 2006 (European Commission 2007) shows that progress made remains uneven.

EU Structural Funds have, to a certain extent, internalised the implications of these arguments. First, Cohesion Fund commitments may be suspended by the Council if public finances depart from the fiscal path foreseen in the national stability and convergence programme in the context of an Excessive Deficit Procedure (EDP). In this context, it has to be highlighted that the co-financing requirement does not imply additional expenditure. Comparing the amount of funds required for co-financing after 2007 to national eligible expenditure in the additionality tables for 2004-2006 indicates that, in the ten new Member States, co-financing can be provided from existing budget lines.

Second, a reference to the key role of national policies for the impact of Structural Funds had been introduced, in particular, in the programming documents 2004-2006 for the new Member States. These included, inter alia, macroeconomic stability, the continuation of privatisation and restructuring, a reduction and re-orientation of state aid, the implementation of mechanisms reducing labour costs, and improving flexibility (and mobility) in the labour market. From 2007 on, the renewed Lisbon Agenda and the implementation of cohesion policy will be formally linked. National strategic documents related to cohesion policy have to demonstrate their links to the national Lisbon strategy. The regulation foresees that a large share of Structural Funds should contribute to the achievement of the Lisbon goals.[6] The earmarking requirement may have a desirable impact on the composition of Structural Funds spending, even if the expenditure classification for earmarking is somewhat ad hoc. While, for example, state aid to large enterprises counts towards Lisbon earmarking for both types of supported regions, investment in important elements of the transport network are not classified as contributing to the Lisbon goals, not even under the Convergence objective. Moreover, earmarking is rather an accounting exercise, as non-compliance will likely be both cumbersome to verify and devoid of sanctions.

Besides the macroeconomic environment, an effective national regional policy is needed for the achievement of real convergence between European regions. Regional policy instruments used by the Member States can be classified mainly into two categories: on the one hand, instruments with a redistributive character, aiming at an equalisation of public financial capacity or living conditions among regions; and, on the other hand, pro-active policy measures aiming at achieving economic development in the poorest regions. However, even if a 'tendency for the policy focus to shift to wealth creation from wealth distribution' (Yuill and Wishlade 2001) can be observed, national regional policies, if compared with the pro-active design of EU Structural Funds, are still redistributive in nature. A mix of fiscal transfer schemes and active regional policy also exists in several incumbent Member States (Davies and Hallet 2001).[7] Fiscal equalisation schemes are also applied in most of the EU-10 countries (in Hungary, Poland, Baltic States, Slovakia – the Czech Republic being an exception) (Slukhai 2003). In Hungary, the rising regional inequalities in the mid 1990s gave rise to domestic allocative regional policy actions, which now need to be coordinated with the strategy followed for the use of EU funds. Poland, on the other hand, relies mainly on EU co-financed regional policy (World Bank 2004).

A further factor of crucial importance for the impact of Structural Funds is a sound institutional and public administration environment. The extent to which EU cohesion policy will be turned into investments enhancing the growth potential of the economy depends on the magnitude of the administrative costs, which divert expenditures from productive uses. At the EU level, simplifications have been repeatedly introduced and, for 2007-2013, the new regulations aim at a further reduction of the administrative burden by emphasising subsidiarity and proportionality. Still, as the final accountability for the use of Structural Funds is in the full responsibility of the European Commission, the trade-off between ensuring accountability and promoting simplicity needs to be recognised. Member States can ease the administrative burden by designing a national implementation system that does not duplicate the EU requirements.

One of the expected effects of Structural Funds is the improvement of administrative capacity due to co-financing of capacity-building measures and the introduction of corresponding legislation. This is of particular importance to the new Member States as their institutional quality is, in general, poorer than that of the old Member States.[8] As of 2007, Convergence regions can also use Structural Funds to enhance their overall public administration capacity. The beneficial impact of these interventions crucially depends on the strategic approach of the actions, as the risk of fragmented or politics-motivated spending cannot easily be ruled out. Also, most of the EU-10 countries are in the process of restructuring the public administration: abundant external support should not prevent structural reforms. Furthermore, it is questionable whether a relaxed budget constraint facilitates downsizing of administrative entities where needed. For the impact of cohesion policy on growth and employment to materialise, these interventions can foster two types of indirect impacts. One, better regulation and legislation can speed up Structural Fund implementation. Two, an improved business environment can expand the leverage effects on private investments.

Table 9.2   Progress with absorption of 2000-2006 Structural and Cohesion Fund commitments by mid 2007, %

	CY	CZ	EE	LV	LT	HU	MT	PL	SI	SK
Structural Funds	41.5	44.5	65.9	65.9	44.4	51.1	60.9	58.0	54.0	55.9
Cohesion Fund	39.8	42.8	43.7	46.8	38.5	36.9	23.2	28.1	38.1	45.0

	EL	ES	IE	PT
Structural Funds	64.4	80.0	86.5	80.9
Cohesion Fund	46.2	65.2	88.4	52.7

Source: European Commission.

Against this background, guaranteeing a substantial absorption of the support from cohesion policy can be seen as one of the crucial challenges for the new Member States. Table 9.2 shows an overall positive picture of absorption. Most new Member States had prepared the contracts for the full amount of their commitments by early 2006. Also, 2006 was the first year when the *n* + *2* rule was binding. However, no significant decommitments took place, as almost every new Member State managed to fully spend the 2004 Structural Fund commitments – albeit partly due to the large advance payments in 2004 and 2005. Lessons show that the shortcomings of procurement procedures and the slow preparatory works of large-scale infrastructure projects could hamper the full administrative absorption of cohesion policy support in 2007-2013.[9]

9.4   ACHIEVING SPATIAL CONCENTRATION

For the achievement of a significant impact on convergence in Europe, cohesion policy must, in the first place, concentrate its scarce financial means – representing about half a percentage point of EU GDP – on those regions and Member States most in need of assistance. Eligibility criteria for the Cohesion Fund and the Structural Funds try to achieve this spatial focus. The Cohesion Fund supports those Member States having, in the reference period, a Gross National Income (GNI) per capita in Purchasing Power Standards (PPS) below 90 percent of the EU average. However, in 2000-2006 only 65 percent of Structural Funds (SF) was allocated to the poorest, so-called Objective 1 regions with a GDP per capita in PPS below 75 percent of the EU average. This has led to strong criticisms and proposals to grant Structural Funds only to poorer Member States, while comparatively rich Member States should support their poor regions from their own financial means and reduce their contributions to the EU budget accordingly (Ederveen et al. 2002; Weise 2002 or Sapir et al. 2003). Concentration through the distribution of the Structural Funds was furthered for 2007-2013. After 2007, the Convergence regions (formally called Objective 1 regions) will receive 76.9 percent of the Structural Funds. Figure 9.1 shows, on the one hand, that these eligibility criteria are instrumental in achieving a spatial focus; on the other hand, it makes clear that also relatively rich countries, well above the EU average, will still receive substantial support. Member States with a per capita GDP in PPS above the EU-25 average will continue to receive 32.85 percent of Structural Fund resources in 2007-2013. This also includes the 5 percent share of Structural Funds devoted to phasing-out support of those regions having lost their Objective 1 status due to the statistical effect of enlargement.[10]

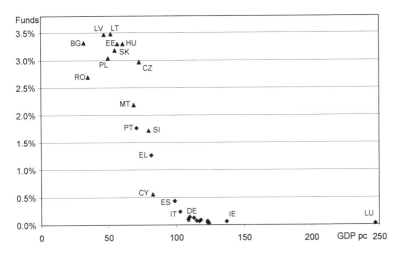

Notes:
Funds: Annual average of financial allocation for Structural Funds and the Cohesion Fund as % of 2007 GDP forecast.
GDP pc: GDP per capita in PPS in 2005, average of EU-25 = 100.
Source: Own calculations based on Eurostat and corresponding European Commission decisions.

Figure 9.1 Per capita GDP and cohesion policy financial allocation by Member States for 2007-2013

A second crucial aspect of spatial concentration of the Funds is the possibility of an equity/efficiency trade-off as, for example, described by the Kuznets-Williamson hypothesis.[11] It postulates a nonlinear, bell-shaped relationship between growth and regional inequalities. In the earlier stages of a country's catching-up process, the maximisation of national growth can be accompanied by a (temporary) rise in inter- and/or intra-regional inequalities, as economic growth is driven by only a few growth poles. Current experience of the new Member States supports this observation as national growth in these countries seems to be largely localised in the most dynamic areas around the capital cities and other major agglomerations where investment, including public investment, is likely to be more productive. After initially increasing inequalities, spillovers from the growth poles may initiate development in the lagging territories as well.

These findings have important implications for regional policy. Namely, consideration should be given to proper sequencing when designing the strategy for EU regional policy because efficiency losses resulting from a focus on equity are likely to be largest in the early phase of the catching-up process. In those countries where the convergence gap is highest, as in most new Member States, more emphasis should be given to national growth, since trying to counteract market forces would be inefficient if not unsuccessful.[12] In those incumbent Member States which have already reached an income level which is closer to the EU average, relatively more focus can be given to the reduction of regional income dispersion. Furthermore, as the theory emphasizes the importance of various spillovers (e.g. knowledge and technology diffusion and migration) in transmitting the impacts of initially spatially-concentrated growth leading to a decline in spatial inequalities, regional policy can at each stage aim at strengthening these mechanisms (Baldwin et al. 2003).

Sequencing and prioritisation have, to some extent, been implemented in the EU-15 cohesion countries. In Ireland, the country with the most impressive growth performance, the main objective since the 1960s has been the maximisation of national growth. It was only towards the end of the 1990s that a specific regional policy emerged, after which more emphasis was given to the reduction of regional inequality. Similarly, in the 2004-2006 period, structural expenditures in the new Member States were mainly focused on national, interregional measures.

Looking at the efficiency-equity trade-off from a micro perspective, models of New Economic Geography explicitly demonstrate that efforts aimed at increasing equity have efficiency costs, since they counteract agglomeration externalities (pecuniary and technological) that foster territorially uneven growth. Moreover, New Economic Geography emphasizes the non-linear effects of interventions, depending strongly on the initial conditions with respect to trade openness, trade costs and the strength of agglomeration forces at play.[13]

Also practical experiences in the EU-15 support this view. The relocation of public enterprises to southern Italy from the 1960s to the mid-1970s with national support under the form of capital grants and wage subsidies did not succeed in enlarging the industrial basis in the South. While clusters have developed in the Centre-North, no similar agglomeration effects can be found in the Mezzogiorno. On the other hand, the promotion of clusters has been a major feature of the Irish development strategy since the 1970s and horizontal and vertical linkages between industries and research centres are promoted in Portugal. As has been argued by some authors (e.g. Midelfart-Knarvik and Overman 2002 and Midelfart 2004), artificially creating comparative advantages has, in most cases, proved to have little impact. Hence, a positive message about the capabilities of regional policy could be that it should build upon existing clusters rather than try to create new ones.[14]

Against the political costs of territorially focusing interventions, it has to be underlined that giving priorities to some regions does not imply a black or white decision. Measures such as intra- and interregional infrastructure investments, policies enhancing the mobility of the labour force and those promoting the diffusion of knowledge can have an important influence on spatial diffusion of growth. In addition, in the EU-10 a range of national measures can be implemented with cohesion policy support, which have impacts both in rural and urban areas.

9.5 THE STRATEGY AND INVESTMENT MIX

EU regional policy is based on a proactive, allocative approach aiming primarily to enhance efficiency and growth in the economy supported. The co-financing of investment that targets the determinants of long-term sustainable growth should improve the availability of public goods (mainly basic infrastructure), enhance human capital, improve the business environment for private investment, and offer investment support.

However, empirical evidence indicates that not all of these investments are equally effective under all circumstances. Rodríguez-Pose and Fratesi (2002) test the design of the development strategies co-financed by the Structural Funds. They regress Structural Funds commitments for each of the four main areas of intervention (infrastructure – business/tourism – human resources – agriculture/rural development) on regional growth in all NUTS 2 and Objective 1 regions for three periods from 1989 to 1999, also taking into account a number of structural variables. They find that agricultural/rural support has a strong immediate effect on growth in Objective 1 regions but this impact vanishes almost immediately and turns negative in later years, suggesting that it fulfils an income support rather than a sustainable development objective. Returns to infrastructure investments in transport and the environment as well as in business/tourism are relatively disappointing, having little or no short-term or medium-term impact. However, for infrastructure, this result may be due to using too short a period for assessing its full impact. Human resources, on the other hand, have both short-term and medium-term impacts if some characteristics of the labour market are controlled for. On the whole, regions with a balanced distribution of funds have performed well, while those with unbalanced strategies (e.g., emphasis on business support or agricultural/rural preferences) have not.

Such results contribute to an understanding of the importance of adequate strategies, such as the investment mix chosen for co-financing as the third condition for an effective regional policy. The choice of investment priorities might also be influenced by rent-seeking activities, information asymmetries and political priorities. These problems are empirically relevant, and their importance is likely to increase with the size of transfers. The cohesion policy regulations include incentives to motivate the Member States to choose projects effectively – such as the principle of co-financing and the performance reserve.[15] However, during the negotiations on the Financial Perspective, the RAMS managed to reach the reduction of national co-financing requirements for 2007-2013, from 25 percent to 15 percent.[16] This might undermine the implemented quality of the investment mix.

As the list of eligible expenditures for EU Structural Funds support is long, and not all eligible expenditures can be regarded as equally effective, the strategy and main areas of support have to be adapted to the needs of the corresponding Member States and regions. Therefore, these support programmes are founded upon a bottom-up approach. Regional and national authorities present development plans, ideally based on a sound analysis of the current situation and involving the relevant actors, which are then negotiated in partnership with the European Commission and adopted as multi-annual programmes. Even if the programmes have to reflect the needs of an individual area, both the theoretical and the empirical economic literature offer some general guidelines for these strategies. Therefore, in the following section, evidence on the effectiveness of different types of investment is first discussed before analysing the strategy chosen for Structural Funds support in the old and the new Member States.

Infrastructure projects (transport, utilities, energy, telecommunication, education and health) are one of the main areas of Structural Funds co-financed investment. While some econometric problems still remain to be resolved, the empirical literature in most cases finds evidence on the growth-enhancing impact of public capital. This impact is usually smaller than the elasticity estimated by Aschauer (1989) (Romp and de Haan 2005), but still indicates the potential for a positive supply-side impact. A relatively abundant literature argues that enhanced endowments in transport infrastructure raise total factor productivity (i.e., via reduced transaction costs for enterprises and by improving workers' labour mobility) and, thus, the growth perspectives of regional or national economies. This is supported by evaluations of Structural Funds programmes and numerous empirical studies.[17] Four main lessons emerge from the literature. First, causation runs both ways: while an adequate public capital stock facilitates growth (its services are used as inputs by almost all productive sectors), growth also creates the scope and demand for further investments. Public investment can create the necessary conditions for growth, but is not sufficient to attain this goal. Second, the returns to such investments are probably high when infrastructure is scarce and basic networks have not been completed, but may be decreasing once a certain threshold has been reached. Third, due to congestion and network effects, the impact of investments on growth is nonlinear. Both theoretical models (see, e.g., Baldwin et al. 2003) and empirical studies (e.g. Bougheas et al. 2000) show a non-monotonic relationship between infrastructure and long-run growth. Fourth and finally, returns to investment are heterogeneous across countries, depending on the quality and quantity of the available capital stock, and on institutional and policy factors. When judging the net effects of the supported infrastructure investments on the society, opportunity costs of other possible uses of the Structural Funds have to be taken into account.

However, theoretical insights from the New Economic Geography raise some concerns for the impact of transport infrastructure (Baldwin et al. 2003; Martin and Rogers 1995; Martin 1999). On the one hand, transport investment to open up interregional trade may, under certain conditions, have the paradoxical effect of concentrating production in wealthier regions, creating welfare gains from agglomeration that also benefit the inhabitants of the lagging region. Intra-regional infrastructure improvements in the lagging territory may, on the other hand, achieve equalising effects at the expense of overall growth and welfare. In addition, the impact of infrastructure investment may be non-linear, due to agglomeration effects. The scarce empirical research finds that concentration may increase due to lower transport costs (Combes and Lafourcade 2001 or Faini 1983). Interregional transport infrastructure in Europe increases the accessibility of growth poles (Vickermann et al. 1999), which may also point to their potential to foster concentration.

Finally, in the competition to attract investment, countries and regions might overinvest. On the other hand, the existence of positive spillovers points to potential underinvestments. This is an area of intervention where Cohesion policy acts in line with the recommendations of the literature on intergovernmental transfers: by supporting and coordinating the creation of networks of European importance, it mitigates both problems.

Besides transport infrastructure, increasing support is given to environmental infrastructure such as waste water treatment plants. Even if the short term contribution of these investments to growth and employment is ambiguous,[18] European Structural Funds contribute, if effectively spent, to the achievement of a long-term sustainable development in all European regions.[19]

Finally, as the discussion of the 'New Economy' has shown (Stierle 2000), not only investment in transport but also in information and communication infrastructure can substantially contribute to productivity and growth. Therefore, investments in information society-related infrastructures are eligible for structural funds co-financing as long as similar investments cannot be expected to be undertaken by private means. ICT investments to remedy market failures represent interventions that promote both growth and dispersion in New Economic Geography models, as they facilitate knowledge and technology spillovers. R&D support, the promotion of technology transfer, and – under specific circumstances – transport investment have similar impacts.

Recent theories of economic growth, in particular the literature on endogenous growth, point to the important role of *human capital*. The result that economies only grow fast if they have high levels of human capital seems to be robust empirically: it is confirmed by cross-country studies such as those by Mankiw et al. (1992), Barro and Lee (1994) and similar studies inspired by these papers.[20] However, studies tend to assess human capital at a very aggregate level without precisely defining the mechanisms through which it influences economic growth. Which specific types of educational and training expenditures are best to be undertaken by policy-makers are thus less clear. A recent study[21] provides policy suggestions, to be adapted to the specific national and regional conditions, in favour of a moderate increase in human capital investment but not in favour of an across-the-board increase in subsidies for post-compulsory education, due to the presence of private incentives for individuals to invest in their own advancement. More important may be the elimination of implicit access barriers to higher education such as liquidity constraints and lower basic skill levels among individuals from disadvantaged backgrounds. In addition, guidance on the most productive types of investments include giving technology-related skills to a broad segment of the population, supporting life-long learning and improving conditions for the accumulation of research-related human capital. As a policy instrument enhancing adaptability, training can facilitate the restructuring that is still ongoing in most of the EU-10 and can mitigate its social costs.

From 2007, interventions in the health sector can be financed from the Structural Funds. While empirical results demonstrate a positive impact on the growth of a healthier working force,[22] the latter may be the result of having developing countries in the sample. Furthermore, external support to the health sector may delay the necessary structural reforms. For the EU-10, other areas of interventions might have a higher rate of return in the short run.

Even if, in the area of the *support for the private business sector*, some parts of the Structural Funds are used to co-finance the provision of technical and business services (mainly to SMEs), as well as of technology diffusion and more market-based forms of investment financing, the co-financing of direct state aid to enterprises remains a quantitatively important area of intervention.[23] Such aid can have significant deadweight losses, displacement or substitution effects which call into question the impact of support and, subsequently, the effectiveness of EU cohesion policy.[24] It can also trigger inefficient competition between regions to attract firms.

Evaluations of state aid are relatively scarce. Nevertheless, the extent of its effects has been assessed by some studies, in nearly all cases concluding that only 10 to 20 percent of the projects are not subject to total or partial deadweight losses.[25] Consequently, co-financing of state aid seems not to be the most effective channel for EU cohesion policy. Therefore, EU cohesion policy should be targeted to those investments where deadweight losses seem lower according to existing studies or where capital market failures may operate: namely in start-up companies, in small businesses and for technological upgrading, research and development and human capital training. Such a focus is mirrored by the Regulations and the Community Strategic Guidelines, although direct state aid is not ruled out.

Structural Fund rules also allow for tackling the negative short-term consequences of industrial restructuring, as opposed to providing state aid to declining industries. Member States may set up a contingency reserve to have quickly accessible resources in place to deal with the consequences of restructuring. Most importantly, in such cases training measures can be relied on to prevent long term structural unemployment, and start-up activities can be supported.

While rural areas will continue to receive support for the diversification of their economic bases under the Structural Funds, a new fund has been established for 2007-2013 to support the agricultural sector and rural development.[26] The economic importance of primary agriculture for the economy as a whole is limited, even in predominantly rural areas within the enlarged EU. In addition, the trends clearly indicate a further decline in the agricultural share in gross value added and its level of employment. Thus, in order to help lagging rural areas, it seems necessary to concentrate funding efforts increasingly outside the agricultural sector. Programming will have to facilitate synergies between rural development support from the Structural Funds and from the EAFRD. Furthermore, as early retirement schemes have few proven effects on the restructuring of the sector, and tend to offset the Community employment strategy by reducing participation rates, these short-term measures may be counterproductive. The lump sum support to farmers in rural areas is neither targeted nor supportive to a positive sectoral restructuring. Moreover, empirical studies[27] indicate that farm investment support could be implemented more efficiently. Finally, it should not be forgotten that this sector already receives substantial financial support from the market and income oriented measures of the Common Agricultural Policy.

Support to *research and development* and to *innovative activities* is gaining ground in the use of Structural Funds. These interventions mix investments in physical and human infrastructure and support to private businesses. The latter entails the promotion of linkages between knowledge production and use. New growth theory highlights the role of these activities in driving total factor productivity growth. Technology has public good characteristics. Its production usually involves large fixed costs, increasing returns and, hence, imperfect competition. Depending on the sources of market failure, different policy recommendations can result.

First of all, a usual argument is that technology producers do not take into account the positive spillovers they generate, hence production support is needed. However, if imperfect competition implies market power of the sellers of innovations, purchases of innovation need to be subsidised. If knowledge production increases the future costs of innovations, an R&D tax could be applied instead of R&D subsidies. Also, it may be argued that no intervention is needed at all. Microeconomic evidence suggests that there are high private returns to R&D investment (Temple 1999; Griliches 1979 and 1992). The implications for social returns are not that clear-cut, as not only positive externalities but also creative destruction and business-stealing impacts may play a role, all of which are difficult to measure or anticipate. Jones (1995a and 1995b) questions the long-run contribution of R&D to growth. However, Temple (1999) concludes that, even if growth effects in the long-run may be absent, R&D is likely to have significant level effects that qualify for the attention of public policy. Geographical proximity plays a key role in the transmission of knowledge through localised technological spillovers: it calls for the spatial concentration of support to R&D and innovation. Areas with low R&D intensity can improve the preconditions for fostering R&D and innovation by education measures.

Besides these areas, Structural Funds also offer co-financing of projects where the link to economic growth and employment is, in most cases, doubtful. For example, a positive impact on regional development will be difficult to find for most small-scale cultural projects or support for sport facilities. Evidence on the economic gains stemming from local economic development initiatives is unavoidably mixed. Finally, despite the importance of administrative capacities as described above, support to the enhancement of public administration capacity has a great potential for being used in an unproductive way.

9.5.1 The Investment Mix in the EU-15 and the New Member States

For the EU-15 Objective 1 regions (see Tables 9.3 and 9.4), there is mixed evidence on whether financial support is shifting over time towards or away from investments that are more conducive to growth and employment. Using very rough categories, the share of basic infrastructure is increasing. However, as Table 9.4 displays, this is not only due to investments in 'concrete' rather than 'brain' as the share of transport infrastructure has been falling recently, but it is also due to a stronger focus on other infrastructures, such as environmental and ICT investments.[28] As Structural Funds can be more easily absorbed by large (infrastructure) projects, Member States might have the incentive to rely on their national means for small projects in the area of human resource development. In fact, national and structural funds show diverging developments for infrastructure and HRD related investments.

Table 9.3 Financial   allocation   of   eligible   public   spending   in Objective 1 / Convergence regions in % of total[29]

	Investment area	EU-15			EU-10	
		1994/ 99	2000/ 06	2007/ 13	2004/ 06	2007/ 13
National without EU co-financing	Infrastructure	51.7	49.2	51.7	58.4	63.3
	Human resources development	28.4	33.6	34.4	19.8	23.8
	Aid to the productive sector	19.9	17.2	13.9	21.8	12.9
National co-financing	Infrastructure	40.3	34.6	49.7	43.3	71.1
	Human resources development	20.2	35.1	28.0	24.4	19.6
	Aid to the productive sector	39.5	30.3	22.3	32.3	9.3

Notes:
Percentage share of the corresponding investment area in total expenditures excluding other spending. National co-financing includes the co-financing of Cohesion Fund projects.
Source: Own calculations based on tables submitted for the verification of additionality of Objective 1 programmes.

For the EU-10, the figures relating to cohesion policy look relatively similar to those of the EU-15 for both 2004-2006 and 2007-2013. The higher share of purely national investments devoted to physical infrastructure investments can be attributed to the higher needs for this form of support among the EU-10. Furthermore, in the EU-10, the share of national resources devoted to aid for the productive sector is relatively smaller than in new Member States, although this may result from the higher absolute size of resources devoted to the other goals.

In the process of Objective 1 programming for the new Member States in 2004-06 and in 2007-2013, the focus was on the main determinants of higher productivity and, in those countries where the labour market situation is a key challenge, on a rapid improvement in the use of human resources. The approach of the new Member States and the Commission was to maximise, in partnership during the negotiations, measures with higher growth and employment potential, to promote concentration, suppress or at least reduce redistributive types of measures and to avoid the creation of distortions in economic activity. Against the background of uneven effectiveness of different investment areas, as highlighted by available evidence, the aim was to select both adequate priorities and an effective mix of measures within each priority. The final results appear in Table 9.4. The apparently similar spending shares for the EU-10 and EU-15 under Objective 1 mask inter-country differences in needs and respective spending allocations for both groups of countries.

In 2004-2006, for regional programmes, the aim was to avoid their mimicking the Community Support Frameworks (CSFs) at the regional level and their dispersing resources into numerous priorities and measures with most likely very little effect on long-run growth and employment. Consequently, an even distribution of the Structural Funds across the whole territory as well as one favouring the most backward regions was avoided. Focus was shifted to investment in areas and urban centres with significant growth potential while providing the necessary infrastructure to allow for their inter-connections and connections with major transit routes. Financing of small-scale regional transport infrastructure was also reduced substantially. The numerous requests for regional/local cultural or sport facilities were deemphasised in terms of financial allocations and made subject to conditions, in particular economic sustainability and significant regional economic impact. This has resulted in an overall scaling down of the regional programmes.

Since the development of human resources is a key to long-term growth, the allocations to the corresponding programmes were increased both where employment is a major challenge, as in Poland, and where higher qualifications are necessitated by the upgrading of economic activity and by the need to activate participation in the labour market. Especially for human resources, the measures have to be tailored to a country's situation. For example, in Hungary, where both unemployment and the labour participation rate are low and where, in some sectors and regions, shortages of highly skilled workers can be observed, the focus shifted to those measures most likely to increase participation and on education and training. In contrast, for example in Poland and Slovakia, where unemployment is a key challenge, measures for social inclusion were granted limited financial allocations to benefit active labour market policies and this support concentrated on groups with the highest possibility of (re)entering the labour market, such as among the young.

Table 9.4   Financial allocation of EU Structural Funds as % of total[30]

	EU-15					EU-10			
	Objective 1 / Convergence			Other objectives		Obj. 1 / Conver.		Other objectives	
	94-99	00-06	07-13	00-06	07-13	04-06	07-13*	04-06	07-13*
Infrastructure	29.8	41.3	50.6	14.1	13.5	41.7	67.3	15.0	16.0
Transport	15.7	19.8	16.1	3.5	1.8	21.6	32.3	4.6	3.0
ICT	1.6	3.5	6.5	1.7	3.3	5.2	5.0	1.2	4.6
Energy	2.3	1.2	2.9	0.4	2.9	1.7	3.2	0.0	0.3
Environment & water	7.5	12.8	13.5	7.5	3.5	4.8	18.3	0.0	3.4
Health & social inf.	1.7	3.9	8.9	0.7	1.0	4.9	6.7	0.9	4.1
Other	1.1	0.0	2.8	0.3	0.9	3.5	2.0	8.3	0.6
Human resources	24.5	23.1	13.4	53.3	56.8	22.3	8.8	62.4	61.9
Productive Environment	41.0	33.8	25.8	29.1	24.3	33.1	17.8	20.6	11.0
Industry and services	19.9	11.3	9.2**	15.8	7.3**	9.8	5.5**	13.6	2.3**
RDTI	3.5	6.0	13.9**	4.5	15.9**	3.0**	10.4**	2.4	8.1**
Agric./rural dev./ fishery	15.2	13.7	n/a	5.1	n/a	16.2	n/a	1.4	n/a
Tourism	2.4	2.7	2.7	3.7	1.0	4.1	1.9	3.2	0.5
Other	4.6	1.8	10.2	3.4	5.5	2.8	6.0	5.6	11.2
Total	100.0	100.0	100.0	100.0	100.0	100.0	100.0	100.0	100.0

Notes:
2007-2013 figures include the financial allocation for the Cohesion Fund.
* Preliminary ex ante figures, based on Operational Programmes under negotiation.
** Figures on these lines not directly comparable to previous periods, due to a change in classification.
Source: Own calculations based on European Commission internal data sources.

Due to the high deadweight and losses from displacement effects of state aid and because of the already high level of state aid in most new Member States (European Commission 2004c), it was, in most cases, agreed to reduce EU Structural Funds support to this area. This resulted – when not counterbalanced by increased support for the business environment, as in the Czech Republic – in a reduction of the competitiveness/enterprise financial allocations, e.g., in Poland and Hungary. Simultaneously, state aid was re-oriented towards SMEs, and targets giving priority to SMEs have been set, for example, in Poland, Hungary and the Czech Republic. All sectoral preferences were suppressed to avoid 'protecting' declining industries or trying to pick up winners by targeting manufacturing or specific 'high-tech' sectors. The remaining policy measures in this priority are thus more focused on soft aid for knowledge, innovation and technology and the business environment.

More emphasis was put on infrastructure improvements as this is regarded as a major impediment to growth in several new Member States. A hierarchy of priorities for the period 2004-2006 was followed with a view to maximising investments with higher returns in terms of enterprise competitiveness while facilitating labour mobility. This has led, depending on each country's situation, to significantly prioritising international and interregional transport infrastructure and to suppressing (or imposing conditions on) aid for regional airports.

Even if agriculture is still of importance for some rural areas in the new Member States, it is questionable whether this sector will be a driving force for growth and employment. In contrast, major restructuring and labour adjustment are still needed in some countries which will add to the expected decrease in the share of agriculture in gross value added and unemployment. Consequently, assistance for agriculture was reduced. Moreover, efforts were made to give higher importance to rural development aimed at offering alternative employment at the expense of state aid for the processing industry and for on-farm investment support.

The same principles were followed in partnership by the Member States and the Commission during the programming for 2007-2013. Due to an increased emphasis on subsidiarity and proportionality, the influence of the Commission has been reduced with regard to the overall financial allocations of the Member States. Still, most of the principles outlined above are mirrored by the 2007-2013 programmes, as new Member States were relying on the experience gained in the previous programming round.

9.6   CONCLUSIONS

As has been shown by impact assessments based on macroeconomic modelling, in spite of its limited financial means, EU cohesion policy can have an important impact on catching-up. However, it can only have significant effects if several conditions are fulfilled, and here experience in recent years shows that room for improvement exists. Among the various factors shaping the effectiveness of Structural Funds in achieving real convergence, particularly against the background of enlargement, the following aspects are important:

- National macroeconomic, structural and regional policies,
- Stronger spatial concentration,
- Better thematic concentration.

Spatial concentration means concentrating Structural Funds on those regions and Member States most in need of them. Despite a step in this direction for 2007-2013, there is scope for further improvements here at the European level. Spatial concentration also means not counteracting market forces in the selection of areas for support. To reduce the equity-efficiency trade-off (i.e., that high catch-up growth might temporarily be accompanied by higher inequalities between regions), a sequencing approach initially emphasising national economic growth and, at a later stage, giving more prominence to addressing regional disparities, could be followed in order to make regional policy more efficient. In parallel, the catching-up process of poorer regions might be accelerated by supporting their growth poles and by building on existing clusters. But one should avoid any attempt to politically achieve a dispersion of economic activities or creation of new clusters against market forces.

Thematic concentration, in turn, means choosing an effective investment mix. The identification and determination of an effective investment mix can only be answered on a case-by-case basis following a sound analysis of the situation in the corresponding Member State and region. However, some general arguments can be made on this point: First, infrastructure endowment can be seen as a precondition for growth, though not as a growth-enhancing investment per se. Second, even if it generally takes time to achieve a needed enhancement of human capital, such enhancements can be regarded as key to long-term growth. Third, aid to the productive sector should be limited to specific projects enhancing the business environment, and support for start-ups and SMEs. Fourth, support for rural areas should take into account the limited and declining importance of agriculture in the process of catching-up, and should be focused on providing alternative employment and development opportunities. Finally, projects of doubtful economic benefit – such as, for example, cultural projects – should not be co-financed.

In order to guarantee the effective use of Structural Funds, the draft regulation proposes further simplifications for the management of Structural Funds in order to reduce administrative problems and costs. In addition, particularly in the new Member States, building up the necessary administrative capacity will be of crucial importance. Indirect and macroeconomic absorption problems, such as the crowding out of national public or private investment, can be avoided or at least contained by programme design and by the setup of the implementation system.

While the new regulation for Structural Funds aims to introduce a stronger regional and thematic concentration, the contribution of EU cohesion policy to real convergence will depend predominantly on Member States' own national and regional policies. The role of regional and national authorities in setting up strategies to support and implement Structural Funds programmes will be of key importance. More broadly, Structural Funds cannot achieve a self-supporting growth led by additional private investment, if national economic policies have not already achieved sound framework conditions.

NOTES

*   The opinions expressed in this chapter are exclusively those of the authors and do not necessarily reflect those of the European Commission, DG Economic and Financial Affairs, by which the authors are employed. The paper is based on a contribution to chapter 2 of the *EU Economy Review 2004* (European Commission 2004). The authors are grateful to Carole Garnier and the participants of the INFER Annual Conference 2005 for valuable comments and suggestions.

1.   See e.g., Fayolle and Lecuyer (2000); García Solanes and María-Dolores (2002) or de la Fuente (2003), although some studies do not find a positive impact such as those by Boldrin and Canova (2001) and Basile and Kostoris Padoa Schioppa (2002).

2.   This is illustrated by Ederveen et al. (2002). Their results, at NUTS II regional level for the period 1981-1996, suggest a negative impact from cohesion policy when factors other than initial productivity and cohesion support are not controlled for. When they are included, then the estimated impact becomes positive and significant. An additional amount of cohesion support in the amount of 1 percent of the GDP leads to an annual increase in the GDP per capita of 0.7 percent.

3.   A short description of these two models with further references also to other models and approaches can be found in European Commission (2004).

    The HERMIN policy externalities are in the middle of the range of estimates in the empirical literature, and QUEST II assumes that the marginal product of private capital is equal to that of public capital. Assumptions of QUEST II on the impact of schooling and R&D investments are more optimistic than those of HERMIN, while HERMIN incorporates more optimistic assumptions on the impact of physical infrastructure investment. For both simulations, EU support is assumed to be terminated at the end of the programming period. For the Baltic countries in QUEST II, the fixed exchange rate regimes are incorporated. As monetary policy does not respond to the inflationary pressures, due to the demand impulse generated by the funds, these countries have to undergo a period of devaluation to restore their competitiveness (In't Veld 2007).

    For more details on the 2007-2013 *ex ante* simulations, see the Fourth Report on Economic and Social Cohesion (European Commission 2007) as well as the paper by John Bradley and Gerhard Untiedt in this volume.

4.   For Objective 1 programmes, Member States agree *ex ante* with the European Commission on a target for national public eligible expenditure that generally should not be lower in real terms than the level achieved during the former programming period. This reflects the difficulty of constructing a counterfactual, but at the same time creates some room for substitution. *Ex-post* verifications for the periods 1994-99 and 2000-06 show that, in most Member States, additionality has at least nearly been met and that this result can be expected as well for the current period (European Commission 2004, table 15 of chapter 2). To further strengthen the enforcement of this principle, in the 2007-2013 programming period a financial sanction is foreseen if the realised national public eligible spending is lower than the agreed baseline. While for 2004-2006, eight out of nine new MS agreed on baselines

exceeding past spending levels (three of them even committed to increases by 10-30 percent), after the introduction of the sanction only three new MS decided to increase their baselines.

Please note that neither additionality nor co-financing requirements imply a necessary increase of overall public spending. Co-financing can be provided from already existing budget lines.

5. See, e.g., Hall and Jones (1999) or Sala-i-Martin (2002) and, for a review, Nicodème and Sauner-Leroy (2004).

6. EU-15 countries are obliged by the regulation to devote 60 percent (75 percent) of funds in Convergence (Regional Competitiveness and Employment) regions to the Lisbon goals. For the EU-10, this remains an informal requirement. As there is significant overlap in the goals of the two policy domains, already in the past, most EU-15 countries had spending profiles satisfying these requirements in non-Objective 1 regions and, under Objective 1, it was nearly reached. Also, Objective 1 spending of the EU-10 in 2004-2006 fell not too far short of the requirement. Under Objective 1 53 percent was dedicated to the present earmarking goals by the EU-15, and 50 percent by the EU-10. Under Objectives 2 and 3, the respective percentages were 77 percent and 61 percent (European Commission).

7. In Germany, for example, estimates on the gross transfer to eastern Germany arrive at €104 billion in 2003 and net transfers representing nearly one third of the eastern German GDP. The main part of these transfers is redistributive, as transfers via the social security system or unconditional grants represent 54 percent and 26 percent of gross transfers respectively. In contrast, only 4 percent of gross transfers are spent for support to the private sector and 10 percent for infrastructure investment (Lehmann et al. 2005).

8. See chapter 2, section 3.2.3 in European Commission (2004).

9. From 2007, Cohesion Fund projects will also be embedded into the same multi-annual programmes as the Structural Fund projects, and the $n + 2$ rule will apply for their commitments. Acknowledging the potential weaknesses in the administrative capacity of the new Member States, in their case until 2010 an $n + 3$ rule will apply for both SF and CF commitments.

10. For these regions, it can be argued that their economic situation has not changed through the purely statistical effect and, therefore, that support has to be continued. On the other hand, allocation of scarce financial means requires prioritisation.

11. See, e.g., section 2.3.2 of chapter 2 in European Commission (2004). For similar conclusions on the basis of various empirical analyses see Funck and Pizzati (2003).

12. De la Fuente (2004) shows that overall efficiency can be increased when EU regional policy follows efficiency considerations, while national policy instruments are used for redistributive purposes.

13. Puga (2002), Baldwin et al (2003). Policy conclusions are mainly derived from models; empirical evidence on the relevance of the conclusions is scarce.

14. On clusters, see Martin and Sunley (2003).

15. The performance reserve was designed to motivate the final beneficiaries. In 2000-2006, 4 percent of the appropriations allocated to each Member State were placed in reserve until 2003, for distribution to the best-performing programmes. Each Member State made proposals to the Commission on the basis of monitoring indicators that it had introduced itself. For heterogeneous results with the implementation of the performance reserve, see European Commission (2004b).

16. Also for the EU-10, non-refundable VAT will become eligible, and private co-financing may contribute towards national co-financing.

17. See, e.g., Moreno et al. (2002), de la Fuente (2003a), del Mar Salinas-Jiménez (2004), or, for a survey, Romp and de Haan (2005).

18. See chapter 6 of the *European Economy Review* 2004 (European Commission 2004).

19. Due to the specific needs of the RAMS in social housing (resulting mainly from the quick deterioration of pre-fabricated estates occupied by low-income tenants), such interventions will become eligible in 2007-2013, although they can take up only a limited share of the spending. The safeguard measures on housing expenditure aim at ensuring that spending contributes to public goals rather than to private interests.

20. Some studies (e.g. Pritchett 1998 or Caselli et al. 1996) using different (panel data) techniques have questioned the link between education and productivity, but recent investigations attribute their negative results to poor data and econometric problems.
21. De la Fuente and Ciccone (2002). See also chapter 3 in the *EU Economy Review 2003* (European Commission 2003).
22. See, e.g., Barro and Sala-i-Martin (2003, chapter 12).
23. However, it is incorrect to assume that EU Structural Funds would mainly distribute state aid, and to conclude, based on this assumption, that Structural Funds are ineffective, as in Midelfart-Knarvik and Overman (2002) or Midelfart (2004).
24. A deadweight effect is if the enterprise would have invested even without support; a displacement effect is if it would have invested anyway but in a different region, and a substitution effect is if a different enterprise would have undertaken the investment.
25. For a literature review including a discussion of the methodologies applied, see Gerling (2002). For empirical studies, applying heterogeneous methodologies and analysing different kinds of aid schemes, see, e.g., Honohan (1998), Barry (2003) and Lenihan (2004) for Ireland, Arup Economics and Planning (2000) for the UK or Gerling (2002) and Ragnitz (2003) for Germany.
26. European Agricultural Fund for Rural Development (EAFRD).
27. See, e.g., studies by Striewe et al. (1996), Ebers (1998) as well as Forstner and Clemens (1998).
28. A possible reason might be that Structural Funds can be more easily absorbed by large projects than by smaller and more complex ones. Consequently, Member States might have the incentive to use structural funds for transport infrastructure projects, such as constructing highways, while using national means for small projects in the area of R&D.
29. Data for 2007/13 are based on the ex ante allocation.
30. Data for 2007/13 are based on the ex ante allocation.

REFERENCES

Arup Economics and Planning (Contractor: Ecotec Research and Consulting Ltd. in association with GVA Grimley and the Centre for Urban and Regional Development Studies, University of Newcastle-upon-Tyne) (2000), *Planning for Clusters*, London.

Aschauer, D. (1989), 'Is Public Expenditure Productive?', *Journal of Monetary Economics*, **3**, pp. 177-200.

Baldwin, R.E., R. Forslid, M. Philippe, G. Ottaviano and F. Robert-Nicoud (2003), *Economic Geography and Public Policy*, Princeton and Oxford.

Barro, R.J. and J.-W. Lee (1994), *Sources of Economic Growth*, Carnegie-Rochester Conference Series on Public Policy, No. 40, pp. 1-46.

Barro, R.J. and X. Sala-i-Martin (2003), *Economic Growth*, Cambridge: The MIT Press.

Barry, F. (2003), 'European Union Regional Aid and Irish Economic Development', in B. Funck and L. Pizzati (eds), *European Integration, Regional Policy, and Growth*, Washington, DC, pp. 135-151.

Basile, R. and F. Kostoris Padoa Schioppa (2002), *Unemployment Dynamics of the 'Mezzogiornos of Europe': Lessons for the Mezzogiorno of Italy*, ISAE, Istituto di Studi e Analisi Economica and ISAE, Istituto di Studi e Analisi Economica.

Beugelsdijk, M. and S. Eijffinger (2003), *The Effectiveness of Structural Policy in the European Union: An Empirical Analysis for the EU-15 during the Period 1995-2001*, CEPR Discussion Paper 3879, London.

Boldrin, M. and F. Canova (2001), 'Inequality and Convergence in Europe's Regions: Reconsidering European Regional Policies', *Economic Policy*, **32**, pp. 207-253.

Bougheas, S., P.O. Demetriades and T.P. Mamuneas (2000), 'Infrastructure, Specialization and Economic Growth', *Canadian Journal of Economics*, **33** (3), pp. 506-522.

Burnside, C. and D. Dollar (2000), 'Aid, Policies, and Growth', *American Economic Review*, **40**, pp. 289-329.

Caselli, F., G. Esquivel and F. Lefort (1996), 'Reopening the Convergence Debate: a New Look at Cross-country Growth Empirics', *Journal of Economic Growth*, **1** (3), pp. 363-389.

Combes, P.-P. and M. Lafourcade (2001), *Transportation Cost Decline and Regional Inequalities: Evidence from France*, CEPR Discussion Paper 2894, London.

Davies, S. and M. Hallet (2001), *Policy Responses to Regional Unemployment: Lessons from Germany, Spain and Italy*, European Commission Directorate-General for Economic and Financial Affairs, European Economy Economic Papers 161, Brussels, available at: http://ec.europa.eu/economy_finance/publications/ /economic_papers/ 2001/ecp161en.pdf.

de la Fuente, A. (2003), 'Does Cohesion Policy Work? Some General Considerations and Evidence from Spain', in B. Funck and L. Pizzati (eds), *Regional Policy for the New EU Members*, World Bank, Washington DC, pp. 155-166.

de la Fuente, A. (2003a), *Infrastructure and Productivity: A Survey*, mimeo, Instituto de Análisis Económico, Barcelona.

de la Fuente, A. (2004), 'Second-best Redistribution through Public Investment: A Characterization, an Empirical Test and an Application to the Case of Spain', *Regional Science and Urban Economics*, 34, pp 489-503.

de la Fuente, A. and A. Ciccone (2002), *Human Capital in a Global and Knowledge-Based Economy*, Report for the European Commission, DG Employment and Social Affairs, Brussels, available at: http://europa.eu.int/comm/employment social/employment_analysis/ conference_en.htm

del Mar Salinas-Jiménez, M. (2004), 'Public Infrastructure and Private Productivity in the Spanish Regions', *Journal of Policy Modelling*, **26** (1), pp. 47-64.

Ebers, H. (1998), *Erfolgskontrolle investiv geförderter landwirtschaftlicher Unternehmen im Bereich der Landwirtschaftskammer Hannover*, Göttingen.

Ederveen, S. and J. Gorter (2002), *Does European Cohesion Policy Reduce Regional Disparities?*, CPB Discussion Paper 15, Den Hague.

Ederveen, S., J. Gorter, R. de Mooij and R. Nuhuis (2002), *Funds and Games: The Economics of European Cohesion Policy*, Den Hague.

European Commission (2003), *The EU Economy Review 2003*, European Economy 6/2003, Brussels, available at: http://ec.europa.eu/economy_finance/publications/ european_economy/the_eu_economy_review2003_en.htm

European Commission (2004), *The EU Economy Review 2004*, European Economy 6/2004, Brussels, available at: http://ec.europa.eu/economy_finance/publications/ european_economy/2004/ee604fullreport_en.pdf

European Commission (2004a), *The 2004 Broad Economic Policy Guidelines BEPGs*. COM(2004)238 final, Brussels, available at: http://ec.europa.eu/economy_finance/ publications/european_economy/2004/comm2004_238en.pdf

European Commission (2004b), 'A Report on the Performance Reserve and Mid Term Evaluation in Objective 1 and 2 Regions', Brussels, available at: http:// ec.europa.eu/regional_policy/sources/docgener/evaluation/pdf/tech_report_en.pdf.

European Commission (2004c), *State Aid Scoreboard, autumn 2004 update*, available at: http://ec.europa.eu/competition/state_aid/scoreboard/2004/autumn_en.pdf.

European Commission (2007), *Growing Regions, Growing Europe, Fourth Report on Economic and Social Cohesion*, available at: http://ec.europa.eu/regional_policy/ sources/docoffic/official/reports/cohesion4/index_en.htm

Faini, R. (1983), 'Cumulative Process of Deindustrialisation in an Open Region: The Case of Southern Italy, 1953 – 1971', *Journal of Development Economics*, **12**, pp. 277-301.

Fayolle, J. and A. Lecuyer (2000), *Regional Growth, National Membership and European Structural Funds: an Empirical Appraisal*, OFCE (Observatoire Français des Conjonctures Èconomiques) Working Paper 00-02, Paris.

Forstner, B. and D. Clemens (1998), 'Einzelbetriebliche Investitionsförderung in Schleswig-Holstein effizient und nachhaltig?', *Bauernblatt für Schleswig-Holstein und Hamburg*, 51/52, pp. 74-78.

Funck, B. and L. Pizzati (2003), *European Integration, Regional Policy and Growth*, The World Bank, Washington, DC.

García Solanes, J. and R. María-Dolores (2002), 'The Impact of European Structural Funds on Economic Convergence in European Countries and Regions', in W. Meeusen and J. Villaverde Castro (eds), *Convergence Issues in the European Union*, London, pp. 61-82.

Gerling, K.M. (2002), *Subsidization and Structural Change in Eastern Germany*, Berlin.

Griliches, Z. (1979), 'Issues in Assessing the Contribution of R&D to Productivity Growth', *Bell Journal of Economics*, **10** (1), pp. 92-116.

Griliches, Z. (1992), 'The Search for R&D Spillovers', *Scandinavian Journal of Economics*, Supplement 94, pp. 29-47.

Hall, R. and C. Jones (1999), 'Why do Some Countries Produce so Much More Output than Others?', *The Quarterly Journal of Economics*, **114** (1), pp. 83-116.

Honohan, P. (1998), *Key Issues of Cost-Benefit Methodology for Irish Industrial Policy*, The Economic and Social Research Institute, General Research Series 172, Dublin.

In't Veld, J. (2007), *The Potential Impact of the Fiscal Transfers under the EU Cohesion Policy Programme*, European Commission Directorate-General for Economic and Financial Affairs, European Economy Economic Papers 283, Brussels, available at: http://ec.europa.eu/economy_finance/publications/ publication9579_en.pdf.

Jones, C.I. (1995a), 'Time Series Tests of Endogenous Growth Models', *Quarterly Journal of Economics*, **110** (2), pp. 495-525.

Jones, C.I. (1995b), 'R&D Based Models of Economic Growth', *Journal of Political Economy*, **103** (4), pp. 759-784.

Lehmann, H., U. Ludwig and J. Ragnitz (2005), 'Originäre Wirtschaftskraft der neuen Länder noch schwächer als bislang angenommen', *Wirtschaft im Wandel*, 5, pp. 134-145.

Lenihan, H. (2004), 'Evaluating Irish Industrial Policy in Terms of Deadweight and Displacement: A Quantitative Methodological Approach', *Applied Economics*, **36** (3), pp. 229-252.

Mankiw, N.G., D. Romer and D.N. Weil (1992), 'A Contribution to the Empirics of Economic Growth', *Quarterly Journal of Economics*, **107**, pp. 407-437.

Martin, P. (1999), 'Public Policies, Regional Inequalities and Growth', *Journal of Public Economics*, **73** (1), pp. 85-105.

Martin, P. and C.A. Rogers (1995), 'Industrial Location and Public Infrastructure', *Journal of International Economics*, **39**, pp. 335-351.

Martin, R. and P. Sunley (2003), 'Deconstructing Clusters: Chaotic Concept or Policy Panacea?', *Journal of Economic Geography*, 3, pp. 5-35.

Midelfart, K.H. (2004), *Regional Policy Design: An Analysis of Relocation, Efficiency and Equity*, CEPR Discussion Paper 4321, London.

Midelfart-Knarvik, K.H. and H.G. Overman (2002), 'Delocation and European Integration: Is Structural Spending Justified?', *Economic Policy*, **35**, pp. 322-359.

Moreno, R., E. López-Bazo and M. Artís (2002), 'Public Infrastructure and the Performance of Manufacturing Industries: Short- and Long-run Effects', *Regional Science and Urban Economics*, **32** (1), pp. 97-121.

Nicodème, G. and J.-B. Sauner-Leroy (2004), *Product Market Reforms and Productivity: A Review of the Theoretical and Empirical Literature on the Transmission Channels*, European Commission Directorate-General for Economic and Financial Affairs, European Economy Economic Papers 218, Brussels, available at: http://ec.europa.eu/economy_finance/publications/economic_papers/2004/ecp218en.pdf.

Pritchett, L. (1998), *Patterns of Economic Growth: Hills, Plateaus, Mountains, and Plains*, World Bank Working Paper 1947, Washington, available at: http://econ.worldbank.org/docs/999.pdf.

Puga, D. (2002), 'European Regional Policies in the Light of Recent Location Theories', *Journal of Urban Economics*, **48**, pp. 286-306.

Ragnitz, J. (2003), *Wirkungen der Investitionsförderung in Ostdeutschland*, Institut für Wirtschaftsforschung Halle, Diskussionspapiere 186, Halle.

Rodríguez-Pose, A. and U. Fratesi (2002), *Unbalanced Development Strategies and the Lack of Regional Convergence in the EU*, ERSA conference papers ersa02p415, available at: http://www.ersa.org/ersaconfs/ersa02/cd-rom/papers/ 415.pdf.

Romp, W. and J. de Haan (2005), 'Public Capital and Economic Growth: A Critical Survey', *EIB Papers*, **10** (1).

Sala-i-Martin, X. (2002), *15 Years of Growth Economics: What Have we Learnt?*, Central Bank of Chile, Working Paper 172.

Sapir, A., P. Aghion, G. Bertola, M. Hellwig, J. Pisany-Ferry, D. Rosati, J. Viñals and H. Wallace (2003), *An Agenda for a Growing Europe, Making the EU Economic System Deliver*, Oxford.

Slukhai, S. (2003), *Dilemmas and Compromises: Fiscal Equalization in Transition Countries*, LGI/OSI, LGI Studies.

Stierle, M.H. (2000), 'New Economy: How Real is the Phenomenon?', in L. Funk, (ed.), *Contemporary Aspects of the Third Way in the New Economy*, Conference Volume of the INFER-Workshop 1-2000, INFER Studies 1, Berlin, pp. 7-30.

Striewe, L., J.-P. Loy and U. Koester (1996), 'Analyse und Beurteilung der einzelbetrieblichen Investitionsförderung in Schleswig-Holstein', in *Agrarwirtschaft*, **45** (12), pp. 423-434.

Temple, J. (1999), 'New Growth Evidence', *Journal of Economic Literature*, **37**, pp. 112-156.

Vickermann, R., K. Spiekermann and M. Wegener (1999), 'Accessibility and regional development in Europe', *Regional Studies*, **33**, pp. 1-15.

Weise, C. (2002), *How to finance Eastern Enlargement of the EU: The Need to Reform EU Policies and the Consequences for the Net Contributor Balance*, DIW Discussion Paper 287, Berlin.

World Bank (2004), *Poland: Directions in Regional Policy*, Report No. 30466 – PL.

Yuill, D. and F. Wishlade (2001), *Regional Policy Developments in the Member States: A Comparative Overview of Change*, University of Strathclyde, European Policies Research Centre, Regional and Industrial Policy Research Paper 45, Glasgow, available at: http://www.eprc.strath.ac.uk/eprc/PDF_files/R46Policies andStrategiesforRegionalDevelopment.pdf.

10. Convergence and Public Investment in Spain: Regional Policies Revisited

Santiago Lago-Peñas and Diego Martínez-López*

10.1 INTRODUCTION

European Union regional policy is becoming increasingly questioned. One key point in the controversy stems from the maintenance of regional disparities despite growing resources allocated to the reduction of territorial income differences. Financial resources devoted to Structural and Cohesion Funds now account for over 30 percent of the total EU budget, more than twice the share they represented in 1988. However, several indicators show a clear retardation of convergence in income per capita after the 1970s (see, among others, López-Bazo et al., 1999; Rodríguez-Pose, 1999; and Sapir et al., 2004). To give an example, out of 30 regions which in 1987 were below 60 percent of the EU average income per capita, 83 percent remained beneath this threshold in 1995 and the remaining 17 percent did not exceed 75 percent (Overman and Puga, 2002). Moreover, the debate has intensified due to the recent enlargement of the EU with new countries which will qualify for Structural Funds. In addition, Member States that are net contributors to the EU budget are reducing their expenditures on development projects.

These points lead to a reconsideration of the objectives and instruments of regional policies, especially in those countries – like Spain – which will lose a significant part of European financing after 2007. Based on the Biehl report (Biehl, 1986), provision of infrastructure has been the central point of the design and implementation of European regional policy during the last two decades. This strategy is based on the idea that investment in infrastructure increases returns from private capital and labor, involving economic growth in areas where public capital has been invested. The relevance of public investment as an instrument of regional policy is especially clear in cases such as Spain or Portugal, where more than 70 percent of the Structural and Cohesion Funds are devoted to public infrastructure projects.

This chapter aims to add new arguments to the debate on the effectiveness of regional policies – mainly based on public investment – using data from Spanish regions. This is an interesting case to be studied for at least two reasons:

1. Since 1986 Spain has been one of the countries that has benefited most from EU regional policy – together with Greece, Portugal and Ireland. Moreover, national regional policy has been strengthened in Spain since the early eighties. And infrastructure investment has become the main tool used in both European and national regional policies (Correa and Manzanedo, 2002). As a result, public investment over Spanish GDP attained one of the highest scores in the OECD area during the eighties and nineties (Sturm, 1998).
2. Statistics at the regional level are better and more detailed in Spain than in Greece or Portugal, due to the intense political and fiscal decentralization in Spain, which has boosted the need for regional statistics.

The main results of the chapter are as follows. First, we have found that regional policies do not seem to favor convergence across Spanish regions during the eighties and nineties. This has occurred despite the redistributive pattern followed by public investment policies and the high degree of private capital mobility across the Spanish regions. Second, we detect a positive correlation between funds devoted to regional policies and human capital accumulation in the poorest Spanish regions. However, this result must be qualified in terms of the type of schooling considered. Finally, we have not found any relationship between regional policy and public R&D spending. On the contrary, a negative link is observed with regard to private innovation activities. This implies that the richer the region, the more intense its effort on R&D expenditures.

The structure of the chapter is as follows. Section 10.2 provides a brief summary of the main issues to be taken into account in regional convergence processes. Section 10.3 offers empirical evidence about the role played by regional policy on many of these growth-affecting factors for Spanish regions. Finally, section 10.4 concludes and suggests some policy implications.

10.2   A SHORT BACKGROUND ON THE DETERMINANTS OF CONVERGENCE

Conventional wisdom suggests that endogenous growth models provide enough scope for government policies aimed at increasing the growth rate of income per capita. While the neoclassical approach usually links the dynamics of income to the existence of decreasing returns to scale and exogenous technical progress, endogenous growth models define the long-term growth rate on the basis of constant returns to scale and without exogenous forces driving transitional dynamics toward a steady-state equilibrium. This framework also permits policy-makers to implement policies affecting long-run growth rates.

Although at a regional level the debate on economic growth presents its own concerns, the determinants of growth and convergence remain unaffected by aggregation level. In this section, we will briefly review the main factors in regional economic growth with the aim of assessing empirically (in the next section) the extent to which regional policy has affected these processes across Spanish regions. We will implicitly use the model described by Funke and Strulik (2005), though our discussion will be extended in some complementary ways. These authors build a two-region endogenous growth model with private capital mobility and a policy rule consisting of a higher provision of public investment in the poor region. The main result of the model is that convergence in income per capita is achieved when both regions have equal access to technology and there is no migration of population from rich to poor regions.

Next we shall briefly discuss the relevance of a number of factors on regional convergence. Among issues considered important, we have chosen to ignore certain aspects of migratory flows. Although unemployment rates in Spanish regions have diverged during the eighties and nineties, several authors have noted that interregional migration has not offset these differences in regional labor markets (Puga, 2002). Thus income redistribution mechanisms – strengthened in Spain since the late seventies – may have discouraged the regional mobility of labor. Moreover, Bentolila (1997) shows a non-linear relationship between unemployment rate differentials and migration. While differences in unemployment rates drive migration flows when the average level of unemployment is moderate, these differences are less relevant when unemployment rates are very high as in Spain during the eighties and nineties.[1] Most empirical papers agree that since the late 1970s net interregional migration rates in Spain have fallen significantly, and so have had little effect on regional convergence (Antolin and Bover, 1997; Bover and Velilla, 2004).

A first issue to deal with is the existence of decreasing returns to scale. As is well-known, the Solow model and its empirical implementation by Mankiw et al. (1992) has predicted that the poorer the region, the higher its growth rate. This neoclassical model includes a force driving economies toward a steady state and thus toward some kind of convergence. Another concern is whether this convergence is conditional or unconditional. Many papers have studied this aspect throughout the last two decades (see Sala-i-Martin, 1996, for a selective survey), and the controversy still continues. On this basis, assuming that regional policy benefits poor regions most, we shall check whether resources devoted to convergence have successfully increased the growth rate of income in these relatively less-developed territories.

Second, several contributions have highlighted the role of public investment in narrowing the gap between high-income and low-income regions (per capita). There are at least two channels through which public investment might affect measures of regional economic growth. One is through the inclusion of public capital as an argument in regional aggregate production functions.[2] The other factor operates through the complementary effects on regional income of public capital expenditures and private investment outlays.[3] Romp and de Haan (2005) have recently surveyed the relationships between economic growth and public capital expenditures. They find the evidence still somewhat inconclusive.

A diversity of findings is also obtained in the case of Spanish regions. While papers such as De la Fuente and Vives (1995), Mas et al. (1995) and De la Fuente (2003) find significant positive effects of public investment on Spanish regional growth, other references do not detect any positive impact. This is the case, for instance, with Mas et al. (1994) over specific periods, Dolado et al. (1994) regarding roads and Spanish provinces, Gorostiaga (1999) with respect to human capital and endogenous technological progress, and González-Páramo and Martínez-López (2003) for a variety of econometric specifications. The wide range of these findings arises not only from sample and specification differences, but also from variant data sources and definitions of variables.[4]

In any event, with regard to regional convergence and public capital provision, the extent to which public investment has followed a regional redistributive pattern should be considered. In the next section, we will examine to what extent the regional allocation of public capital has favored poorer regions, and whether or not this spending has tracked the behavior of private investment expenditure.

A third issue addressed is the degree of private capital mobility across different economies. In particular, Barro et al. (1995) attribute the speed of convergence to private capital mobility: the more perfect the capital markets, the higher the speed of convergence. This finding appears to apply in a regional context as long as political barriers are absent and if regional policies succeed in attracting private capital to less developed areas. While a high level of private capital mobility is expected for regional samples, to the best of our knowledge no previous studies have examined the issue for Spanish regions.[5]

A fourth determinant of convergence is given by the consideration of human capital as a factor of production. Ever since the seminal papers on this subject by Uzawa (1965) and Lucas (1988), human capital investment has been seen as a way of relaxing the constraint of decreasing returns to scale, and hence as a force sustaining long-term per capita income growth. However, even after acknowledging the theoretical issues involved in the transition to a steady state with accumulating human capital (see Barro and Sala-i-Martin, 1995, for more details), human capital variables seem often to be insignificant or even negative in their regressed effects on economic growth and convergence (Caselli et al., 1996). This striking result can be partially explained by the poor quality of human capital data, which yields measurement errors and negative bias in derived estimates (De la Fuente and Domenech, 2001, 2002). Adjusting for this problem makes the effect of education on per capita income growth positive and quite sizable. On the basis of this renewed evidence, we evaluate the redistributive effects of the territorial allocation of human capital investment across Spanish regions.

Finally, technological progress serves as a crucial variable for sustaining the long-term growth rate of income per capita, both under neoclassical exogenous growth models and under a newer generation of endogenous growth models. At first view, R&D investment could be seen as similar to investment in other assets such as private capital, yielding growth in income per capita but subject to decreasing returns to scale. However, there is more to this story. First, if the cost of R&D investment declines (or is at least non-rising) with the level of technology available for an economy, we would find increasing (or at least constant) returns to scale due to positive externalities generated by existing technology (Romer, 1990). Under such circumstances, economies would be unlikely to converge over time.

Alternatively, technological progress may have public good properties. If so, such progress would lead to convergence as long as lagged economies can imitate leading economies at lower R&D cost (Grossman and Helpman, 1991). Of course, this success is conditional on assumptions about the gap between leader and follower economies, the cost of adapting new technologies, the nature of property rights and patents, etc. (Barro and Sala-i-Martin, 1995). In general, however, R&D investment tends to boost growth of income per capita, assuming some minimum threshold level of R&D expenditures. On these grounds, the regional allocation of R&D investments becomes a relevant basis on which to assess economic convergence in a regional context. Our empirical analysis of the Spanish case in the next section supports this view.

10.3 EMPIRICAL EVIDENCE FROM SPANISH REGIONS

Spain has followed a similar pattern to other European countries in terms of regional convergence: a clear convergence in income per capita up until the late 1970s, and thereafter convergence came to a sudden stop (López-Bazo et al., 1999). There are at least two explanations of this phenomenon. The first is that regional labor productivity showed weak convergence during the 80s and 90s (Goerlich et al., 2002). The second is, as already noted, the unequal behavior of regional labor markets, in which – without migratory flows – excess labor in poor regions does not migrate to meet the demand for labor in more rapidly growing regions.

A first look at regional convergence in Spain is provided in the following manner. Instead of estimating a standard convergence equation, changes in GDP and population are separately analyzed. As known, the aim of regional policy is convergence through higher GDP growth rates in the poorest regions. Actually, achieving convergence through migration is not a goal of regional policy. After analyzing GDP and population, then changes in the most important productive inputs (infrastructure investment, private capital investment, R&D expenditures, and human capital accumulation) under an assumption of capital mobility are examined to evaluate the effectiveness of past regional policies.

A more direct analytical approach might be employed, based on the estimated effects of public capital on economic growth. However, such an approach encounters two problems. First, estimates of the effects of public capital investment on growth are usually made using uniequational frameworks such as convergence equations (with public capital as a factor conditioning steady-states) and aggregate production functions (with public capital as an additional input). Both procedures fail to capture the full effects of public capital on the accumulation of other inputs, mainly private capital, which are so relevant to European regional policy. Alternative approaches such as VAR models or estimates for cost and factor demand functions do account for the likely complementarity between public and private capital, but regional aspects are not properly treated in the former, and convergence results are difficult to analyze in the latter. Second, with regard to international samples, evidence of the effects of public capital on growth and convergence is still inconclusive for Spain, as we briefly showed in the previous section.

For all these reasons, we have chosen a simpler approach. Our aim is not to test directly the effect of public investment on growth, but to study how regional policy – mainly based on public capital provision – has influenced the regional distribution of Spanish GDP, along with its effects on other factors important to economic growth.

GDP and Population Regional Shares

Has regional policy affected Spanish economic geography? In order to answer this question the following equation is estimated:

$$\Delta Y_i = \alpha + \beta \cdot FUNDS_i + \varepsilon_i$$

where ΔY_i is defined as changes in regional shares on Spanish GDP between years t and $t + s$:

$$\Delta Y_i = \left(\frac{Y_{it+S}}{\sum_{j=1}^{17} Y_{jt+S}} \right) - \left(\frac{Y_{it}}{\sum_{j=1}^{17} Y_{jt}} \right)$$

The idea is to compare regional shares just before (year t) and after $(t + s)$ the implementation of regional policies. Variable $FUNDS_i$ is the per capita regional financing received by region i between $t + 1$ and $t + s$. As an alternative endogenous variable, changes in population have been used:

$$\Delta P_i = \left(\frac{P_{it+S}}{\sum_{j=1}^{17} P_{jt+S}} \right) - \left(\frac{P_{it}}{\sum_{j=1}^{17} P_{jt}} \right)$$

Finally, the rates of change in GDP and population are used as an explained variable.

Due to data constraints, our analysis focuses solely on the period 1983-1999. Correa and Manzanedo (2002) provide accumulated data on both Spanish and European regional policies for periods 1983-1989, 1990-1999 and the whole period 1983-1999.[6] In particular, they offer figures on per capita funds received by Spanish regions and expressed in real terms (Table 10.1). Correlation between resources received in both subperiods is very high (r = 0.87), but they are significantly more relevant in the nineties. Standardized data are used in econometric estimates. GDP and population data are taken from FBBVA (2000) for 1999 and from FBBVA (1999) for 1981 and 1989.[7] Changes are expressed in percentage.

Table 10.1 Regional policy in Spain

Period	1983-1999	1983-1989	1990-1999	1983-1999	1983-1989	1990-1999
Andalucía	2.97	0.90	2.08	1.35	1.44	1.31
Aragón	2.13	0.51	1.61	0.96	0.82	1.02
Asturias	3.02	0.59	2.44	1.37	0.95	1.54
Baleares	0.88	0.30	0.58	0.40	0.49	0.37
Canarias	3.05	0.83	2.22	1.38	1.33	1.40
Cantabria	2.40	0.47	1.93	1.09	0.75	1.22
Castilla y León	3.25	0.83	2.42	1.47	1.33	1.53
Castilla-La Mancha	3.76	1.07	2.69	1.70	1.72	1.70
Cataluña	1.06	0.38	0.69	0.48	0.61	0.43
Comunidad Valenciana	1.67	0.37	1.30	0.76	0.60	0.82
Extremadura	4.70	1.44	3.26	2.13	2.32	2.06
Galicia	3.57	0.79	2.79	1.62	1.26	1.76
Madrid	0.74	0.28	0.46	0.34	0.46	0.29
Murcia	2.40	0.54	1.87	1.09	0.87	1.18
Navarra	1.17	0.27	0.90	0.53	0.43	0.57
País Vasco	1.47	0.54	0.93	0.67	0.87	0.59
La Rioja	1.30	0.34	0.96	0.59	0.55	0.61
Spain	2.21	0.62	1.58	1.00	1.00	1.00

Notes: Figures in thousands of 1986 euros (the first three columns) and standardized with Spain = 1.00 (the remaining columns).
Source: Correa and Manzanedo (2002).

In order to expand the sample and take advantage of the availability of information on regional policy for two subperiods, the following specification has been also estimated:

$$\Delta Y_{it} = \alpha + \beta \cdot FUNDS_{it} + \gamma \cdot D_t + \lambda \cdot FUNDS_{it} \cdot D_t + \varepsilon_{it} .$$

Variable D is a dummy variable, with a value of 1 for observations corresponding to the period 1990-1999 and 0 for those corresponding to 1983-1989. Two cross-sections are then used, passing from 17 to 34 observations. The first cross-section relates changes in GDP shares between 1981 and 1989 with regional funds received during 1983-1989. The second one relates changes in GDP shares from 1989 to 1999 with data on regional funds received during 1990-1999. Coefficients for variable D and *FUNDS D* allow for changes in the impact of regional policy. In particular, while the effect of regional policy on GDP shares during the eighties is captured by coefficient β, the marginal effect of variable *FUNDS* during the second period is $\beta + \lambda$.

Econometric results are shown in Table 10.2. Specification tests did not reveal problems in this respect. For the whole period 1981-1999 there is a negative but scarcely significant (p-value = 0.23) relationship between changes in GDP shares and regional funds received (column 1). In other words, regional policy would have not helped to increase GDP shares corresponding to subsidized regions during the eighties and nineties. When the sample is split into two, results are interesting (column 2). While the relationship is positive but not significant for the eighties, it is negative and significant for the nineties, when regional policy is stronger. The null hypothesis $\beta + \lambda = 0$ should be rejected according to a Wald test (p-value = 0.02). On the contrary, regional policy is not related to changes in regional population shares (column 3). Combining both changes in population and GDP shares, column 4 clearly shows that Spanish regions did not converge.

Table 10.2 Regional policy and changes in population and GDP, 1981-1999

	ΔY	ΔY	ΔP	$\Delta Y - \Delta P$
Intercept	0.20	−0.05	0.02	−0.07
	(0.28)	(0.65)	(0.92)	(0.73)
FUNDS	−0.19	0.05	−0.02	0.07
	(0.23)	(0.61)	(0.91)	(0.69)
D		0.29	−0.12	0.17
		(0.06)	(0.68)	(0.55)
*FUNDS*D*		−0.27	−0.11	−0.16
		(0.05)	(0.66)	(0.51)
R^2	0.09	0.18	0.02	0.02
Observations	17	34	34	34
White (*p*-value)	0.48	0.61	0.28	0.60
RESET (*p*-value)	0.36	0.35	0.23	0.09

Notes:
Below each coefficient appears, in parenthesis, the *p*-value corresponding to standard *t*-statistic.
White is the White's test on the null hypothesis of homoscedasticity.
RESET is the Ramsey's test on the null hypothesis of no specification errors.

What these results suggest is that regional policy and *ex post* redistribution could have prevented interregional migration from the poorest to the richest regions, but did not change the spatial distribution of Spanish GDP in favor of less developed regions. Our findings here are in agreement with those of other papers (see, for instance, De la Fuente, 2002). Of course, there are positive experiences. Some of the most heavily-subsidized regions (Andalucia and Canarias) have increased their GDP shares. But this behavior is offset by negative trends in regions like Galicia, Asturias, Castilla-La Mancha, and Castilla y Leon.

Public and Private Capital

According to data from FBBVA (2005), the net stock of capital in the Spanish economy rose substantially from 1982 to 1999. While non-residential private capital (K) grew by 66 percent, productive public capital (G) grew by 103 percent.[8] Have these figures involved significant changes in the regional distribution of physical capital? In order to answer this question, the following econometric specification was estimated:

$$\Delta CAPITAL_{it} = \alpha + \beta \cdot FUNDS_{it} + \gamma \cdot D_t + \lambda \cdot FUNDS_{it} \cdot D_t + \varepsilon_{it}$$

The endogenous variable is the change in regional shares of, alternatively, public and private capital (G and K). They are defined in the same way as GDP and Population regional shares were before, but with $t = 1982$. Moreover, the exogenous variables are the same as before. Estimates are reported in Table 10.3.

Table 10.3 Regional policy and evolutions of public productive capital and private productive capital stocks, 1982-1999

	ΔG	ΔK	$\Delta G - \Delta K$
INTERCEPT	−0.51	0.18	−0.69
	(0.10)	(0.51)	(0.05)
FUNDS	0.51	−0.19	0.70
	(0.06)	(0.46)	(0.03)
D	0.32	0.46	−0.14
	(0.46)	(0.25)	(0.78)
*FUNDS*D*	−0.34	−0.41	0.07
	(0.37)	(0.23)	(0.87)
R^2	0.12	0.19	0.28
Observations	34	34	34
White (p-value)	0.69	0.16	0.75
RESET (p-value)	0.32	0.44	0.20

Note: See Table 10.2.

The relationship between regional funding and the accumulation of productive public capital is found to be positive, but it seems to be stronger in the first period than in the latter period. According to the two Wald tests, the hypothesis $\beta = 0$ could be rejected at the 10 percent level, but not the hypothesis $\beta + \lambda = 0$ (p-value = 0.50). Results for private capital are the opposite. Private capital has tended to increase more rapidly in richer regions, especially in the nineties: the hypothesis $\beta + \lambda = 0$ is clearly rejected (p-value = 0.02). In column 3 the endogenous variable is the difference in growth rates corresponding to productive public capital and private capital. In this case, the ratio G/K has clearly grown faster in less developed regions in both periods. These results show that the territorial allocation of public investment (in relation to private investment) has followed a redistributive pattern (González-Páramo and Martínez-López, 2003; De la Fuente, 2004), in line with policy rules set in models such as that of Funke and Strulik (2005).

Capital Mobility

Another factor potentially affecting the effectiveness of regional policies is the degree of private capital mobility across regions. Here there exists a complementary relationship between public and private capital, so that a higher public investment effort in the poor regions should be accompanied by private capital flows towards these regions, thereby increasing their growth rates. Paradoxically, previous references have not addressed or tested this hypothesis.

The assumption of perfect capital mobility across Spanish regions has been tested. In accord with Feldstein and Horioka (1980), our analysis focuses on the relationship between gross saving and investment rather than data net of depreciation for two reasons. First, gross saving is what really flows between regions. Second, measurement errors in depreciation rates would bias parameter estimates. Our baseline econometric specification is as follows:

$$\left(\frac{I}{Y}\right)_{it} = \alpha_i + \beta_t \cdot \left(\frac{S}{Y}\right)_{it} + \lambda_t \cdot D_t + \mu_{it}$$

Where $(I / Y)_{it}$ is the ratio of gross private non-residential investment over Gross Domestic Product (GDP) in region i and year t, $(S / Y)_{it}$ is the share of gross regional private saving over regional GDP, and D_t is a dummy variable that values 1 in year t and 0 otherwise. Individual fixed-effects (α_i) and time fixed-effects (λD_t) are included in order to deal with heterogeneity.

Data for regional saving have been available since 1991. Moreover, to compare data for both investment and saving, the sample must be reduced to the years 1991, 1993, 1995, 1996, 1997 and 1998. The data source for saving and GDP in 1991 and 1993 is again FBBVA (1997), and for saving and GDP in 1995-1998 is Alcaide (2003), while investment data were taken from FBBVA (2005). Ratios are expressed in percentage terms.

Table 10.4 Regional mobility of private capital

	(1)	(2)	(3)	(4)
Intercept				11.90
				(0.00)
(S/Y)	0.10			
	(0.02)			
$(S/Y) \cdot D_{1991}$		0.22	0.20	0.22
		(0.00)	(0.00)	(0.00)
		[0.00]		
$(S/Y) \cdot D_{1993}$		0.16	0.11	0.16
		(0.05)	(0.00)	(0.05)
		[0.04]		
$(S/Y) \cdot D_{1995}$		0.10	0.03	0.10
		(0.20)	(0.62)	(0.19)
		[0.17]		
$(S/Y) \cdot D_{1996}$		0.05	−0.00	0.05
		(0.48)	(0.94)	(0.49)
		[0.47]		
$(S/Y) \cdot D_{1997}$		0.01	−0.05	0.01
		(0.87)	(0.41)	(0.91)
		[0.90]		
$(S/Y) \cdot D_{1998}$		−0.00	0.01	−0.01
		(0.92)	(0.89)	(0.88)
		[0.92]		
R^2	0.870	0.881	0.876	0.881
Observations	102	102	102	102
$\hat{\rho}$	0.15	0.11	0.12	0.11
	(0.14)	(0.29)	(0.23)	(0.27)
Hausman (p-value)	0.94			
λ_{LM}(p-value)		0.30	0.35	
LM (p-value)		0.00		

Notes:
All estimates include time fixed-effects. Estimates (1) to (3) include individual fixed-effects. Estimate (4) includes individual random-effects. In the case of estimate (3) FGLS is used to correct groupwise heteroskedasticity. Below each coefficient appears, in parenthesis, the p-value corresponding to standard *t*-statistic and, in brackets, that corresponding to White's *t*-statistic. LM corresponds to a Lagrange multiplier test on the null hypothesis of cross-section homoscedasticity. λ_{LM} is the statistic corresponding to a Lagrange multiplier test on the null hypothesis of contemporaneous uncorrelation of residuals. Hausman is the statistic corresponding to the test on the null hypothesis of exogeneity of (S/Y).

Estimates in Table 10.4 are aimed at testing for a statistical relationship between regional savings and investment, as high capital mobility would suggest. Both individual and time fixed-effects are statistically significant. Serial autocorrelation is not problematic.[9] Finally, the potential endogeneity of the saving ratio has been also tested using a Hausman test. The corresponding p-value is very high and then the null hypothesis of exogeneity is not rejected.[10]

According to estimates reported in column (1), the value of $\hat{\beta}$ for the whole sample is positive and significant but very low (0.10). Moreover, according again to Feldstein and Horioka (1980), it should be taken into account that with perfect regional capital mobility, an increase in the savings rate in region i could cause a rise in investment in all regions (including, of course, region i). Therefore, perfect mobility would be compatible with low values of β.[11]

On the other hand, there is a lack of structural stability of coefficient $\hat{\beta}$ over time. In column (2) of Table 10.4 the following specification is estimated:

$$\left(\frac{I}{Y}\right)_{it} = \alpha_i + \beta_t \cdot \left(\frac{S}{Y}\right)_{it} \cdot D_t + \lambda_t \cdot D_t + \mu_{it}$$

It includes interactions between the savings ratio and the variable D_t in order to capture time differences in $\hat{\beta}$. This coefficient drops over time from 0.22 to 0. Autocorrelation is not a problem.[12] On the contrary, while contemporaneous correlations may be discarded according to the results from a LM test, groupwise heteroskedasticity was detected using another LM test.

In column (3) the Feasible Generalized Least Squares (FGLS) estimator to deal with groupwise heteroskedasticity is used.[13] While results are similar, estimates of parameter β are lower than in column (2) (0.20 in 1991 and 0.10 in 1993). Finally, in column (4) individual fixed effects are replaced by random effects. Results are also analogous to those shown in column (2). In sum, this battery of results reveals a high degree of capital mobility across Spanish regions.

Human Capital

Despite the empirical problems noted in Section 10.2 with regard to the effect of human capital on growth, there are few doubts that investment in education (defined broadly) is an important growth-enhancing factor. Human capital has significantly improved between 1982 and 1999 in Spain. While total activities (H1) increased by 24 percent, the number of them with at least secondary schooling (H2) rose by 184 percent, and the accumulated growth of actives with universitary schooling (H3) was 230 percent.[14]

Using H1, H2, and H3 as alternative explained variables, the same model as that for physical capital is estimated. Data for all Spanish regions and the period 1982-1999 are used:

$$\Delta H_{it} = \alpha + \beta \cdot FUNDS_{it} + \gamma \cdot D_t + \lambda \cdot FUNDS_{it} \cdot D_t + \varepsilon_{it} \, .$$

The endogenous variable is defined as the change in regional shares of, alternatively, H1, H2 and H3. These shares are defined in the same way as the regional shares of variables G and K. Exogenous variables are also the same. Econometric estimates are reported in Table 10.5.

Table 10.5 Regional evolution of human capital, 1982-1999

	ΔH1	ΔH2	ΔH3
INTERCEPT	−0.19	−1.02	−0.28
	(0.48)	(0.03)	(0.62)
FUNDS	0.17	1.01	0.28
	(0.48)	(0.02)	(0.59)
D	0.64	0.54	−0.41
	(0.10)	(0.41)	(0.62)
*FUNDS*D*	−0.59	−0.57	0.36
	(0.08)	(0.31)	(0.61)
R^2	0.11	0.20	0.06
Observations	34	34	34
White (p-value)	0.42	0.85	0.29
RESET (p-value)	0.92	0.06	0.50
$\beta + \lambda = 0$ (p-value)	0.07	0.25	0.18

Notes:
Below each coefficient appears, in parenthesis, the p-value corresponding to standard t-statistic. White is the White's test on the null hypothesis of homoscedasticity. RESET is the Ramsey's test on the null hypothesis of no specification errors. H1 is active population; H2 is active population with, at least, secondary schooling, H3 is active population with universitary schooling.

According to the results shown in column 1, active population has tended to increase faster in richer regions during the 1990s (p-value = 0.07). On the contrary, column 2 shows that active population with at least secondary schooling has risen faster in poorer regions during the eighties (p-value = 0.02), but the results are less clear during the nineties. While the coefficient for the 90s ($\beta + \lambda$) is also positive, its statistical significance is low according to a Wald test (p-value = 0.25). Finally, coefficients for *FUNDS* in column 3 are also positive but not very significant. Corresponding p-values are 0.59 for the 80s and 0.18 for the 1990s. In sum, the average educational levels in the active population have tended to grow faster in poorer regions.

R&D Expenditures

Differences in technological levels can be another potential cause of divergence among regions. Therefore the relationship between R&D expenditures and regional funding is explored. While R&D expenditure &D grew in all Spanish regions,[15] the question is whether that growth has been faster or slower in subsidized regions. To address this question, a basic model including individual fixed effects and a time trend t is estimated. The coefficient of the interactive term $FUNDS_i \cdot t$ serves to test for the existence of differences correlated to the amount of regional funds received:

$$\left(\frac{RD}{Y}\right)_{it} = \alpha_i + \beta \cdot t + \lambda_t \cdot FUNDS_i \cdot t + \mu_{it}$$

Data for regional R&D expenditures over regional GDP are from INE (2004) and correspond to Spanish regions during the period 1987-1999.[16] Data for Madrid are excluded because they behave as outliers; Madrid concentrates a large number of both private and public R&D activities, because this region is the headquarters of many public offices and significant private firms: in 1987 Madrid accounted for 44 percent of total Spanish R&D expenditure. Data for *FUNDS* correspond again to the accumulated per capita resources received by each region from the regional policy in the course of the period 1983-1999.

Econometric results are shown in Table 10.6. Using the same test as above, contemporaneous correlation and groupwise heteroskedasticity were detected. Moreover, previous estimates revealed residual autocorrelation. In order to deal with those problems, the Prais-Winsten estimator, assuming a common AR(1) process, and Panel Corrected Standard Errors (PCSE) are used.[17] According to the estimates (column 1), total R&D expenditures have risen less rapidly in regions receiving more funds, but the statistical significance is very low (p-value = 0.29). These results change when public and private R&D expenditures are separately analyzed. The path followed by public R&D expenditures is positively related to the amount of regional funds received, but statistical significance is only marginal (p-value = 0.19). On the contrary, private R&D expenditures significantly drop with the level of funds (p-value = 0.00). This implies that private R&D expenditures are progressively concentrated into the richest regions. Estimated coefficients also reveal that public and private expenditures have grown at similar average rates.[18]

The question now is: do regional differences in private R&D expenditures result from different behaviors of high and mid-high technology firms across the national territory or, by contrast, are they a consequence of structural divergences among Spanish regions? Using data on High Technology Indicators by INE, it is easy to see in Table 10.7 that there is no positive correlation between regional GDP per capita and regional expenditure on innovation activities in high and mid-high technology sectors[19] (measured as a ratio over turnover and, alternatively, over sales of products) over the period 2000-2001.[20]

Table 10.6 Regional evolution of R&D expenditures over GDP, 1987-1999

	Total	Public	Firms
t	0.027	0.010	0.018
	(0.00)	(0.04)	(0.00)
FUNDS*t	−0.003	0.003	−0.007
	(0.29)	(0.19)	(0.00)
R^2	0.97	0.89	0.96
Observations	208	208	208
$\hat{\rho}$	0.31	0.51	0.37
λ_{LM} (p-value)	0.00		
LM (p-value)	0.00		

Notes:
All estimates include individual fixed-effects and the Prais-Winsten estimator to correct for serial autocorrelation is used. Below each coefficient appears the p-value corresponding to the PCSE t-statistic. LM corresponds to a Lagrange multiplier test on the null hypothesis of cross-section homoskedasticity. λ_{LM} is the statistic corresponding to a Lagrange multiplier test on the null hypothesis of contemporaneous uncorrelation of residuals.

In other words, territorial criteria are not an important determinant of the behavior of firms belonging to sectors with a high technological content. These firms may well make greater R&D expenditures in lagged regions than in richer regions. Therefore, we can surmise that the results in Table 10.6 are more closely related to the sectoral specialization of regions (i.e., different relative sizes of high technological content sectors over the total regional output) than to an explicit influence of the territory on these firms' investment decisions. Indeed, the percentage of the regional GVA produced by high and high-mid technology firms is about 3 percent for the five least developed regions, while this ratio increases up to 9 percent in the case of the five most developed regions in the year 2000. As these sectors are more prone to invest in innovation, this may partially explain why regions in which these sectors dominate are those in which R&D expenditures are higher relative to per capita GDP. This finding conforms to that pointed out by De la Fuente (2002), who attributes regional per capita income differentials to sectoral factors. Our results support this finding, especially in sectors with high technological content, especially on the growth rate of income.

At this point, one must acknowledge that not all the potential variables involved in growth processes have been analyzed. But on the basis of our empirical results and the relevant literature on growth-enhancing public policies since the late 1990's (see, for instance, Boldrin and Canova, 2001, and the subsequent literature), we find no reason to question the effectiveness of current regional policies intensively based on infrastructure investment, due to their lack of impact on regional convergence and on relevant variables such as human capital and R&D expenditures.

Table 10.7 Technological effort in the high and mid-high technological
Sectors

	R & D	R & D	GDP per
	Turnover	*Sales*	capita
Andalucía	96.4	99.1	74.3
Aragón	42.2	39.0	106.2
Asturias	69.3	73.0	85.6
Baleares	50.0	85.8	125.5
Canarias	282.6	765.5	94.7
Cantabria	24.8	22.2	96.3
Castilla y León	71.5	56.9	92.2
Castilla-La-Mancha	114.3	109.2	80.6
Cataluña	86.0	81.2	119.9
Comunidad Valenciana	58.5	54.4	95.9
Extremadura	184.2	181.3	64.2
Galicia	35.1	35.4	79.1
Madrid	181.3	248.4	134.5
Murcia	96.9	82.0	85.3
Navarra	62.7	52.2	126.0
País Vasco	148.3	136.7	124.2
La Rioja	101.0	86.1	114.6
Spain	100.0	100.0	100.0
Correlations with GDP per capita	−0.024	−0.005	1

Note: Average and standardized values for 2000-2001, Spain=100.
Source: INE (2004).

10.4   CONCLUSIONS AND POLICY IMPLICATIONS

The redefinition of European regional policy is considered here, with respect to two particular issues. On the one hand, there is only weak evidence for regional convergence between regions receiving Structural Funds and the most developed areas in the EU, as highlighted by previous papers. On the other hand, the recent enlargement of the EU by admitting new countries with relatively low levels of per capita GDP increases the importance of establishing the likelihood of convergence. Moreover, net contributor countries appear reluctant to increase the Community Budget for financing development policies in new Member States. A more efficient use of resources for regional policies seems to be important.

This chapter aims to make a contribution to this issue. Using data from Spain we find that the concentration of economic activity in the richest regions has not changed in spite of an implementation of regional development policies during the 1980s and 1990s. In fact, the resources devoted to promoting convergence among regions have advanced the pace of physical and human capital accumulation in poor regions. In addition, private capital mobility (very high during the studied period) has not been an obstacle for convergence. In contrast, R&D expenditures do not seem to have had a close, positive relationship with regional policy. While private firms have spent more on innovation in high income regions, the territorial allocation of public R&D expenditures has not specifically targeted poor regions. Moreover, we have adduced more evidence that sectoral factors play a role in the explanation of regional income differentials, with particular regard to R&D investment spending.

Two different – but compatible – interpretations of the empirical evidence can be offered: either insufficient resources have been devoted to regional policies; or regional policies have not been optimally designed. Regarding the first interpretation, there is little realistic chance of a significant increase in the allocation of financial resources for regional development. Spanish regional policy might be able to compensate for some cuts in European funds (Utrilla, 2004), but is not likely to be able to increase total funds for this purpose. Hence looking for more efficient regional policy options appears more realistic as a means to improve performance in terms of convergence.

To this effect, there are a number of challenges which should be faced by both European and Spanish regional policy makers:

1.   Higher levels of efficiency in the allocation of public funds is a priority. *Ex ante* cost-benefit analyses should play a crucial role in deciding which spending programmes are to be continued, and in determining the optimal balance between development spending on

infrastructures, training and R&D. Moreover, the current legal controls on the use of public and private grants seem inadequate. *Ex post* controls on the efficiency of expenditures in all areas should also be strengthened to avoid the refinancing of programmes showing poor results.

2. Public and private R&D investment should aim to achieve several objectives at European, national and regional levels. First, overall expenditures in this area ought to be increased. According to OECD data, the EU invests 1.9 percent of its GDP in R&D, which percentage falls almost to 1 percent in the case of Spain. Additional efforts are clearly needed to meet the Lisbon target of close to 3 percent (Kok, 2004). A significant part of public R&D spending in the EU and Spain, relative to that in the US, is rooted in the inadequate R&D spending of private companies. Stimulating private investment in R&D through tax credits, and a more effective conversion of knowledge into commercially-viable innovations were proposed in the *Sapir Report* (Sapir et al., 2004). But these measures are no panacea: while the Spanish tax system is comparatively generous with regard to R&D spending, the level of R&D investment by Spanish firms is lower than the European average. For this purpose, a closer look at the relationships between universities and firms in the US could provide some useful lessons for redesigning European R&D systems (Veloso et al., 2003). Moreover, there is a mixed body of evidence on the promotion of innovation at the regional level (in terms of creation of clusters, of the links between local universities and firms, and with respect to the integration of world-wide networks of knowledge, etc.) that is worth further analysis.[21] Second, as long as there is significant underinvestment by firms in backward regions, regional policy and subcentral governments with powers in this field (as in Spain) should pay more attention to the promotion of R&D activities. The controversy over whether public R&D spending increases private R&D investment is currently being debated in academic and policy circles as well (David et al., 1999). While innovation policies across Europe have sought to develop better linkages between public and private R&D (Howells, 2005), this complementary relationship is influenced by the capacity of the private sector to initiate and absorb public R&D investment funding (Oughton et al., 2002).

3. The *Sapir Report* also advocates an increase in total investment on higher education to 3 percent of GDP. In 2000, USA spent 2.9 percent, the EU 1.4 percent and Spain 1.3 percent (OECD, 2003). Econometric results show that the proportion of the active population with secondary education has tended to rise faster in backward

Spanish regions. Empirical evidence on the regional distribution of actives with university schooling is less favorable for poorer than for richer regions. Moreover, data from Hernández-Armenteros (2004) show that the ratio between public resources granted to universities and the number of students is significantly lower in the less developed regions.22 The financing system of Spanish public universities (private educational institutions in Spain are still quantitatively marginal) is based on grants from regional governments (around 75 percent of total revenues), and fiscal equalization is very strong in Spain at the regional level. Therefore, differences in per capita public spending are not adequately explained by divergences in the financial capacity of regions; they are better explained by political preferences on public spending composition. Clearly, backward regions should make additional efforts themselves to promote their own economic and social development. Of course, increasing financial resources is not enough to improve the quality of education, as shown in the meta-study by Hanushek (2003). But implementing reforms aimed at promoting excellence – as proposed in the *Sapir Report* – is much easier with additional funding. Moreover, regional efforts made to promote human capital accumulation should take more into account the particular needs of regional productive systems and regional clusters.

4.   Finally, a worse performance in the labour market is found in poor regions, where unemployment rates are higher than in more dynamic areas. A closer interaction between training activities financed by regional policy and by firms would also be an aid to convergence.

Of course, there are other ways to deal with regional disparities, such as switching the focus of EU development policy from regions to Member States (Sapir et al., 2004; De la Fuente, 2004). In fact, the major advances in convergence across the European Union have been in terms of national economies. This solution would imply that Structural Funds should be allocated according to national criteria (such as Cohesion Funds), and their redistribution within countries would use mainly instruments of *ex post* personal income redistribution, namely taxes and grants to households. But this solution involves an acceptance of a higher spatial concentration of GDP, employment and population (and therewith of voters and political power) in some regions relative to others. Furthermore, such a policy recommendation may be very difficult to implement in highly decentralized European states such as Spain, with strong regional political cleavages and regionalist political parties.[23]

NOTES

* We thank Javier Rodero, Joan Rossello, Albert Sole-Olle, participants at XII Spanish Meeting of Public Economics, at 7th INFER Annual Conference: Regional Economics: New challenges for theory, empirics and policy, and at III Jornadas de Macroeconomía de Castilla-La Mancha, for their helpful comments on an earlier version, and Carmen García for her research assistance. Santiago Lago-Peñas acknowledges the financial support from the Centro de Estudios Andaluces, and both authors the financial support from the Spanish Ministry of Education and Science (project SEC 2006-04803). The usual disclaimer applies.

1. For example, let there be two regions, A and B. Unemployment rate in region B is five percentage points higher than in region A. Incentives for migration from B to A will be much stronger when the unemployment rate in A is 3 percent than when it is 15 percent.
2. For a general survey of this literature see Sturm (1998).
3. Flores de Frutos et al. (1998) obtain a positive relationship for the Spanish economy as a whole, and Martínez-López (2006) confirms that when the sample consists of Spanish regions.
4. Caramés and Lago-Peñas (2000) show this variability in results with data from the 17 Spanish regions during the period 1984-1993. In particular, they compare results using data from the Instituto Nacional de Estadística versus FBBVA; using total private GDP versus no primary private GDP; and using basic econometric specifications of the aggregate production function versus those including human capital.
5. Recently, Rodríguez et al. (2007) have found empirical evidence on the link between the speed of convergence and the degree of private capital mobility across Spanish regions.
6. Hereafter, $t = 1982$ and $t + s = 1999$. Homogeneous data for Spanish regional policy before 1983 are not available. Spain enjoys European regional funds since 1986. Data comprise all kind of aids included under the label of regional policy: Structural and Cohesion Funds, General and Particular Funds of the Spanish regional policy (FCI, ZUR, ZPE, etc.); see Correa and Manzanedo (2002) for details. Homogeneous data for the budgetary package 2000-2006 are not available.
7. Data for GDP in 1982 are not available. Information from the Instituto Nacional de Estadística (INE) is not used due to methodological changes in 1986 and 1995. In any case, we have also estimated correlations between *FUNDS* and ΔY_i using data from the INE. Changes in regional GDP shares corresponding to two periods were used: 1981-1999 and 1981-2005. Correlations were also negative but not significant.
8. Productive capital includes roads, hydraulic infrastructures, ports, urban infrastructures, motorways and airports.
9. Assuming a common AR(1) process with the same ρ_i and using OLS residuals (e_i), the following consistent estimator for panel data was estimated: $\hat{\rho} = \sum_{i=1}^{n} \sum_{i=2}^{t} e_{it} \cdot e_{it-1} / \sum_{i=1}^{n} \sum_{i=2}^{t} e_{it}^2$. The hypothesis of common autocorrelation coefficients was verified by using a Wald test. Estimated parameter is low (0.15) and only marginally significant (p-value = 0.14).
10. In order to test exogeneity, residuals from an auxiliary regression (Z_{it}) were incorporated into the main regression. Auxiliary regression was:
$(S/Y)_{it} = \alpha_i + \delta \cdot (S/Y)_{it-1} + \gamma \cdot (I/Y)_{it-1} + \lambda_t \cdot D_t + \varepsilon_{it}$.
Endogeneity is discarded when the t-statistic corresponding to Z_{it} in the main regression is not significant.
11. 'The value of β would only be of the order of magnitude of its share of total world capital. True value of β would thus vary among the OECD countries but would average less than 0.10' (Feldstein and Horioka, 1980, 318).
12. Significance of AR(1) parameter is now very low (p-value = 0.29).
13. In column (2) robust t-statistics for OLS estimates are also reported.
14. Source for data on human capital is the IVIE.
15. For the whole country, R&D expenditures over GDP grew from 0.64 (in 1987) to 0.88 (in 1999).
16. Data before 1987 are not available

17. See Beck and Katz (1995). The Prais-Winsten transformed regression estimator fits a linear regression that is corrected for first-order serially-correlated residuals. Usual standard errors are replaced by Panel Corrected Standard Error (PCSE) estimates for linear cross-sectional time-series models. When computing the standard errors and the variance-covariance estimates, the disturbances are assumed to be heteroskedastic and contemporaneously correlated across panels.
18. For a region receiving average funds ($FUNDS = 1$), the coefficient for the time trend in the equation corresponding to public expenditures is $0.010 + 0 = 0.010$. It is $0.018 - 0.007 = 0.011$ in the second case.
19. The list of high and mid-high technology sectors can be seen on www.ine.es, selected in agreement with the methodology proposed by the OECD.
20. We consider the average values for the two years in order to mitigate the volatility of data corresponding to regional spending on innovation activities. The results are not sensitive to the exclusion of Madrid.
21. Volume 34, Issue 8, Pages 1123-1282 Volume (2005) of Research Policy offers a good review about many of these issues.
22. For instance, the three regions with the lowest per capita GDP in 2002 had the worst ratios. Defining the Spanish average as 100 percent, Extremadura spent 70.80 percent, Andalucia 83.04 percent, and Galicia 85.44 percent.
23. See Gunther et al. (2004, chapter 6) for a discussion on the decentralization of politics in Spain since the late 1970s.

REFERENCES

Alcaide, J. (2003), 'El ahorro nacional en el período 1995-2002. Estadísticas y análisis del ahorro regional y provincial', *Cuadernos de Información Económica* 176, pp. 40-79.

Antolin, P. and O. Bover (1997), 'Regional migration in Spain: the effect of personal characteristics and of unemployment, wage and house price differentials using pooled cross-sections', *Oxford Bulletin of Economics and Statistics*, **59** (2), pp. 215-235.

Barro, R.J., N.G. Mankiw and X. Sala-i-Martin (1995), 'Capital mobility in neoclassical models of growth', *American Economic Review*, **85** (1), pp. 103-115.

Barro, R.J. and X. Sala-i-Martin (1995), *Economic Growth*, Cambridge, MA: The MIT Press.

Beck, N. and J.N. Katz (1995), 'What to do (and not to do) with time-series cross-section data', *American Political Science Review*, **89**, pp. 634-647.

Bentolila, S. (1997), 'Sticky labor in Spanish regions', *European Economic Review*, **41** (3-5), pp. 591-598.

Biehl, D. (ed.) (1986), *The Contribution of Infrastructure to Regional Development*. Final Report of the Infrastructure Studies Group to the Commission of the European Communities.

Boldrin M. and F. Canova (2001), 'Inequality and convergence in Europe's regions: reconsidering European regional policies', *Economic Policy*, **32**, pp. 207-253.

Bover, O. and P. Velilla (2004), 'Migrations in Spain: Historical background and current trends', in K. Zimmermann (ed) *European Migration: What do we Know?*, Oxford, CEPR and Oxford University Press.

Caramés, L. and S. Lago-Peñas (2000), 'La inversión pública autonómica y el crecimiento de las regiones españolas', in L. Caramés (ed), *Gasto público autonómico*, Santiago de Compostela: EGAP, pp. 113-137.

Caselli, F., G. Esquivel and F. Lefort (1996), 'Reopening the convergence debate: a new look at cross-country growth empirics', in *Journal of Economic Growth*, **3**, pp. 363-389.

Correa, M.D. and J. Manzanedo (2002), *Política regional española y europea. Período 1983-1999*, Documentos de Trabajo, SGFCC-2002-05, Dirección General de Presupuestos, Madrid, Ministerio de Hacienda.

David, P.A., B.H. Hall, and A.A. Toole (1999), 'Is public R&D a complement or substitute for private R&D? A review of the econometric evidence', NBER Working Paper 7373, Cambridge, MA: National Bureau of Economic Research.

De la Fuente, A. (2002), 'On the sources of convergence: A close look at the Spanish regions', *European Economic Review*, **46**, pp. 569-599.

De la Fuente, A. (2003), 'El impacto de los Fondos Estructurales: convergencia real y cohesión interna', *Hacienda Pública Española*, **165**, pp. 129-122.

De la Fuente, A. (2004), 'Second best redistribution through public investment: a characterization, an empirical test and an application to the case of Spain', *Regional Science and Urban Economics*, **34**, pp. 489-503.

De la Fuente, A. and R. Domenech (2001), 'Schooling data, technological diffusion and the neoclassical model', *American Economic Review*, **91** (2), pp. 323-327.

De la Fuente, A. and R. Domenech (2002), 'Human capital in growth regressions: how much difference does data quality make? An update and further results', CEPR Discussion Paper 3587, London.

De la Fuente, A. and X. Vives (1995), 'Regional policy and Spain: Infrastructure and education as instruments of regional policy: Evidence from Spain', *Economic Policy*, **20**, pp. 11-54.

Dolado, J.J., J.M. González-Páramo and J.M. Roldán (1994), 'Convergencia económica entre las provincias españolas', *Moneda y Crédito*, **198**, pp. 81-131.

FBBVA (1997), *Renta Nacional de España y su distribución provincial 1993. Avance 1994-1995.*

FBBVA (1999), *Renta Nacional de España y su distribución provincial 1993. Serie homogénea. Años 1955 a 1993 y avances 1994 a 1997.*

FBBVA (2000), *Renta Nacional de España y su distribución provincial. Año 1995 y avances 1996-1999.*

FBBVA (2005), *El Stock de capital en España y su distribución territorial (1964-2002).*

Feldstein, M. and C. Horioka (1980), 'Domestic saving and international capital flows', *The Economic Journal*, **90**, pp. 314-329.

Flores de Frutos, R., M. Gracia-Díez and T. Pérez-Amaral (1998), 'Public capital stock and economic growth: an analysis of the Spanish economy', *Applied Economics*, **30**, pp. 985-994.

Funke, M. and H. Strulik (2005), 'Growth and convergence in a two-region model: the hypothetical case of Korean unification', *Journal of Asian Economics*, **16** (2), pp. 255-279.

Goerlich, F.J., M. Mas and F. Perez (2002), 'Concentración, convergencia y desigualdad regional en España', *Papeles de Economía Española*, **93**, pp. 17-39.

González-Páramo, J.M. and D. Martínez-López (2003), 'Convergence across Spanish regions. New evidence of the effects of public investment', *Review of Regional Studies*, **33** (2), pp. 65-86.

Gorostiaga, A. (1999), '¿Cómo afectan el capital público y el capital humano al crecimiento?: Un análisis para las regiones españolas en el marco neoclásico', *Investigaciones Económicas*, **22** (1), pp. 95-114.

European Regional Policy

Grossman, G.M. and E. Helpman (1991), *Innovation and Growth in the Global Economy*, Cambridge, MA: The MIT Press.

Gunther, R., J.R. Montero and J. Botella (2004), *Democracy in Modern Spain*, New Haven: Yale University Press.

Hanushek, E. (2003), 'The failure of input-based schooling policies', *Economic Journal*, **113**, pp. 64-98.

Hernández-Armenteros, J. (ed.) (2004), *La Universidad española en cifras: 2004*, Madrid: CRUE.

Howells, J. (2005), 'Innovation and regional economic development: a matter of perspective', *Research Policy*, **34** (8), pp. 1220-1234.

INE (2004), *La estadística de I+D en España: 38 años de historia.*

Kok, M.W. (ed.) (2004), *Relever le défi: la stratégie de Lisbonne pour la croissance et l'emploi*, available at: http://europa.eu.int/comm/lisbon_strategy/pdf/ 2004-1866-FR-complet.pdf.

López-Bazo, E., E. Vayá, J. Mora and J. Suriñach (1999), 'Regional economics dynamics and convergence in the European Union', *The Annals of Regional Science*, **3**, pp. 343-370.

Lucas, R.E. (1988), 'On the mechanics of development planning', *Journal of Monetary Economics*, **22** (1), pp. 3-42.

Mankiw, N.G., D. Romer and D. Weil (1992), 'A contribution to the empirics of economics growth', *Quarterly Journal of Economics*, **107**, pp. 407-437.

Martínez-López, D. (2006), 'Linking public investment to private investment. The case of Spanish regions', *International Review of Applied Economics*, **20** (4), pp. 411-423.

Mas, M., J. Maudos, F. Pérez and E. Uriel (1994), 'Disparidades regionales y convergencia en las Comunidades Autónomas', *Revista de Economía Aplicada*, **4**, pp. 129-148.

Mas, M., J. Maudos, F. Pérez and E. Uriel (1995), 'Public capital and convergence in the Spanish regions', *Enterpreneurship and Regional Development*, **7**, pp. 309-327.

OECD (2003), *Education at a Glance: OECD Indicators*, Paris.

Oughton, C., M. Landabaso and K. Morgan (2002), 'The regional innovation paradox: innovation policy and industrial policy', *Journal of Technology Transfer*, **27**, pp. 97-110.

Overman, H.G. and D. Puga (2002), 'Unemployment clusters across European regions and countries', *Economic Policy*, **17**, pp. 115-147.

Puga, D. (2002), 'European regional policies in light of recent location theories', *Journal of Economic Geography*, **2**, pp. 372-406.

Rodríguez, J., D. Romero and D. Martínez-López (2007), *Persistence in Inequalities Across Spanish Regions*, University Pablo Olavide, mimeo.

Rodríguez-Pose, A. (1999), 'Convergence or divergence? Types of regional response to socio-economic change', *Tijdschrift voor Economische en Sociale Geografie*, **90**, pp. 363-378.

Romer, P.M. (1990), 'Endogenous technological change', *Journal of Political Economy*, **98** (5), pp. 71-102.

Romp, W. and J. de Haan (2005), *Public Capital and Economic Growth: A Critical Survey*, European Investment Bank Papers 2.

Sala-i-Martin, X. (1996), 'Regional Cohesion: evidence and theories of regional economic growth and convergence', *European Economic Review*, **40**, pp. 1325-1352.

Sapir, A., P. Aghhion, G. Bertola, M. Hellwig, J. Pisany-Ferry, D. Rosati, J. Viñals and H. Wallace (2004), *An Agenda for a Growing Europe*, Oxford: Oxford University Press.

Sturm, J.E. (1998), *Public Capital Expenditures in OECD Countries. The Causes and Impact of the Decline in Public Capital Spending*, Cheltenham, UK and Northampton, MA, USA: Edward Elgar.

Utrilla, A. (2004), *Los instrumentos de la solidaridad interterritorial en el marco de la revisión de la política regional europea. Análisis de actuación y propuestas de reforma*, Instituto de Estudios Fiscales, Documento de Trabajo 3/04.

Uzawa, H. (1965), 'Optimal technical change in aggregative model in economic growth', *International Economic Review*, **6**, pp. 18-31.

Veloso, F., J.A. Tavares, N. Vasconcelos, P. Ferreira and P. Conceiçao (2003), *Investir no futuro. Relaçoes universidade industria em Portugal e nos Estados Unidos da América*, Lisbon: Gradiva.

11. European Cohesion Policy and the Spanish Economy

Simón Sosvilla-Rivero and José A. Herce*

11.1 INTRODUCTION

Since it joined the then European Community (EC) – today's European Union (EU) – on 1 January 1986, the Spanish economy has experienced a strong stimulus based on several factors. Among these factors we can cite the liberalisation, both internal and external, that entry to the EU implied the massive reception of structural aid, participation in the co-ordination of macroeconomic policy at the beginning, and the later adoption of the euro and the stability plan. It is not necessary to carry out a sophisticated and rather difficult macroeconomic evaluation to conclude that without all of these stimuli, the Spanish economy would be in a less favourable position than it is in today.

Among the factors cited above are the structural and cohesion aid that Spain has received since its incorporation, especially after the Structural Funds were reformed in 1987. The expressions 'Delors Package' I (1989 to 1993) and II (1994 to 1999), and 'Agenda 2000' (2000 to 2006) have been widely used over the Spanish economy's recent history, as well as the expression 'Cohesion Fund' (since 1993), to identify the overall regional community policy. In what follows, we shall refer to the structural and cohesion aid, or more plainly community aid, to denote the aid of one or the other type of fund, and will use the term cohesion policy to group together all the EU aid programmes oriented towards territorial equilibrium, less developed regions and economic and social cohesion, independently of whether they come from the Structural Funds or the Cohesion Fund. Most often we will refer to these aids as the Community Support Frameworks (CSF).

This chapter uses a methodology, tested by the authors on several past contributions, that conducts a macroeconomic evaluation of the effects of the aid packages on the aggregated economy based on several indicators such as final production, income per capita, employment, the rate of unemployment and productivity. The controversies about this community policy call for a careful analysis of its effects on the Spanish economy. We will look at the whole economy over the period 1989-2006, although we divide this period into programming sub-periods. Our evaluation is based on the observed evolution (and a projection up to a given year) of the chosen indicators, from which we deduce the effects on community aid using the HERMIN model of the Spanish economy. Proceeding in this way, we develop a counterfactual scenario that we compare with the observed (and projected) trends. This counterfactual method will always be limited since, had the community aid not been available, other developments and alternative policies could have taken place. Therefore, the effects attributed to community aid cannot be understood as benefits that the Spanish economy would not have sought through other alternative policies in the absence of this assistance. It cannot be denied, however, that the community cohesion policy has been beneficial for Spain in many regards.

In Section 11.2 we describe European regional policy in detail, and we offer a quantification of the cohesion aid that Spain has received or will receive during the period 1989-2006. In Section 11.3 we briefly discuss the methodology used, and in Section 11.4 we address the principal effects of the structural and cohesion community aid received by Spain during the relevant period, and we compare this with the situation that would have occurred in the absence of this aid. Finally, Section 11.5 provides some concluding remarks.

11.2   EUROPEAN COHESION POLICY TOWARDS SPAIN

The European Regional Development Fund (ERDF), the centrepiece of the European Union's regional policy, was established in 1975, but it was not until 1985 (when Spain and Portugal were admitted to the then European Community) that regional income differences became a priority issue on the community's agenda. The European Social Fund (ESF) had existed since 1969, and agricultural policy was financed by the European Agricultural Guidance and Guarantee Fund (EAGGF), whose Guidance Section was assimilated into the Structural Funds Programme during the early 1990s. In 1987 the Structural Funds were reformed and the amount granted within them was increased considerably in order to adapt the programme to general objectives that remain in place. The Financial Instrument for Fisheries Guidance (FIFG) itself became a structural fund with the adoption of the Agenda 2000 that same year. The Cohesion Fund, created in 1993 and directed toward member states below 90 percent of per capita EU-wide GDP completes the array of aid instruments under what has become known as EU cohesion policy.

The balance of resources from the overall community budget were a great benefit to Spain due to the primary terms of the implied flows, going back to the early 1990s with a net balance of close to 6 billion euros per year in its favour. The structural and cohesion aid received by Spain has been of a similarly significant magnitude, and Spain has been the country that has most benefited, in absolute terms, from the EU's cohesion policy. As we shall show in the analysis that follows, the macroeconomic impact of this aid has been both substantive and enduring in its effects. In Table 11.1 we detail the community aid that has been provided to Spain by both the Structural Funds and the Cohesion Fund by programming period and functional category. In order to carry out our evaluation, we have classified the aid into the following categories: public investment in infrastructure; aid for private productive investment; and investment in human resources. We have used information on actual expenses for the years 1989-1999 (Correa and Manzanedo, 2002), whereas for the programming period 2000-2006, we have simply used the amounts envisaged in the Agenda 2000 plan (Ministerio de Hacienda, 2001).

Table 11.1 Community aid received by Spain, by programming period and aid category for the period 1989-2006 (in million euros, at 1999 prices)

Programming period	Infra-structure	Production aid	Human capital	Total
Delors I (1989-1993, per year)	1 382.08	500.71	1 110.14	2 992.93
Delors II (1994-1999, per year)	3 135.74	835.82	2 049.41	6 020.97
Agenda 2000 (2000-2006, per year)	3 436.29	1 369.17	1 856.09	6 661.55
Annual average 1989-2006	2 765.49	950.15	1 713.32	5 428.96
Total aid 1989-2006	49 778.90	17 102.64	30 839.80	97 721.34

Sources: Correa and Manzanedo (2002), Ministerio de Hacienda (2001) and own computations.

Within this schema, the total amount of community aid destined for Spain over the period 1989-2006 is found to be 97 721.3 million euros at 1999 prices, of which 84 935.9 million correspond to the Structural Funds and 12 785.4 million to the Cohesion Fund. As can be seen in Table 11.1, over this period an average of 51 percent of the aid is dedicated to infrastructures

(49 778.9 million euros), which represents an annual average over the period of 2 765.5 million euros. The next most important category is the aid destined to enhance human capital of 30 839.8 million euros, or 31.6 percent of the total CSF, representing an annual average over the period 1989-2006 of 1 713.3 million euros. Finally, we have 17 102.6 million euros dedicated to productive aid to firms, 17.4 percent of the total aid package, representing an annual average over the period 1989-2006 of 950.15 million euros.

In Figure 11.1 we show the CSF as a percentage of Spanish Gross Domestic Product (GDP) for each programming period, at 1999 prices. As can be seen in this graph, the CSF would have provided a positive shock on the economy equivalent to 0.65 percent of annual real production over the period 1989-1993, which increases to 1.17 percent for 1994-1999, and to 1.05 percent of annual GDP over the rest of the period. Over the entire period 1989-2006, the annual average of CSF as a percentage of real GDP has been 0.98 percent. We can also note in the graph the relative importance of each functional shock received by the Spanish economy in each period.

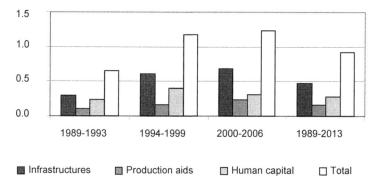

Figure 11.1   CSF received by Spain as a percentage of GDP by programming period and category of aid - 1989-2006 (annual average)

11.3   METHODOLOGY

As we have mentioned already, in order to evaluate the macroeconomic effects of the CSF we use the HERMIN model that was developed by FEDEA in Spain,[1] The Economic and Social Research Institute in Ireland, and the *Universidade Católica Portuguesa* in Portugal.[2]

The HERMIN model has been used on several occasions to compare the structural characteristics of the European periphery economies (Bradley, Modesto and Sosvilla Rivero, 1995a and 1995b) to evaluate the macroeconomic effects of the Community Support Frameworks (Bradley, Herce and Modesto, 1995; Herce and Sosvilla Rivero, 1994) or the Single European Market (Barry et al., 1997), as well as the aging of population (Herce and Sosvilla Rivero, 1998) and the effects for the Spanish economy of the eastern enlargement of the European Union (Martín et al., 2002).

The HERMIN model is a conventional Keynesian type model in which expenditure and distribution of income generate the standard expenditure-income mechanisms. However, the model also incorporates several neoclassical characteristics, mostly associated with the supply side of the model. Thus private sector production is not determined exclusively by demand, but rather is also influenced by competitiveness in costs and prices, within a context of firms acting to minimise productive costs (Bradley and FitzGerald, 1998). The model incorporates a constant elasticity of substitution (CES) production function, in which the capital/labour ratio responds to the relative prices of these factors. Finally, the inclusion of a Phillips curve mechanism in the wage negotiation procedure introduces further relative price effects into the model. Thus, the HERMIN-Spain model not only captures the structural characteristics of the Spanish economy, but it also incorporates supply aspects that are specially designed to model in an appropriate manner the types of shocks whose impact we are attempting to examine (Bradley, Modesto and Sosvilla-Rivero, 1995a).

Since our final objective is to identify and to model the channels through which CSF can affect the Spanish economy, we distinguish between demand and supply effects in our analysis.

From the demand side, the projects financed by community aid imply a stimulus for the economy through increased public spending that directly impacts demand and production, with further effects on employment, income, prices and wages. The supply-side effects of the increased capacity – in infrastructure, private capital and human capital – operate through lower costs, higher productivity and increased competitiveness, stimulating production, reducing imports and increasing exports. As income increases, we also note the inflationary pressure that originates in the demand side of the model.

In the study we have grouped the possible effects according to three types of aid programmes:

a)   Public investment in infrastructures: The primary effect appears in the lower costs of transport and other communication services, that reduce production costs sufficiently to stimulate long term increases in both output and employment (see, for example, Gramlich, 1994).

b)   Investment in human resources: This programme increases the efficiency and productivity of the labour force, thereby reducing the costs of existing firms, increasing the quality of their products, and providing incentives for the creation of new firms that can then take advantage of these efficiency and productivity improvements.

c)   Aid for productive investment: The objective of this type of aid is designed to stimulate private activities that are considered productive and desirable, in order to increase production, exports and employment.

We assume that the economic effects of each programme manifest first as stimuli to aggregate demand and then as supply externalities as the extra productive capacity they create becomes operational. In the case of externalities we attempt to capture the effects by modifying the key equations in the model (mainly the production functions and the demands for factors).[3] In particular, we take into account two types of externality that are derived from each of the three programmes on which the CSF is based: the first is the increase in the productivity of private factors, and the second is related to the increase in the quality of the goods and services supplied by the private sector.

With respect to the first type of externality effects, consider the following CES production function:

$$O = A \left\{ \delta \left[\exp(\lambda_L t) L \right]^{-p} + (1 - \delta) \left[\exp(\lambda_K t) K \right]^{-p} \right\}^{-(1/p)}$$

where O, L and K represent, respectively, GDP, employment and the stock of capital; where A is a scale parameter; $1/(1 + \rho)$ is the elasticity of substitution; δ is a parameter of factor intensity; and λ_L and λ_K are the rates of technical change attributable to labour and capital, respectively.

Externality effects can be incorporated by making the scale parameter endogenous, for example, as a function of public investment in infrastructure ($KGINF$), human capital (KH) and private capital (K), in the following way:

$$A_t = A_0 (KGINF_t / KGINF_0)^{\eta_1} (KH_t / KH_0)^{\eta_2} (K_t / K_0)^{\eta_3}$$

where the subindexes t and 0 denote the accumulated stock with and without CSF, and η_1, η_2 and η_3 represent the corresponding elasticities. In this way, each of the CSF programmes exerts its own specific influence through this first channel based on the productivity and accumulation of private and public inputs.

The second type of externality operates both directly through the effect of each programme on improving the quality of industrial production (which in turn increases the exterior demand for these goods), as well as indirectly through the increased flows of foreign direct investment derived from the availability of a more qualified labour force and better infrastructures (Porter, 1986) and the resulting modernisation of production techniques and equipment within participating firms and their greater propensity to export (Alonso and Donoso, 1994). In order to capture this type of externality, we relate the growth in the stock of infrastructure, the increase in human capital and the greater endowment of private sector capital due to the different programmes associated with European aid, to the measure of external demand used by the HERMIN model, *OW* (a key variable in the determination of the level of production in the tradeables sector), in the following way:

$$OWX = OW \times (KGINF_t / KGINF_0)^{\eta_1} \times (KH_t / KH_0)^{\eta_2} \times (K_t / K_0)^{\eta_3}$$

In our empirical application we adopt the following values for the different elasticities: $\eta_1 = 0.20$, $\eta_2 = 0.07$ and $\eta_3 = 0.10$. These values are approached gradually as the different investments within the CSF package mature. The value used for the elasticity $\eta_1 = 0.20$ is based on the estimations of Bajo-Rubio and Sosvilla-Rivero (1993) and Argimón et al. (1994). The value for the elasticity $\eta_2 = 0.07$ was taken from the estimates of the social return from education and professional training in Spain obtained by Corugedo et al. (1992). This elasticity is actually the estimated coefficient for the education variable in a model that attempts to explain the net wage earned by a worker in his or her current job, and it corresponds to the internal rate of return for education proposed by Mincer (1974). Finally, the value of the elasticity $\eta_3 = 0.10$ was chosen based on detailed field evidence on the effects of the Community Support Framework 1989-93 (Herce, 1994).

The introduction of supply effects into a conventional econometric model amounts to an ad hoc attempt within a treatment that has yet to be fully explored. To be conservative, we have taken only the most moderate values for the elasticities suggested in the previous literature, and in the simulations we have allowed their effects to mature progressively. Consequently, the results for the supply effects of European structural aids will depend on both the size of the externalities and their rate of maturation.

11.4   SIMULATION RESULTS

In this section we present the results for the estimated effects of the CSF on the Spanish economy over the period 1989-2006. The effects are compared with the situation that would have existed without this aid (as the benchmark scenario). The approach adopted reflects the fact that if a particular economy has not 'improved' in its absolute level of performance in spite of having received CSF grants, this outcome does not necessarily imply that the aid received was ineffective, since the economy could feasibly have been in an even worse position in the absence of this assistance.

11.4.1   Effects on Real Output and its Rate of Growth

Given that the main objective of the European Structural and Cohesion Funds is to promote economic and social convergence, we shall focus our attention initially on the impact on real GDP at factor cost, a common measure of the final production of goods and services in an economy, net of the influence of taxes. In Figure 11.2 we present the results for each programming period in terms of this variable for three simulations: the first shows only the demand effects; the second only takes into account the supply effects; and the third considers their combined effects.

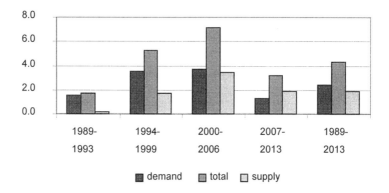

Figure 11.2   Effects of the CSF aids on real production: percentage difference with respect to real GDP without aids (average values for each period)

Demand effects stem from the impact of aid on aggregate economic demand, that is, on the industries that provide goods and services, equipment, etc., that benefit directly from this shock, which impact then works through the entire economy by means of inter-industry relationships and demand-income interactions. In addition to these demand effects we also have supply effects derived from an increased productivity of private factors of production which now enjoy an improved endowment of infrastructures, human capital, etc.

As can be seen in Figure 11.2, the demand (or Keynesian) effects have, on average, increased *the level* of real GDP over the period 1989-1993, corresponding to the so-called 'Delors I' package, by an average of 1.54 percent over the benchmark scenario. We can translate this into the statement that the indicator in question, without the CSF and *ceteris paribus*, would have been lower than its observed value by 1.54 percent. The 'GDP gap' induced by the demand effects of the CSF would have increased, according to our estimates, to 3.51 percent during the period 1994-1999 (or Delors II package), and to 3.71 percent over the financial period envisaged by the Agenda 2000, 2000-2006. On the other hand, the supply effects have been unfolding more progressively, since we have included (as is common in the literature) a gradual externality effect. It can be seen that over the period 1989-1993 there was an average increase of 0.19 percent over the benchmark scenario (no CSF), which has increased gradually to 1.76 percent over the period 1993-1999 and then to 3.41 percent for 2000-2006. This effect is produced in a progressive manner so long as the installed infrastructural, private and human capital is maintained by the appropriate replacement investment which would not necessarily be financed by the CSF programmes. In our calculations, this maintenance has been assumed to occur at the same time as the programmes of investment in each period supersede those of the previous periods. Overall, as can be seen in Figure 11.2, the total effects (both demand and supply) would have reached an average difference over the benchmark scenario of 1.73 percent for 1989-1993, which is increased to 5.27 percent for the period 1994-1999, and then to 7.11 percent for 2000-2006. Finally, the results of our simulations suggest that, on average over the total period 1989-2006, the demand effects of the community aid would have increased real GDP over the period by 2.88 percent compared to the situation without CSF, while the supply effects would have been 1.86 percent. Thus, the overall effect of the CSF aid is that Spanish real GDP is 4.74 percent higher today than would have been the case without the CSF. By the end of the last programming period, in 2006, the level of the Spanish GDP was most likely be about 7 percent higher than would it would have been without the structural and cohesion aid, with about half of this result due to the supply externalities.

Table 11.2 displays the results of the simulation in terms of average changes in the level of real GDP (at 1999 prices) for each of the different programming periods (1989-1993, 1994-1999 and 2000-2006). Comparing the results for the scenario combining both demand and supply effects with that of the benchmark scenario without CSF, we estimate an average difference in real production over the period 1989-1993 of 7.817 million euros at 1999 prices. On the other hand, the results obtained for the second period (1994-1999) suggest an average increase in real production of 25.814 million euros (again at 1999 prices). Finally, if we extend our period of analysis up to the year 2006, the results of our simulations suggest an expansion in average real production between the two scenarios of 42.025 million euros (at 1999 prices). Over the entire period of analysis (1989-2006) the Spanish economy would have experienced an increase in the value of goods and services produced of 25.692 million euros at 1999 prices maintained year by year all through the period.

Table 11.2 also reports the annual growth rate of GDP (cumulative) for the period 1988-2006 (including the impact of Agenda 2000). As can be seen, we estimate that in the scenario without CSF aid, the Spanish economy would have grown in real terms over the period 1988-2006 at an annual cummulative rate of 2.37 percent, compared to the figure of 2.75 percent in the scenario with CSF. In other words, the structural and cohesion community aid would have allowed the Spanish economy to grow at almost 0.4 percentage points above its growth rate in the absence of CSF. Of this effect, almost half can be attributed to the supply or externality effects, and the rest to the demand effects.

Table 11.2 Spanish GDP with and without structural and cohesion aids (CSF), (annual averages, billion euros at 1999 prices)

	Without CSF	Including only supply effects	With CSF (both supply and demand effects)
Annual average GDP, period 1989-1993	450.3	451.2	458.2
Annual average GDP, period 1994-1999	483.9	492.2	509.7
Annual average GDP, period 2000-2006	591.0	610.5	633.0
Annual average GDP, period 1989-2006	511.2	521.2	536.9
Annual growth rate 1988-2006	2.37%	2.57%	2.75%
Id. Differences w.r.t. first column	–	0.20%	0.38%

11.4.2   Effects on per capita income and convergence to EU-15

Table 11.3 presents the results in terms of real per capita income, proxied by per capita GDP. As can be seen in the table, for the programming period 1989-1993 the results of our simulations suggest that per capita annual income was, on average, 200 euros greater than what it would have been without CSF (at 1999 prices). Over the second programming period (1994-1999), the difference increases to 654 euros (at 1999 prices), and this increases to 1 027 euros for the final period (2000-2006). Finally, over the entire period analysed (1989-2006), we obtain an average difference of 638 euros at 1999 prices between the scenarios with and without structural and cohesion aids.

Table 11.4 shows the relative situation of income per-capita between Spain and the average of the European Union of 15 (EU-15) before May 2004 in terms of purchasing power parity (PPP) and expressed as index numbers with a value of 100 for the average of EU-15 for each year. As can be seen, in 1988 Spain's per capita income was only 74.34 percent of the average of the EU-15.

The results of our simulations suggest that by the end of the first programming period the Spanish economy had achieved an index that was greater by 1.88 percentage points than what would have been the case without CSF, a real convergence result. This difference is elevated to 3.55 percentage points for the second programming period.

Table 11.3 Effects of CSF on the real per capita income in Spain
(annual average, in euros at 1999 prices)

	Without CSF	Only including supply effects	With aid (both supply and demand effects)
Period 1989-1993	11 555.38	11 577.31	11 755.73
Period 1994-1999	12 279.41	12 490.96	12 933.56
Period 2000-2006	14 444.04	14 920.06	15 471.19
Period 1989-2006	12 811.21	13 059.17	13 448.94

As far as the forecast for the year 2006 is concerned, our results indicate that the difference in the index between the scenarios with and without CSF could be 5.78 percentage points, with the relative Spanish per capita income being 90 percent of the EU-15 average, quite a real progress by any standard.

From a dynamic point of view, Table 11.4 shows that without the investments corresponding to the CSF, the process of real convergence would have advanced more slowly, both between 1993 and 1999 (2.13 percentage points compared to 0.46) as well as between 1993 and 2006 (10.56 percentage points compared to 6.66).

Table 11.4 Relative per-capita income in Spain (PPP adjusted, EU-15=100)

	With CSF	Without CSF	Difference
Index in 1988	74.34	74.34	0.00
Index in 1993	78.83	76.95	1.88
Index in 1999	83.54	79.99	3.55
Index in 2006	89.39	83.61	5.78
Average index for period 1989-1993	77.78	76.45	1.33
Average index for period 1994-1999	80.22	76.21	4.01
Average index for period 2000-2006	86.76	81.00	5.76

Source: Own calculations using the HERMIN-Spain model, and using the series from the AMECO database (DG ECFIN, EU Commission).

In terms of average values per budgeting period, the simulations indicate that the difference in relative income between the scenarios with and without CSF is 1.33, 4.01 and 5.76 percentage points for the periods 1989-1993, 1994-1999 and 2000-2006 respectively. This implies that real convergence has advanced by 2.55 percentage points between the first and the second periods, and by 6.49 percentage points between the first and the third. This compares with the figures of 1.23 percentage points that would have been achieved between 1989-1993 and 1994-1999, and 4.97 percentage points between 1989-1993 and 2000-06 had no aid been given.

11.4.3   Effects on Employment and the Unemployment Rate

Employment is dealt with in Figure 11.3, which shows the percentage deviations in the number of employed persons with respect to the benchmark scenario (without structural and cohesion aid). As the graph shows, the demand (or Keynesian) effects alone have implied an average stimulus to the level of employment over the period 1989-1993 of 1.41 percent over the benchmark scenario, of 3.17 percent over the period 1994-1999, and then of 3.32 percent for the period 2000-2006. The total effects (including both demand and supply effects) point to an increase in the number of employed persons over the period 1989-1993 of 1.22 percent compared to the situation that would have been achieved without the CSF.

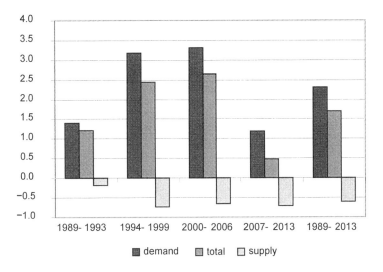

Figure 11.3   Effects of CSF on employment (% difference with respect to the employment level without CSF)

This difference increases to 2.43 percent and 2.66 percent for the periods 1994-1999 and 2000-2006, respectively. This seemingly contradictory result is attributable to the greater endowment of public infrastructures, private capital and human capital that has been achieved due to the CSF, which has raised the productivity of private factors of production sufficiently that a relatively smaller quantity of labour is required now to produce the same amount of goods and services. Finally, our simulations imply that, on average over the period 1989-2006, the demand effects of the CSF have raised the level of employment by 2.60 percent, while the supply effects have been to reduce it by 0.53 percent. Thus, the overall effect of the CSF has been that employment has been only 2.07 percent greater than what would have occurred without the CSF.

In Table 11.5 we offer the results in terms of the number of jobs created under the different scenarios. As can be seen, the CSF has allowed, on average, 154 thousand jobs to be created or maintained over the period 1989-1993. For the period 1994-1999 the results of the simulations suggest that the average number of employed persons in Spain would have been 317 thousand less had no European aid been given at all. For the last programming period we get a difference between the scenarios with and without CSF of 429 thousand jobs. Finally, over the entire period of analysis (1988-2006) the difference in the average number of employed persons between the two scenarios is 299 thousand. These jobs could have been either created or maintained under alternative programmes to those corresponding to the CSF, but, *ceteris paribus*, can be attributed to it and overall imply a significant employment effect.

Table 11.5 Effects of CSF on employment (in thousands)

	Without aid	With aid	Difference
Employment in 1989	12 546.23	12 638.23	92.00
Employment in 2006	17 375.56	17 783.46	407.91
Annual average employment for period 1989-1993	12 599.74	12 753.27	153.53
Annual average employment for period 1994-1999	12 881.22	13 198.29	317.07
Annual average employment for period 2000-2006	16 211.51	16 640.64	429.13
Annual average employment for period 1989-2006	13 998.43	14 297.06	298.63
Id. its annual growth rate	1.98 %	2.11 %	0.13 %

Source: Own calculations based on the results of the HERMIN-Spain model using the Spanish Labour Force Survey (EPA) employment series for 1989-2003, projected to 2006.

Table 11.6 Effects of CSF on the rate of unemployment (a)

	With aid	Without aid	Difference (b)
Rate of unemployment in 1989	17.31	17.24	−0.07
Rate of unemployment in 2006	10.09	9.97	−0.12
Average rate of unemployment in period 1989-1993	18.28	18.16	−0.12
Average rate of unemployment in period 1994-1999	20.99	20.73	−0.26
Average rate of unemployment in period 2000-2006	11.36	11.21	−0.15
Average rate of unemployment in period 1989-2006	16.64	16.47	−0.17

a) As a percentage of active population.
b) A negative sign means a reduction in the rate of unemployment due to CSF.

This result translates directly into effects on the rate of unemployment in the economy over the period, as shown in Table 11.6. In this table we see the rates of unemployment that would have been registered in Spain under each of the alternative scenarios (with and without CSF). As can be seen, this aid has allowed the rate of unemployment to be reduced by 0.12 percentage points over the first programming period, 0.26 percentage points over the second period, and 0.15 percentage points over the third one. The average reduction in the rate of unemployment over the entire period 1989-2006 has been 0.17 percentage points. This process shows a progressive deceleration as the increased capitalisation in the economy (infrastructures, private capital and human capital) produced by the CSF implies an increase in the productivity of labour which offsets the stimuli that the demand effects have upon employment and the rate of unemployment.

11.4.4 Effects on the Productivity of Labour

In Figure 11.4 we present the results for the apparent productivity of labour, or GDP per worker, expressed as an index with value 100 in 1988, for different years over the period 1989-2006.

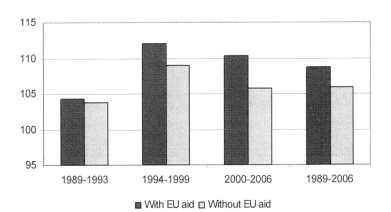

*Figure 11.4   Effects of the CSF on the productivity of labour
(Index with base of 100 in 1988)*

As can be seen, the value of the index of the apparent productivity of labour has increased due to the CSF over the period 1989-1993 by approximately 1.2 percentage points compared to the scenario without community aid. In 1999, during the operation of the Delors I and II packages, the index of productivity reached 4.5 percentage points above the case of no structural and cohesion aid, and in 2006, after the Agenda 2000, the accumulated total gain in the index of productivity is 4.8 percentage points. Over the entire period of analysis (1988-2006), the average increase is 3 percentage points. The total accumulated gain of 4.8 points represents 23.5 percent of the increase in the index over the period 1988-2006, which would therefore be what we can attribute to the operation of the community structural and cohesion aids.

In terms of the annual rate of growth of the index of labour productivity over the period, we can see that the community aid has contributed 0.24 percentage points to the average growth rate over the period of 0.62 percent per year, which is 39 percent of the total rate of productivity growth. In other words, the Spanish economy has followed a modest trajectory in labour productivity growth over the period, with some notable ups and downs. However, the CSF appears to have had a positive net contribution to the maintenance of overall productivity growth that without the aid, *ceteris paribus*, would have been even more modest.

11.5 CONCLUDING REMARKS

The Spanish economy has benefited from important macroeconomic effects attributable to the substantive structural and cohesion aid provided under the EU's Community Support Frameworks (CSF) that it has received since 1989. In this chapter we have provided quantitative estimates of these effects on such variables as GDP, employment and per capita income in the Spanish economy from 1989, when the so-called 'Delors I Package' began, through 2006, when the last programming period, Agenda 2000, ended.

To summarise the results, the community aid has allowed the average real rate of growth of the Spanish economy since 1989 to be about four tenths of a percentage point above what it would have been in absence of the CSF. The aid has also provided for about a third of the 15 percentage points that the Spanish per capita income has gained with respect to the EU-15 average over the period of analysis. These results are similar to those obtained in earlier studies, although for shorter periods of analysis, both by the current authors and by other authors (de la Fuente, 2003). These results are presented with the caution that they are expressed in terms of a 'counterfactual' analysis, since we cannot know what would have happened had the CSF not been provided. Additionally, we should also consider the possible crowding-out effects that structural aid may have on private initiatives (de la Fuente 2003), and the debatable overall efficiency of the regional community policy (Canova, 2001). But on the whole, we believe that for Spain the structural aid packages have had a significantly positive effect on its economic growth and development.

NOTES

*   The authors thank Francisco Pérez-Bermejo for his assistance in the creation of the data base used in this chapter. Financial support from Ministerio de Ciencia y Tecnología (CICYT grant SEC2002-01892) and from the Real Instituto Elcano for International and Strategic Studies is gratefully acknowledged. The views expressed here are those of the authors and do not necessarily reflect those of the institutions they are affiliated. The usual disclaimer applies.
1.   See Herce and Sosvilla-Rivero (1995) for a more detailed description of the Spanish version of the model, and Herce and Sosvilla-Rivero (1994) for an exposition of the macroeconomic treatment of the Community Support Frameworks.
2.   We owe credit to John Bradley at the Economic and Social Research Institute (Dublin) who more than a decade ago developed the HERMIN modelling framework for Ireland, Greece, Spain and Portugal. This framework has been extended also to some of the new EU Member States.
3.   The concept of externalities in production is central to the recent developments in the theory of endogenous growth, offering a more adequate representation of the process of economic growth by extending neoclassical growth theory to include the role of human capital, public capital and technology (see, for example, Sala-i-Martin, 1990).

REFERENCES

Alonso, J.A. and V. Donoso (1994), *Competitividad de la Empresa Exportadora Española*, Madrid: ICEX.

Argimón, I., J.M. González-Páramo, M.J. Martín and J.M. Roldán (1994), 'Productividad e infraestructuras en la economía española', in *Moneda y Crédito*, **198**, pp. 207-241.

Bajo-Rubio, O. and S. Sosvilla-Rivero (1993), 'Does public capital affect private sector performance? An analysis of the Spanish case, 1964-1988', *Economic Modelling*, **10**, pp. 179-185.

Barry, F., J. Bradley, A. Hannan, J. McCartan and S. Sosvilla-Rivero (1997), *Single Market Review: Aggregate and Regional Aspects: The Cases of Greece, Ireland, Portugal and Spain*, Luxemburg: Office of Official Publications of the European Communities.

Bradley, J. and J. FitzGerald (1988), 'Industrial output and factor input determination in an econometric model of a small open economy', *European Economic Review*, **32**, pp. 1227-1241.

Bradley, J., J.A. Herce and L. Modesto (1995), 'The macroeconomic effects of the CSF 1994-99 in the EU periphery: An analysis based on the HERMIN model', in *Economic Modelling*, **12**, pp. 323-333.

Bradley, J., L. Modesto and S. Sosvilla-Rivero (1995a), 'HERMIN: A macroeconomic modelling framework for the EU periphery', *Economic Modelling*, **12**, pp. 221-247.

Bradley, J., L. Modesto and S. Sosvilla-Rivero (1995b), 'Similarity and diversity in the EU periphery: A HERMIN-based investigation', *Economic Modelling*, **12**, pp. 313-322.

Canova, F. (2001), *Are EU policies fostering growth and reducing regional inequalities?*, CREI-Universitat Pompeu Fabra opuscle 8, available at: http://www.econ.upf.es/crei/research/opuscles/op8ang.pdf.

Correa, M.D. and J. Manzanedo (2002), *Política regional española y europea*, Ministerio de Hacienda, General Budgetary Office working paper SGFCC-2002-05.

Corugedo, I., E. García and J. Martínez (1992), 'Educación y rentas. Una aplicación a la enseñanza media en España: Una nota', *Investigaciones Económicas*, **16**, pp. 299-304.

de la Fuente, A. (2003), 'Does Cohesion Policy Work? Some General Considerations and Evidence from Spain', in B. Funck and L Pizzati (eds), *Regional Policy for the new EU members*, World Bank, Washington, DC, pp. 155-166.

Gramlich, E.M. (1994), 'Infrastructure Investment: A Review Essay', *Journal of Economic Literature*, **32**, pp. 1176-1196.

Herce, J.A. (co-ordinator) (1994), *Evaluación del Marco de Apoyo Comunitario 1989-93*, mimeo, FEDEA.

Herce, J.A. and S. Sosvilla Rivero (1994), 'The effects of the Community Support Framework 1994-99 on the Spanish economy: An analysis based on the HERMIN model', FEDEA working paper 94-10R.

Herce, J.A. and S. Sosvilla Rivero (1995), 'HERMIN Spain', *Economic Modelling*, **12**, pp. 295-311.

Herce, J.A. and S. Sosvilla Rivero (1998), *Macroeconomic consequences of population ageing in Spain: A preliminary evaluation*, Paper presented to the XIIth Annual Conference of the European Society of Population Economics, Amsterdam.

Martín, C., J.A. Herce, S. Sosvilla-Rivero and F.J. Velázquez (2002), *European Union Enlargement. Effects on the Spanish Economy*, La Caixa Economic Studies 27, available at: http://papers.ssrn.com/sol3/papers.cfm?abstract_id=329123.

Mincer, J. (1974), *Schooling Experience and Earnings*, New York: National Bureau of Economic Research.

Ministerio de Hacienda (2001), *Marco Comunitario de Apoyo 2000-2006 para las Regiones Españolas del Objetivo 1*, Madrid: Ministerio de Hacienda. An English summary can be downloaded at http://europa.eu.int/comm/regional_policy/funds/prord/document/resu_en.pdf.

Porter, M. E. (1986), 'Competition in global industries: A conceptual framework', in M.E. Porter (ed.), *Competition in Global Industries*, Boston: Harvard Business School Press, pp. 15-60.

Sala-i-Martin, X. (1990), 'Lecture notes on Economic Growth (I): Introduction to the literature and the neoclassical model'; NBER working paper 3563, Cambridge, MA: National Bureau of Economic Research.

Index